SCRIPTURALIZING REVELATION

Society of Biblical Literature

Semeia Studies

Gerald O. West, Editor

Editorial Board

Number 80

SCRIPTURALIZING REVELATION

AN AFRICAN AMERICAN POSTCOLONIAL
READING OF EMPIRE

Lynne St. Clair Darden

SBL Press
Atlanta

Copyright © 2015 by SBL Press

Library of Congress Cataloging-in-Publication Data

Darden, Lynne St. Clair.
    Scripturalizing Revelation : an African American postcolonial reading of empire / Lynne St. Clair Darden.
        p. cm. — (Semeia studies ; Number 80)
    Includes bibliographical references and index.
    ISBN 978-1-62837-088-1 (hardcover : alk. paper) — ISBN 978-1-62837-087-4 (pbk. : alk. paper) — ISBN 978-1-62837-089-8 (electronic)
    1. Bible. Revelation—Postcolonial criticism. 2. Bible. Revelation—Black interpretations. 3. Postcolonial theology. 4. Black theology. 5. Bible. Revelation. I. Title.
    BS2825.52.D37 2015
    228'.06—dc23   2015005192

Cover photograph:
Harriet Powers, American, 1837–1910
Pictorial quilt (detail)
American (Athens, Georgia), 1895–1898
Cotton plain weave, pieced, appliqued, embroidered, and quilted
175 x 266.7 cm (68 7/8 x 105 in.)
Museum of Fine Arts, Boston
Bequest of Maxim Karolik, 64.619

Printed on acid-free, recycled paper conforming to
ANSI/NISO Z39.48-1992 (R1997) and ISO 9706:1994
standards for paper permanence.

St. Clair Elizabeth Darden
(alpha)

and

Ava Sophia LaPene
(omega)

CONTENTS

ACKNOWLEDGMENTS

I owe a debt of gratitude to a host of people who have helped me complete this journey. First and foremost, I would like to thank Stephen D. Moore for his keen navigational skills that allowed me to finish this, my first solo passage, safe and sound. He charted a steady course throughout and provided me with a reliable compass that never failed to point me in the right direction. I consider myself very fortunate to have been an apprentice to such an ace helmsman, who taught me how to cast my own sails, to glide with the wind, and to maneuver skillfully over the rough currents. I am extremely grateful to my Semeia Studies editors, Gay Byron and Gerald West, and also to Althea Spencer-Miller, Melanie Johnson-deBaufre, and Abraham Smith for their insightful suggestions that helped me to rechart certain sections of this monograph in order to avoid particularly stony roads.

I thank the staff, my fellow faculty colleagues, and the administration at the Interdenominational Theological Center for their support of my research. I am particularly grateful to Drs. Randall Bailey, Reginaldo Braga, Riggins Earl, Temba Mafico, Beverly Wallace, Henry Whelchel, and Mark Lomax for their support of my research grant proposal that was approved by my institution. I appreciate Eric Thomas, my research assistant, for his impeccable work on my monograph. I am indebted to the Fund of Theological Education for continuing networking support for FTE fellows. I thank Vincent L. Wimbush for his mapping of African Americans and the Bible project and his guidance of my work while at Union Theological Seminary, New York.

I am especially indebted to Dennis Yi-Shin Kuo and Daniel Hunt, who were my lifesavers when I was tossed into the eye of the storm toward the end of my journey. Their steady hands provided me with the opportunity I needed to finish. I could not have completed my travels without their expertise. I am grateful for the assistance and friendship of Kathie Brown, Ernie Rubinstein, and Suzanne Sellinger. I thank them for being safe havens of solace and will remember fondly my days spent in their offices at Drew University.

Many colleagues and friends supplied me with food and water to nourish both body and soul: Margaret Aymer, Randall Bailey, Reginaldo Braga, Temba Mafico, Vanessa Lovelace, Daniel Shin, Rose Ellen Dunn, Maria Iannuzzi, Sharon Jacob, Jennifer Kaalund, Michelle Mapp, Jea Sophia Oh, Susan Rosario, Alma Tuitt, and Robert Wafula. I cherish the camaraderie and I consider the many gatherings, lunches, and dinners we have shared as sunny, breezy, smooth-sailing days.

Most of all, I thank my family for their love, encouragement, support, patience, and their understanding that sacrifices had to be made in order to complete this project. I thank my brother, Joseph Darden, and my son, Damian LaPene, for carrying some of the load so that I was not too exhausted when approaching the last leg of my journey. I thank my granddaughter, Ava LaPene, for being such a good little traveling companion on those many occasions when she went along with her Na-Na to do research. And I thank my mother, the late St. Clair Darden, who was the light tower that made visible the way home and whose homing pigeons always seemed to find me, no matter where I was. Her keen curiosity and passion to learn new things, her persistent drive and courage to live life to the fullest, and her dedication to serving others are qualities she made sure to instill in me. These qualities provided the fortitude, determination, and stamina I needed to complete this wonderful journey.

PREFACE

In this reading of the book of Revelation I examine John the Seer's rhetorical strategy, in general, and his use of imperial cult ritual in the heavenly throne room scenes, in particular, through the lens of an African American scripturalization that is framed by the concepts of signifyin(g) and cultural memory, and supplemented by postcolonial theory.[1] The purpose of this scripturalization is to unveil the complex cultural negotiations involved in the construction of a Christian identity. The scripting will propose that John the Seer's signifyin(g) on empire demonstrates that he is well aware of the oppressive nature of Roman imperialism on the lives of provincial Asia Christians. This is made evident throughout the text by his fierce, nonaccommodating stance toward participation in imperial ritual that supports an imperial ideology.

Yet, ironically, John reinscribes imperial processes and practices. Seemingly, no matter how determined he is in his persuasion to disconnect the Christian communities from the religio-political manipulations of empire, his hybrid[2] identity disallows him. John's colonized construction as "almost the same but not quite like" has resulted in the production of a resistance strategy that is a "blurred copy" of the hegemonic tactics of the Roman Empire that entail violent disruption and displacement.

This scripturalization of the book of Revelation fused with postcolonial theory is directed to the contemporary African American community as a cautionary warning of the potential danger of reinscribing the oppressive elements of an American empire. This is not to say that this reading supports a postliberation or postracial sentiment, that the two great beasts of society—racism and sexism—are no longer threats to a holistic and affirming society. What this reading does maintain, however, is that

---

1. The work of Henry Louis Gates Jr. (1988) will frame, in part, the reading strategy.
2. Cultural hybridity is defined as an identity construction formed by the "cross-breeding" of two cultures.

African American biblical scribes must speak to the community's vulnerability to the subtle ways of the beasts by addressing a fuller scope of the complexity of African American identity. By neglecting to reflect on and write about the issues and concerns of a growing segment of African Americans who are carving an upper niche in American politics, economy, education, and finance, African American biblical scribes may find themselves unintentionally feeding the beast.

Abbreviations

AARAS	American Academy of Religion Academy Series
BibInt	*Biblical Interpretation*
BibInt	Biblical Interpretation Series
BR	*Biblical Research*
BSOAS	*Bulletin of the School of Oriental and African Studies*
EJIL	Early Judaism and Its Literature
HTR	*Harvard Theological Review*
Int	*Interpretation*
JBL	*Journal of Biblical Literature*
JFSR	*Journal of Feminist Studies in Religion*
JITC	*Journal of the Interdenominational Theological Center*
JRS	*Journal of Roman Studies*
JSNT	*Journal for the Study of the New Testament*
JSNTSup	Journal for the Study of the New Testament Supplement Series
LCL	Loeb Classical Library
NTS	*New Testament Studies*
SemeiaSt	Semeia Studies
StABH	Studies in American Biblical Hermeneutics
SymS	Symposium Series
WBC	Word Biblical Commentary

INTRODUCTION: "AT LAST"

On January 20, 2009, the day after Martin Luther King Day, the people of this nation witnessed the swearing in of Barack Hussein Obama as the forty-fourth president of the United States. This was a momentous day for all Americans, but particularly so for African Americans. I think it is safe to say that many of the African Americans who lined the Washington Mall on that blustery winter day, or watched and/or read about the event, would have never dreamed that, in their lifetime, one of their own would call the White House "home."

The Obama presidential inauguration was the climax of memorial communal events that began with his announcement on February 10, 2007, of his candidacy for president of the United States. His campaign slogan, "Yes We Can!" would resound from African American pulpits, barbershops, beauty salons, restaurants, schools, and street corners. The slogan instilled a sense of unbounded possibility and inspired a people who for generations have wrestled with various forms of displacement and disruption, including enslavement, disenfranchisement, exploitation, segregation, and racism.

Appropriately, the song "At Last," which was the song that Barack and Michelle Obama danced to at the Neighborhood Inauguration Ball, signified a community that had finally found "a dream that they could speak to, a dream that they could finally call their own." The dream was no longer deferred. Despite its fuzziness on a hot, hazy day in August 1963, Martin Luther King Jr. had caught a glimpse of the dream in the distance. Alas, he did not live to see the dream become a clear reality. However, forty-six years later, African Americans were back on the mall en masse, front and center, fully participating in arguably *the* most important civic ritual performance in America—the president's inauguration address and the celebratory festivities that followed.

The inauguration ritual is an important function in American society because it serves to legitimate the authority of the president as leader and as high priest (Fairbanks 1981). As Robert Bellah states,

> The separation of church and state in America has not denied the politi-
> cal realm a religious dimension. Although matters of personal religious
> belief, worship, and association are considered to be strictly private
> affairs, there are, at the same time, certain common elements of reli-
> gious orientation that the great majority of Americans share. These
> have played a crucial role in the development of American institutions
> and still provide a religious dimension for the whole fabric of Ameri-
> can life, including the political sphere. This public religious dimension
> is expressed in a set of beliefs, symbols, and rituals that I am calling the
> American civil religion. The inauguration of a president is an important
> ceremonial event in this religion. It reaffirms, among other things, the
> religious legitimation of the highest political authority. (1967, 3–4)

The ritual event serves to reaffirm a sacred narration of nation grounded
in biblical metaphor that shapes the American ethos. It reiterates a myth
of origin that is based on the dual biblical themes of chosenness and conquest, and is informed by the belief that the discovery, founding, and
growth of the nation are guided by divine providence. The presidential
inauguration ceremony is the prime moment to reinforce the notion of
being that monumental "city on the hill" that God has ordained to be the
beacon of light for the entire world.

Since the interweaving of the biblical text with social meaning serves
to justify institutionalized power and the differentiation of groups based
on class, gender, and race, American civic ritual, prior to Obama's advent,
marginalized the majority of African Americans. Instead of merely participating on the periphery, African Americans developed and performed
practices that reflected their particular version of the nation's narration.[1]
For example, the public celebration speeches by blacks in the nineteenth
century recycled the biblical narratives to challenge the system of chattel
slavery, not to depict America as "the beacon of light to the nations." The
recontextualization of America's sacred narration relied on a Euro-American calendar of events, yet transformed and reordered the civic rituals in
both function and meaning.

---

1. Performative practice is defined as a repetitious, recursive strategy in which
people, not necessarily unified in their beliefs or by their willingness to be represented
by the national identity, take part in producing national culture differently through the
integration with, or the enunciation of, the national story or identity. See Bhaba 1994.
Also see Runions 2002.

Therefore, the African American sacred narration is a counternarration to a racist ethos that is also grounded in biblical imagery and was first articulated by the enslaved and free descendants of Africans as a means for "talking back." The mimicking or copying of the rhetorical tools of their oppressors thoroughly mocked the Euro-American self-construction. By learning to speak the alien tongue, they were able to claim a level of power within the context of domination. In possessing a shared language, a shared culture, they were able to construct new cultural identities and find a means to create political and communal solidarity (hooks 1994, 170). Through the strategic use of this rhetorical device, the community slowly morphed into ambivalent African Americans, inaugurating a double-consciousness construct that would be the hallmark of their cultural identity—a cultural identity that simultaneously adopts and adapts, embraces and resists, mimics and mocks, the dominant American ethos.

The African American sacred narration has been revised and retold in various ways and dimensions in response to significant communal events that have occurred throughout the centuries. This particular watershed moment in history, in which there is a mass participation of African Americans in the civic ritual performance of the status quo, signals: (1) a key point for renarration and thus reshaping communal identity, and (2) a shift in the dominant social paradigm. Barack Obama's rise as president of the United States signifies that a growing segment of the African American community is weaving a niche in the inner fabric of American sociopolitical and economic structures.

New Challenges for the African American Community

The Scripture verse that Obama alluded to in his 2009 inaugural address, 1 Cor 13:11, served to re-present the nation's sacred narration. He said:

> We remain a young nation, but in the words of Scripture, the time has come to set aside childish things. The time has come to reaffirm our enduring spirit; to choose our better history; to carry forward that precious gift, that noble idea, passed on from generation to generation: the God-given promise that all are equal, all are free, and all deserve a chance to pursue their full measure of happiness. (Obama 2009)

Of course, the idea of transformation must inevitably be orated in light of such a major development in American political history. He continued on,

For we know that our patchwork heritage is a strength, not a weakness. We are a nation of Christians and Muslims, Jews and Hindus—and non-believers. We are shaped by every language and culture, drawn from every end of this Earth; and because we have tasted the bitter swill of civil war and segregation, and emerged from that dark chapter stronger and more united, we cannot help but believe that the old hatreds shall someday pass; that the lines of tribe shall soon dissolve; that as the world grows smaller, our common humanity shall reveal itself; and that America must play its role in ushering in a *new era of peace.*[2]

Here Obama signifies the African American counternarration that challenged the Euro-American myth of origin, provoking and challenging America into realizing the potential of an American dream that benefits all. Yet he also transformed the tradition by extending it past the narrow confines of simply a black and white America. His narration included voices that have been excluded, but have always influenced the story in extremely important ways. Obama's narration of nation pointed to a new direction that America is moving toward: it alluded to the fact that the African American and other communities will continue to make great strides in the future.

However, with this shift in the paradigm that provides such potential for increasingly larger numbers of African Americans to play important roles in forging a more equal and just society for a greater number of citizens, there also is the potential for increasingly large numbers of African Americans to get caught up in the prevalent status quo and to neglect the need to continue to challenge an ethos that is founded on hierarchical racial, ethnic, class, and gender categories. At this pivotal moment, when, the narrative has at last reached the twist in the plot, will the new story line be a disappointing repetition of the old? Will the community comply with the dominant ethos and simply construct another group as the epitome "other" in order to fill the void that has been made by their advancement? Will the counternarration eventually collapse into a myth of origin that no longer mocks the dominant narration, but instead mimics it by affirming social stratification resulting in inequality, economic exploitation and injustice?[3]

---

2. Obama 2009, emphasis added. The last two lines echo the sentiment of the Pax Romana, except the world is getting smaller in Obama's rhetorical spin and with Augustus the world was expanding.

3. I posit that Barack Obama's second inauguration speech (2013) hints at the

In order to avoid this potential peril, I suggest that African American biblical scribes must continue to expose the community to what lurks in the darkness by challenging and provoking the dominant system, and to become more diligent in cautioning the community to the subtle adherence of the oppressive elements of the dominant culture. In this way, scholars will better represent the inherent ambivalence of African American identity. The task of the African American biblical scribe in the twenty-first century and beyond is to open the eyes of the community to the challenges and pitfalls involved in accommodating to a social, political, and economic system that is founded on social inequality, exploitation, and an unfair distribution of wealth.

It is this potential danger inherent in the shift in the African American matrix that serves as the motivation to produce an African American reading of the book of Revelation that addresses the broader issues, concerns, and challenges that the African American community must encounter and overcome in the twenty-first century.

I will attempt to take on this challenge in my implementation of an African American scripturalization of Revelation that is undergirded by the theoretical concepts of Henry Louis Gates Jr.'s signifyin(g) (Gates 1988), cultural memory (Halbwachs 1975; Nora 1989), and postcolonial theory (Bhabha 1994) to suggest that John's colonized, hybridized construction as "almost the same but not quite like" the colonizer (Roman Empire) has resulted in a blurred copy of the colonizer that is made evident by his mimicry of certain aspects of imperial culture, behavior, and manners.

An important aspect of John's signifyin(g) strategy relies on shaping the cultural memory of his community as he connects the past with the present and the future. Thus the images he conjures both allude to and signify on the various power structures of the ancient past, as well as the axis of power in his day, the Roman Empire. However, I will argue that John's signifyin(g) is a contradiction because he seemed to have simply reconfigured and reenacted imperial policy/propaganda to establish his future Christian empire called the new Jerusalem. His signifyin(g) remained fixated on constructing

---

collapsing of a narrative that no longer mocks the dominant narration but accommodates or mimics the prevalent American ethos. His rhetorical strategy for the second inauguration speech places emphasis on a people who once existed as half slave and half free (or black and white), who are now unified as "We, the People," and who are committed to a sacred narration of manifest destiny that presents the United States as the leader of the free world. See ch. 3 below for the fleshing out of this argument.

an ethos established by cycles of war, conquest, and revolt; and paralleled by cycles of worship, ritual, and mythmaking.

I argue that John's mimicry of the ideological assumptions and methods of constructing empire is due, to a certain degree, to his being a member of a society that demanded participation in the rituals of empire. Ritual performance caused participants to connect with imperial codes, implicitly and explicitly, that, in turn, modified their behavior. In addition, I suggest that John's denial of his own ambivalent, hybrid construction, his repression or nonrealization of his own fragmentation, his own double-consciousness, may be the cause for his contradictory stance toward empire.

I hope that this volume will also contribute generally to a New Testament scholarship that is presently preoccupied with negotiating the meaning of the biblical texts in relation to the context of imperial Rome as, for example, the numerous works by Richard Horsley on Paul and empire, and the relatively new discipline of postcolonial biblical criticism attest.[4] These works have been extremely important in highlighting the imperial ideology embedded in the texts, aptly illustrating similar resistant strategies employed by ancient and modern colonized communities, and persuasively positing the texts as a subversion of the imperial agenda. However, there is a significant lack in the scholarship that explicitly investigates the intricacies involved in the construction of a colonized, or "double-consciousness," identity that is the result of the contact between unequal political powers. Therefore, in this volume I attempt to respond to that need by analyzing how John the Seer's colonized identity is constructed by images of empire in the book of Revelation through the lens of an African American scripturalization supplemented by postcolonial theory.

MAPPING THE PROJECT

In chapter 1 I discuss the academic interpretive task known as African American biblical hermeneutics that emerged as a subfield in biblical studies as a result of the black power/black liberation movements in the 1970s (Brown 2004, 16–17). Although the methodological approaches of

---

4. See, e.g., Horsley 1997, 2003, 2006; Carter 2001, 2008; Runions 2002; Moore and Segovia 2007. See ch. 2 below for a fuller discussion.

African American biblical exegetes are diverse and vary from the modern method of historical criticism and all that the approach entails—source criticism, redaction criticism, rhetorical criticism—to the postmodern methods of reader-response, deconstruction, ideological criticism, and so on, their point of departure is set in a particular hermeneutical key. African American biblical hermeneuts are mainly interpreters of liberation whose overall objectives are: (1) to expose and confront Eurocentric ideological interpretations, (2) to recover the presence of blackness in the biblical texts, and (3) to articulate liberation from a history of dominant interpretations that have been instrumental in the oppression/suppression of African Americans (Brown 2004, 20–22).

However, many African American biblical scholars, particularly womanist biblical scholars, do not adopt a homogeneous articulation of liberation from an overtly oppressive sociopolitical system since (1) greater numbers of African Americans are moving into positions of political and economic power, and (2) overt oppression is becoming much more subtle as it moves more and more underground. Because of these shifts in the sociopolitical ethos, more complex enunciations of the biblical story must be produced in order to better address the intricacy of an entangled cultural identity. Therefore, in this chapter I will discuss the need for a reconfiguration of African American biblical hermeneutics that addresses the broader dimensions of identity formation.

Thus the second section of chapter 1 situates African American scholars in a global community of cultural-critical scholars who emphasize the importance of contemporary social location in the production of meaning. A comprehensive examination of the cultural-critical paradigm is made in juxtaposition to the historical-critical paradigm, analyzing and critiquing the dominant approach to biblical scholarship. I will then propose a renaming of African American biblical hermeneutics/interpretation to that of "African American scripturalization." The change in name signifies a shift in the discipline's approach that allows for a fuller representation of the diversity and complexity of African American identities. In this chapter I introduce the concept of cultural memory to the proposal as being useful in moving past the understanding of a homogeneous or monolithic communal identity formation because the remembrance of the distant past as held by a people depends on a given social and historical context (see Halbwachs 1975; Nora 1989). Thus I develop the idea of African American scripturalization as a site of memory, both a receptacle and carrier of cultural memory.

The third section of the chapter discusses the theorization of an African American reading strategy as suggested by Vincent Wimbush that is influenced by Henry Louis Gates Jr.'s articulation of "signifyin(g)." Although the concept can take on a broad dimension, signifyin(g), according to Gates, is rhetorical indirection, doubling, figuration, pastiche, parody, and irony that is made evident when one speaker or writer repeats another's structure by a fairly exact repetition of a given narrative or rhetorical structure. (For example, the African American sacred narration can be said to be "signifyin[g]" on the American narration of nation. This example will be fully fleshed out in ch. 3.) The notion of signifyin(g) is particularly applicable to the reading of Revelation as it is obvious that all of the above rhetorical devices can be clearly illustrated throughout this text.

The last section of the chapter revisits the work of four African American biblical scribes—Charles Copher, Cain Hope Felder, Vincent Wimbush, and Cheryl Kirk-Duggan—whose approaches represent the versatility of African American scripturalization, which ranges from corrective historical criticism to a contemporary cultural engagement with the biblical narratives.

In chapter 2 I examine the development of postcolonial studies, discuss its potential as a supplementation to African American scripturalization, and provide an overview of postcolonial theory as conceptualized by Edward Said, Gayatri Spivak, and Homi Bhabha. Bhabha's postcolonial theoretical concepts of hybridity, ambivalence, and mimicry will set the hermeneutical key for the African American scripturalization of Revelation. His theoretical gestures will serve to articulate a cultural location of the in-between space, which refers to the site of conflict, interaction, and mutual assimilation that involves every encounter between cultures. According to Bhabha, this is a site of negotiation that can be either "consensual or conflictual as it confounds our definition of tradition and estranges any immediate access to an originary identity or a 'received tradition'" (1994, 3). Therefore, I will illustrate that cultures can never be defined independently because of this continual exchange that produces mutual representation of cultural difference. Supplementing postcolonial theory with the African American engagement with the Bible reveals that domination never involves the simple imposition of one culture onto another, but is a constantly shifting space that creates possibilities for subversion and collusion (Bhabha 1994, 5). Bhabha's theoretical language will aid in displacing the notion of a homogenized communal identity and assist in evincing the complexity of identity construction. I will argue that the fusion of postcolonial theory with African American scripturalization blends smoothly in ironing out the knotty dimensions of a double-consciousness hermeneutical tradition. Both disciplines are interested in: (1) attempting to explore issues of re-presentation, essentialism, and nationalism; (2) providing alternative enunciations of the myth of origin; (3) critiquing how the West uses the concept of the Other and vice versa in the construction of identity; and (4), with reference to womanists and postcolonial feminists, critiquing patriarchy as it aligns with the imperial agenda, including white feminist ideology. Both disciplines enhance one another. Whereas postcolonial theory contributes to African American scripturalization by resituating it out of its local cultural context and placing it into a broader global conversation, African American scripturalization is ideally situated to address issues in relation to the (neo)imperial practices of the United States that postcolonial theory presently does but rarely, choosing instead to limit the discipline mainly to aspects of British imperialism/colonization.

In chapter 3 I provide a comprehensive cartography of the development of the African American narration of nation, which is presented as an emancipatory act of double-consciousness, a bifocal vision that revolves around a countermemory. I will suggest that the praxis is, paradoxically, an ambivalent yet sustaining praxis that constructs a positive identity while enunciating a dissent with the American ethos. I will illustrate that this communal tradition began in early colonial and antebellum periods when the enslaved and disenfranchised African's appropriation of Christian Scripture was used to carve out the creation of an internal space of value and order while simultaneously creating a suitable outlet of protest and indignation toward an external, chaotic world. While the early Euro-Americans' identification with the exodus story focused on the success of freedom of the Israelites from Egyptian rule, the enslaved African, being a few pages back in the story, focused on the hope of freedom from a cruel oppression. As the early Euro-Americans have escaped from Egypt and are now on an errand of destiny to (control) the "promised" land, the enslaved Africans' construction countered with the Joseph story, accusing the early Euro-Americans of selling their fellow brothers and sisters into a destiny of chattel slavery. Biblical rhetoric and allusion, whether expressed in song, sermon, or speech, served to sustain human dignity and to protect the honor of the enslaved Africans as they denounced an inhumane sociopolitical system. I maintain that the African American hermeneutical tradition is a hybrid hermeneutic that simultaneously mimics and mocks the Euro-American hermeneutical tradition. It is a signifyin(g) tradition that is produced as a result of an ambivalent identity construction that, in turn, narrates a national myth that differs from the dominant version. Whereas Euro-Americans view the American myth as being realized, the African American's narration of nation provokes and challenges America into realizing the potential of an American myth that benefits all.

In chapter 4 I apply the concepts of African American scripturalization to the general observations on the book of Revelation to illustrate how this approach opens the text to a broader analysis. This is a vital step because the standard scholarship on Revelation that is based on the historical-critical paradigm must be deconstructed. I adamantly maintain that if this is not done, standard scholarship will muffle the perspective of an African American scriptualization. Therefore, in this chapter, using a call-and-response format (with the call being the standard scholarship perspective and the response being that of an African American scripturalization approach), I examine the text in order to illustrate that John's signifyin(g) on the Roman Empire attempts to construct a narration of nation as a response to a people's cultural memory that has been traumatized during years of bondage and continued discrimination. However, John's hybrid construction disallows him from disconnecting from an oppressive ethos that has become part of his identity construction. John seemingly is split between an urge toward Christianity—conceived in cultural terms—and the continued presence of imperial ideas. John is affected by the complexities of identity construction in the ancient world that are produced by the double movement of shifting away from "Roman" constructions while simultaneously shifting toward (re)appropriating the ideological, theological, linguistic, and textual forms of Roman imperial power. The chapter will examine John's mimicry of the ideological processes of empire, in spite of his fierce nonaccommodating stance toward the participation in the imperial cult, the religio-political system that divinely sanctioned the Roman Empire.

In chapter 5 I will attempt to illustrate the more complex dimensions of a marginalized identity by analyzing the images of the heavenly throne room scenes throughout the text in general, and in Revelation 4 and 5 in particular, to argue that John's reinscription of imperial ideology is evident by his mere transference of imperial ritual to the heavenly sphere. John's reuse of imperial rituals that have supported an oppressive imperial ideology results in continued marginalization. Therefore, I contend that the exploitative sociopolitical tactics of empire are transferred into yet another symbolic order sustained by ritual performance. I compare the work of Brian Blount and Clarice Martin on Revelation to my approach in order to highlight the difference between an African American interpretation driven by the concepts of black liberation theology and an African American scripturalization underscored by postcolonial theory. Blount's work applies African American religious and sociopolitical circumstances to the reading of Revelation (2005a, 2009a). His reading contends that Revelation was written out of the context of a suffering community that is forced to assimilate into an oppressive society. Martin (2005) performs a womanist critique of ancient Roman slavery and imperial ideology through the lens of the African American experience and compares the seer's fierce rhetorical responses to those of the Signifying Monkey, who uses language tropes with defiance in order to subvert the domination of the Lion's hegemonic claims to powers. However, to date, few African American scholars have yet to apply a sustained postcolonial theoretical analysis to their interpretive task that will allow for a broader engagement of the Bible from multifaceted communal locations (S. Smith 2014).

In chapter 6 I conclude the work by discussing the implications of this African American scripturalization of Revelation.

1

AFRICAN AMERICAN SCRIPTURALIZATION: SIGNIFYIN(G) AND CULTURAL MEMORY

Deep down in the jungle so they say
There's a signifying monkey down the way
There hadn't been no disturbin' in the jungle for quite a bit
For up jumped the monkey in the tree one day and laughed
"I guess I'll start some shit."

— Henry Louis Gates Jr., *The Signifying Monkey*

The Indian resists curiosity by a stony silence. The Negro offers a feather-bed resistance. That is, we let the probe enter, but it never comes out. It gets smothered under a lot of laughter and pleasantries. The theory behind our tactics: "The white man is always trying to know into somebody else's business. All right, I'll set something outside the door of my mind for him to play with and handle. He can read my writing but he sho' can't read my mind. I'll put this play toy in his hand, and he will seize it and go away. Then I'll say my say and sing my song."

— Zora Neale Hurston, *Mules and Men*

INTRODUCTION

African American biblical scholars generally engage in a hermeneutical key that is, to use a term first made popular by Edward Said, *contrapuntal*[1] to the Euro-American ideological framework. Thus the primary objective of African American biblical scholars is to analyze the texts as a corrective to a discipline that privileges a Euro-American epistemology and ethos. These interpreters typically aim to counter Euro-American biblical

---

1. *Contrapuntal* is a term that Said used to convey a manner of reading that aims to "give emphasis and voice to what is silent or marginally present or ideologically represented" (1993, 66). I further discuss this term and its limitations in ch. 2.

scholarship by: (1) exposing oppressive white supremacist interpretations, (2) recovering the presence of blackness in the biblical texts that has been eradicated by Euro-American scholarship, and (3) reconstructing a history of dominant interpretations that have been instrumental in the oppression of African Americans. In approaching this task, African American biblical scholars have mainly adhered to a hermeneutic of liberation, striving to revive a diasporan community that has been burdened by displacement, slavery, disenfranchisement, marginalization, and persistent racism.

African American biblical hermeneutics with its focus on liberation hermeneutics has made vital contributions to the biblical guild based on the use of this emancipatory framework. This is particularly the case when liberation hermeneutics is fused with complementary theoretical and methodological approaches that effectively reflect new forms of relevant and constructive praxis. Thus the field is extremely "interdisciplinary friendly," which allows for the cultivation of a vast analytical repertoire.[2] In addition to the resources of black liberation theology and womanist theology, ideological criticism, narrative criticism, African American literary criticism, African American history and religious studies, postmodern criticism, and postcolonial theory are just a few of the methodological tools that complement this scribal activity.

A variety of methods are used because scholars recognize that there is an increasing need to better address the complexity of cultural identity. As a segment of the community continues to move steadily into the center of American society, scholars are aware of the potential of that group's estrangement from within the community as well as the possibility of discrimination against other groups that are deemed to be less powerful. African American biblical scholars recognize the necessity of expanding their objectives in response to these compelling challenges in order to continue to be productive and meaningful voices. This, of course, does

---

2. The versatility of African American biblical scholars is evident by a glance at any SBL annual conference program. In addition to their own sessions on African American biblical hermeneutics, where scholars showcase their interpretive abilities focusing on cultural location in which they utilize a variety of multidisciplinary approaches, these scholars also participate in the broader sessions that focus on the more traditional historical exegeting of specific biblical texts. In these general sessions, African American scholars often frame their analysis to be more consistent with the expectation of a wider audience. This hermeneutical flexibility displays the "double" location of the African American biblical scholar.

not mean to advocate for a postliberation or postracial sentiment, that the two great beasts of American society—racism and sexism—are no longer threats. What this does mean, however, is that African American biblical scholars are very aware that they will be held accountable for the community's falling sway to the more subtle tactics of the beast of classism by failing to address a fuller scope of African American identity construction. This chapter, therefore, is a call for the reframing of African American biblical hermeneutics that addresses the broader dimensions of cultural identity without forsaking the key issues and concerns of African American biblical scholars on race and gender.

The Establishment of the Cultural Studies Paradigm

Beginning in the early 1980s, an influx of scholars of color and women besieged the well-fortified walls of the biblical guild. These scholars spearheaded an "other" way of reading text by utilizing a variety of critical reading strategies that focused on contemporary cultural context and social location being influenced by the two reading approaches that had emerged in the discipline in the 1970s—literary criticism and sociocultural criticism.[3] Social-scientific criticism makes use of models of the social sciences, notably sociology and cultural anthropology. Both of these criticisms offered significant alternative approaches to historical biblical criticism, the traditional paradigm of biblical scholarship.

The fresh array of scholars that entered the field at the end of the twentieth century challenged the historical-critical method by claiming that it lacked theoretical sophistication. The method's requirement of only a practical expertise resulted in an inadequate analytical orientation. In addition, historical critics failed to display a self-reflection on how their approach conformed to or differed from literary criticism since the artifacts they excavated were textual.

Thus the cultural-critical paradigm was established based on the interrelationship between the text and—in the words of Fernando F.

---

3. Literary criticism makes use of a variety of methods drawn from literary theory, contemporary rhetorical theory, structuralism, deconstruction, psychoanalytic theory, and reader-response criticism, approaches that tend to give priority to the role of the reader in the construction of meaning. The social-scientific method treats the biblical text as a cultural product in which inscribed social and cultural codes are decoded in order to reconstruct the world behind the text.

Segovia, one of the leading pioneers of this paradigm—"real" or "flesh-and-blood readers" (Segovia 1995b, 9, 10).[4] This explicit focus on social location shifted the discipline from the exclusive gaze of Western male theologians/scholars that defined the historical-critical method as "discerning" the truth by neutral observation and as *the* way of interpreting the biblical texts.

A Discussion via Juxtaposition:
Historical Criticism and Cultural Criticism

Through the several methods that constitute the historical-critical paradigm (source criticism, form criticism, redaction criticism, tradition criticism, and textual criticism), historical-critical scholars perform a thorough excavation of textual artifacts in their various languages, gathering an extensive collection of the historical data available regarding authorship and specific time and place of composition. Historical scholars believe that only by the rigorous application of the various methods mentioned above can a meaning be reproduced that is univocal and value-free.

Adherents of the cultural-critical paradigm are extremely ambivalent about this learned and extensively detailed paradigm that never explicitly ventures beyond the horizon of the original audience (Segovia 1995a, 11). They are wary of the paradigm's primary interest in discerning the theological meaning embedded in the text without comprehensively weighing the complex sociopolitical agendas, concerns, and issues that lurk in the shadow of the text's message. For cultural-critical scholars, this points to the fact that the historical paradigm is a biased excavation. This is made evident by the selection of material that the historical-critical scholar chooses to focus on from the vast amount of historical data available. The claim of an objective historical criticism is, in fact, a camouflaged subjectivity.

This camouflaged subjectivity was greatly informed by Friedrich Schleiermacher's philosophical hermeneutics, an Enlightenment-influenced contribution based on the mode of reconstruction and integration

---

4. No work by a biblical scholar, especially a scholar of color, interested in cultural biblical criticism can avoid referencing Fernando F. Segovia, Oberlin Graduate Professor of New Testament and Early Christianity at Vanderbilt Divinity School in Nashville, Tennessee. His two seminal essays on social location and biblical interpretation are 1995a and 1995b. See also Bailey et al. 2009, 3–43.

of the reader (Waetjen 1995, 77; see Thiselton 1992, 204). Schleiermacher's main distinction was the suggestion that interpretation is an "art of under-standing," an act of living, feeling, and intuiting being human. It is both a comparative and an intuitive/divinatory activity combining the objective, grammatical operation of moving from the part to the whole and the subjective/psychological reconstruction of the author's thought. That is, the finished expression, the grammatical expression, is penetrated by the interpreter, and the intellect and psyche of the author are reconstructed. In addition, if identification with the original audience is possible, then the interpreter knows everything that is necessary to reproduce an objective meaning (Schleiermacher 1998, vii). According to Schleiermacher, only by "deadening ourselves" can the reconstructed composition take place. He suggested the ability to intuit the mind of another because there is a commonality, an affinity, between the author and the interpreter.[5]

Cultural-critical scholars unmask the historical-critical goal of reproduction by revealing that: (1) we can never "deaden ourselves" in order to "transform ourselves into another person" because (2) we live in the world of the present, not the past, and (3) we bring to the text certain preconceptions and presuppositions; furthermore, (4) these preconceptions/presuppositions are consequences of our particular cultural and social location; therefore, (5) it is inevitable that the cultural/social location will inform the production of meaning, and so (6) historical interpreters can, at best, merely reconstruct the *possibilities* of the ancient writer's preconceptions/presuppositions *and* only by way of a contemporary historical mediation.[6]

---

5. Central to Schleiermacher's theory is the linguistic nature of communication in general. There is no understanding without language. Language falls into a combination of general patterns—grammatical (the objective aspect) and psychological (the subjective aspect). The principle upon which Schleiermacher's articulation rests is that of the hermeneutical circle. Understanding is circular. The circle as a whole defines the individual part, and the parts together form the circle. It is within this circular, dialectical relationship between the whole and the parts that meaning emerges. Therefore, the hermeneutical circle requires an attempt on the part of the interpreter to position himself or herself with the author, and at the same time to distance himself or herself from the author in order to make new sense of the text or utterance in the context of the linguistic system.

6. This is exactly how the ancient writers constructed meaning. For instance, the authors of the Gospel narratives shaped Jesus' activity around their own immediate imperial context in relation to their community's experience of imperial domination.

Cultural-critical scholars argue that "any text that has been separated from its original context and subsequently has become a piece of universal tradition requires integration into the readers' contemporary situation" (Waetjen 1995, 78).[7] In other words, because a "flesh-and-blood" reading activity involves living in the present as well as reading the past—a reading based on doubling, one might say—cultural context and social location must necessarily factor in when constructing meaning. Thus historical mediation is based on a direct application to contemporary context. The particular meaning uncovered will be directly related to a contemporary reality that is in "partnership" or "solidarity" with the ancient text. In this way, the ancient biblical text is thrust forward into another horizon that is influenced by the cultural specificity of the interpreter. The recasting of the text is indicative of the text's capacity in every age to satisfy individual and communal yearning.

The development of the cultural-critical paradigm and the multiple reading strategies this paradigm supports—contextual hermeneutics, feminist interpretation, deconstructive criticism, ideological criticism, postcolonial criticism, and various combinations of the above—signifies an unraveling of prevailing Western philosophical thought. This shift dismantles the reductive tendency of the historical-critical paradigm and unleashes a multitude of compelling and potentially transformative meanings. The result of approaching the text by way of cultural and social location is an enhanced understanding of the work Scripture does in constructing communities and individuals as new meanings are produced based on the propositions of the cultural-critical paradigm.

THE PARADOX OF CULTURAL-CRITICAL SCHOLARSHIP

One must acknowledge, however, that despite the vital contributions of cultural-critical scholarship, the historical-critical paradigm continues to strike the major hermeneutical key in North American/European biblical scholarship. Therefore, many cultural-critical scholars continue to employ the prevailing methods that define biblical studies. However, when these methods are adapted strategically and used in conversation

---

7. Although this articulation is similar to Hans-Georg Gadamer's integration, the emphasis of the term when applied to a cultural hermeneutic is not on the unveiling of a single, objective true meaning, but on the possibility of the construction of multiple meanings.

with interdisciplinary theories and models, the reductive assumptions are countered. This is particularly the case for the pioneers of the cultural-critical paradigm, whose scholarly socialization was, in large part, dependent on employing the historical-critical model as an exegetical device—and to some extent, this continues to hold true to this day, although with somewhat more creativity due to a wider reception of the interrelationship between text and context and the incorporation of theoretical models in historical biblical scholarship.

Lifting Our Voices: African American Biblical Scholarship

African American biblical scholars share a common cultural context that informs their reading of the biblical texts—a collective cultural memory of what I term "the strangeness of home." By this I mean a communal experience of institutionalized marginalization by a society that sanctioned a racist and sexist ideology as its dominant ethos while it simultaneously conceived itself as a "democratic" nation.

According to Hebrew Bible scholar Leslie R. James, the intention of African American biblical scholars is to disclose "the role of the Bible in the cause of Black freedom, humanization, identity reconstruction, agency, culture, economic and political self-determination and sovereignty, nation building, and integration" (2010, 15). Thus, as mentioned above, the critical framework of African American scholarship focuses on the identification of biblical passages that have special relevance to the community, the identification of biblical passages that have been used to keep the community in a marginal location, and the need for further attention to the history of interpretation within African American religious and cultural traditions (Bailey 2003, 1).

Womanist Biblical Hermeneutics

Although this monograph's discussion applies to the field of African American biblical scholarship as a whole, it is appropriate here to mention womanist biblical hermeneutics, the disciplinary area in which African American female scholars explore issues and concerns that are important to women of African descent.[8] Although African American women

---

8. The term *womanist* was coined by Alice Walker (particularly 1983). The term

adhere to the main objectives of the discipline, they include the analysis of gender and class, in addition to race, in their work. As Clarice Martin states, "African American women's struggles comprise the constitutive elements in their conceptual and interpretive horizon and hermeneutics for experiences of oppression, like all human experience, affect the way in which women code and decode sacred and secular reality" (1990, 42; see Weems 1991; Jones-Warsaw 1994; Gafney 2006; St. Clair 2007). Womanist scholars strive to unmask the specific agendas, cultural biases, ideological motivations, and political influences that produced the texts in their final form, as well as the history of interpretation that accompanies these texts by the modern reader.

Howard Thurman's grandmother, an ex-slave, serves as a good example of womanist interpretation:

> "During the days of slavery," she said, "the master's minister would occasionally hold services for the slaves. Also, the white minister used as his text something from Paul. 'Slaves be obedient to them that are your masters … as unto Christ.' Then he would go on to show how, if we were good and happy slaves, Christ would bless us. I promised my Maker that if I ever learned to read, and if freedom ever came, I would not read that part of the Bible." (Thurman 1949, 30–31)

Womanist scholars represent the voice of women who have experienced discrimination in the dominant society and in their own community. In addition, womanist scholars tend to voice a wider concern for advocating just treatment for all members of marginalized communities, not just for peoples of African descent.

Black Liberation Theology as Theological Impetus for African American Biblical Scholarship

It is the fundamental principles of black liberation theology as conceptualized by James Cone that influence African American biblical interpretation,

---

is meant to connote the audacious behavior of African American women. Womanist theology as conceived by Kate Cannon, Jacqueline Grant, and Delores Williams has played an extremely influential role for womanist biblical scholars. See Cannon 1985; Grant 1989; D. Williams 1987. Williams's seminal work (1993) focuses on the Hebrew Bible characterization of Hagar as a typology of the experience of African American women. See also Townes 1993.

especially in its nascent stage, including to a certain extent womanist biblical hermeneutics. Black liberation theology was conceived as a response to the sociopolitical circumstances of the African American community in the 1960s. The theology contends that European and American cultures have corrupted Christianity, and the result is a mainstream faith-based empire that serves its own interests, not God's. Black liberation theology asks whose side God should be on—the side of the oppressed or the side of the oppressors.

The theology is doubly influenced by the ideals of the mainstream, integrationist civil rights movement and the radical, nationalistic thoughts of the black power movement. The black power movement (1966) grew out of the civil rights movement that had steadily gained momentum through the 1950s and 1960s. Many young African Americans considered the civil rights movement as an important contribution toward equality in racial status, yet held the suspicion that the movement was geared too much toward embracing Euro-American sensibilities and ideology. For years, the leaders claimed, blacks had been trying to aspire to white ideals of what they should be. The time had come for blacks to set their own agenda, putting their needs and aspirations first. This meant reclaiming African heritage and embracing African diasporic cultural traditions.

Kwame Touré (né Stokely Carmichael), a founder of the black power movement, and his coauthor Charles Hamilton commented that in an age of decolonization, the situation of Africans in America should be considered as a unique case of internal colonialism: "black people in this country form a colony, and it is not in the interests of the colonial power to liberate them.... They stand as colonial subjects in relation to the white society. Thus institutional racism has another name: colonialism" (Carmichael and Hamilton 1967, 5). Therefore, they considered liberation not only as the fight against racism and white supremacy, but also as the struggle for freedom from colonialism.

The formation of the black power movement marked a division in the ideological grounding of the communal quest for liberation from an oppressive system. While both movements of the 1960s developed their strategies on the issue of race and social inequality in the United States, the black power movement urged the need for African Americans to close ranks before entering the open society. In addition, the black power movement expressed a strong hermeneutic of suspicion toward Western Christianity, as it was understood to be just another form of legitimating white supremacy. Cone acknowledges that the black power movement "forced black clergy to raise the theological question about the relation between black faith and white religion," and that "black power shook black clergy out of their theological complacency" (1986, 105).

The different ideological strategies of these two integral yet opposite movements is a key illustration that the political maneuverings within the African American community are based on the complexity and ambiguity of a fragmented identity construct. Both movements in one way or another addressed the double-consciousness (or ambivalent) nature of African American identity, an identity that is simultaneously resistant to a racist nation, yet also embracing the potential benefits that nation has to offer.[9] Black liberation theology attempts to reconcile the ideological impetus of both movements in its theological construction.

Basing his logic on a binary opposition, which is the hallmark of the Western way of knowing, Cone posits that if racism is the negative social issue that the theology investigates, then an affirmation of African American humanity is its obvious counterpoint. So, within the confines of the contemporary African American experience of oppression, black liberation theologians articulate the effects/affects of racism on the lives, psyches, and spirits of African Americans (Brown 2004, 16–17).

The theology is dependent on the appropriation of the biblical narratives, particularly the Gospel narratives, as the basis for its articulation on issues of oppression and social injustice. In its nascence, black liberation theology had been relatively effective in the use of African American traditions as a source for theological construction; however, it had not been nearly as effective in the incorporation of the biblical narratives. This is because when black liberation theology made its debut in the scholarly arena there were only a handful of African American biblical scholars. The lack of African Americans in the biblical field exposed a deficit in black liberation theology's objectives. Because of its double nature as a Christian theology in which there is an intermingling of contemporary and ancient contexts, there was a vital necessity for African American biblical scholars to take part in this theological-cultural-political enterprise. Thus a small cadre of biblical scholars began to engage the implications of black liberation theology beginning in the early 1980s.[10] Since

---

9. See Cone 1991. He details the double nature of African American identity through the analysis of the religio-political thinking of Martin Luther King Jr. and Malcolm X.

10. Although Leon Wright is believed to have been the first African American to

then, biblical scholars have vocalized more than ever before their understandings of what it means to be African American and Christian (see
Bailey 2010; Myers 1991; Weems 1991).

Cain Hope Felder describes the concerns of these scholars in the
introduction of the seminal volume on African American biblical hermeneutics, *Stony the Road We Trod: African American Biblical Interpretation*:

> Having traveled the "long road" of being trained and credentialed to teach
> Bible in higher education, African American scholars have testimonies
> of record that are at times disturbing and at other times exhilarating.
> These testimonies inform the ranging presuppositions of their writings.
> They are collected here with a memory of how all the authors individu-
> ally survived variegated assaults upon their history, identity, and sense
> of integrity as African Americans trying to make sense of the history of
> biblical interpretation as well as their evolving socio-political context in
> a nation invariably resistant to their highest social ideals. (Felder 1991, 3)

Exploring ways in which they could assist the cause of black liberation,
African American biblical scholars began to articulate the primary objectives of an emancipatory reading of Scripture and began interpreting the
text as a corrective to a method that privileges a Euro-American epistemology and ethos.[11]

A Lacuna in African American Biblical Hermeneutics/Interpretation

I suggest that the time has come for the hermeneutical approach to be
more intentional in exposing the broader dimensions of African American identity and with it the broader cultural challenges of the community.

---

receive the doctorate in New Testament, graduating from Howard University in 1945,
the number of African Americans presently in the field of biblical studies is still relatively small. Out of six thousand full members of SBL, fewer than a hundred are African American. And although their numbers almost tripled from twenty-six in 1995 to
approximately eighty in 2013, there are only eleven women with a doctorate in New
Testament and Early Christian Origins. See Bailey 2000, 707, for a listing of scholars,
including the institutions that trained them, as of 2000. See appendix to Blount 2009b,
559–60, which provides an up-to-date listing of African Americans who hold doctor-
ates in NT studies.

11. An examination of the work of key African American scholars is discussed in
the last section of this chapter.

African American biblical scholars need to begin taking into consideration the new challenges that African Americans face as a segment of the community progresses steadily into the center of American society. As mentioned earlier, this is certainly not to say that I advocate a postliberation or postracial sentiment. Yet I do resonate with Elonda Clay's query: "If the signifier liberation is not updated throughout changing conditions and contexts across various historical moments, does this not make the concept vulnerable to mutating into mere legitimation?" (2010, 317). Therefore, I am suggesting that African American biblical scholars may find themselves unintentionally feeding the beast if they do not broaden their inquiry. The discipline must now begin to caution the community about the potential danger of reinscription. Therefore, the time has come to reframe the reading strategy with new theoretical concepts that will allow for this articulation to be expressed.

The discussion in this chapter attempts to move toward a revitalization of African American biblical hermeneutics by: (1) renaming the enterprise; (2) purposing a reframing of the literary strategy with a theorization influenced by the work of Vincent Wimbush and by extension Henry Louis Gates Jr.; and (3) incorporating the aspects of cultural memory.[12]

Renaming African American Biblical Hermeneutics as African American Scripturalization

In an attempt to bring a fresh critical analysis to the discipline, I suggest that the first step is to rename African American biblical hermeneutics as African American scripturalization. According to Grey Gundaker, the term *scripturalization* signifies "the re-contextualization or the re-cycling of sacred text in which a community's past is remembered and its future prophetically witnessed in the present."[13] The term is derived from the understanding that a sacred text cannot be separated from its context and a community cannot be separated from its scriptures. Therefore, it

---

12. The discussion in this chapter is the first part of a two-part proposal. The second half of the proposed reconfiguration will be discussed in the following two chapters, which focus on the supplementation of postcolonial theory.

13. Gundaker 2008. In addition, see Wan 2008; Newman 1999. Newman lays out a similar definition of the term *scripturalization* in her introduction, although the term is located in an historical-critical mode and not a contemporary contextual understanding. Yet the use of the term is the same for both authors.

is through the process of scripturalization that the formation, deformation, and reformation of a community is made possible (Wimbush 2000b; Love 2000). For Vincent Wimbush, African American scripturalization as a body of commemorative action "lies not in interpretation of (the culturally overdetermined) sacred texts but in the construction and manipulation of 'world,' and of meanings in relationship to ... such texts" (Wimbush, 2000, 21–22).[14]

African American scripturalization is meant to connote this understanding directed toward a specific cultural identity. The term implies for me, therefore, a shift from the "interpretation" of texts, as the term "African American biblical hermeneutics" or "African American biblical interpretation" denotes, to the more activating sense of "writing" texts, thereby suggesting the production of a scribe whose pen is an active agent in the conceptualization and reconceptualization of a community and its praxis.

African American scripturalization signals: (1) resistance to homogenization; (2) sensitivity to patterns of imperialism, neocolonialism, and globalization; (3) a fluidity that offers a more complex theorization of identity construction (e.g., the postcolonial concepts of hybridity, ambivalence, and mimicry/mockery are extremely useful in the supplementation of this reading strategy, which will be illustrated in chaps. 2 and 3); and (4) this fluidity makes possible for a broader conversation that includes African American communities that are not necessarily situated in the conservative, mainstream black church, as well as providing a means for a wider engagement with the international field of biblical scholars. However, at the same time, the renaming continues to gesture to the field's vital contribution to biblical scholarship: the explicit focus on and critique of the dynamics of race and ethnicity in the United States.

THEORIZING AFRICAN AMERICAN SCRIPTURALIZATION

The second step to the revitalization of the discipline is to undergird it with a literary theoretical orientation. In the nascent stages of the enterprise there were no attempts to apply an African American literary theory to the reading of texts. Any such theorization would have probably been shunned by African American scribes at that time because: (1) primarily

---

14. This sense is similar to the notion of intertextuality. As Julia Kristeva claims, intertextuality is both contextual as well as textual. Just as the memory of a text is in its intertextuality, so is it for the act of scripturalization. See Kristeva 1980.

they were (and still are) clergy and theologians of the black church whose tenets include the belief that the Bible should be framed by theological concepts and not secular, abstract, literary concepts (Hoyt 1991); and (2) the texts were analyzed in the manner in which African American scribes had been taught in conservative Euro-American seminaries, albeit through a black contextual/theological lens.[15] Thus the majority of scribes leaned toward the theological and historical, and not the theoretical, in their biblical exegetical work.

However, a few scribes worked in an interdisciplinary manner in the early stages of the discipline. For instance, womanist scribes incorporated the concept of black feminist thought as developed by African American sociologist Patricia Hill Collins in their work, which continues to be an extremely provocative framework for their scripturalizing.[16] Collins's work is valuable because she understands gender, race, and class not merely as distinctive systems of oppression, but as part of an overarching, dominant structure. Following the thought of Kimberle Crenshaw, Collins positions the categories of race, class, and gender as interwoven systems of oppression. By investigating the intersectionality of race, class, and gender oppression, the focus of analysis shifts from merely describing the similarities and differences between these oppressive systems to a greater attention on how they interlace. This is a radical paradigmatic shift that allows for the domination of African American women to be understood as being structured by a system in any given sociohistorical context.

Womanists were not the only scribes to incorporate critical theory. Randall Bailey's early endeavors to produce an Afrocentric biblical interpretation used feminist biblical scholarship as a model to help him develop his emancipatory method of scripturalization (2010). From his adaptation of the feminist method, he was eventually able to develop a method of scripturalizing the African presence in the Bible as being from the "south, militarily strong, politically mighty, wealthy, wise, and the standard of valuation for ancient Israel and the Early Church" (Bailey 2010, 20). Also, the advent of ideological criticism has greatly influenced Bailey's scripturalizing, which seeks to use the African American story as a strategy for reading.

---

15. For example, the work of Charles Copher, which I discuss below.
16. See P. Collins 1990.

Bailey understands scripturalization as praxis and transformation that is central to African American scholarship. Thus he is of the opinion that postcolonial theory's focus on active involvement and transformation of the self complements the objective that is central to a scholarship that is responding to an ideology that justified slavery, disenfranchisement, and segregation (Bailey et al. 2009, 3–43). His recent work, in partnership with two scholars who are very involved in postcolonial biblical criticism, Tatsiong Benny Liew and Fernando Segovia, focuses on the development of a minority criticism in which "the crossing of racial-ethnic minority lines helps highlight the arbitrariness of race-ethnicity and hence may create a space to confound dominant racialization processes by forming an alliance that comes close to being a new racial-ethnic group" (Bailey et al. 2009, 14).

Bailey, Liew, and Segovia claim that Patricia Hill Collins's rejection of binary thinking also corresponds to the situation of racial-ethnic minorities, and they suggest that her theoretical concepts are useful in articulating a minority criticism. They write, "racial-ethnic minorities in the U.S.—going back to Du Bois's 'double consciousness'—are also amenable to accepting 'the both/and conceptual stance' that Collins highlights for and in black feminist thought" (2009, 16–17).

A broader dimension in the analysis of Scripture is also taking shape at the Institute of Signifying Scriptures (ISS), housed at Claremont Graduate University under the direction of Vincent Wimbush. Wimbush's research at ISS has branched off entirely from the hegemonic historical-critical paradigm of the biblical guild, in which, he claims, cultural critics have been held hostage for too many years. Instead, a multidisciplinary orientation that investigates the textures of Scripture expressed in various contemporary communal media is emphasized.[17] The research at ISS is an extension of the African Americans and the Bible research project that Wimbush directed at Union Theological Seminary in New York City and was grounded in a multidisciplinary approach investigating how sacred

---

17. Because of this shift in methodology, the credentials of the students in the graduate program at ISS are in religious studies, not biblical studies, although ISS presents papers at both AAR and SBL. This suggests that the hegemony of the historical-critical paradigm is still in place in the biblical guild. However, progress continues to be made in the guild—Wimbush served as SBL president in 2010. I take his appointment as an indication that this radical orientation is considered an important way of approaching texts even by way of the historical-critical method.

texts are negotiated in the construction of identity, both communal and individual. The project culminated in the African Americans and the Bible Conference in 1998, and the conference essays were published in *African Americans and the Bible: Sacred Texts and Social Textures* (Wimbush 2000a).

Wimbush's introductory essay in that volume, "Reading Darkness, Reading Scriptures," ponders how putting African Americans at the center of the study of the Bible might affect the study of the Bible. What impact might it have on the politics of the conceptualization and the structuring of the academic guild? What are the ramifications of construing the Bible on bases other than European cultural presumptions? (Wimbush 2000b, 2).

His proposal to theorize a reading strategy is an important step forward in broadening the critical dimensions of African American scripturalization. In *Theorizing Scriptures*, Wimbush calls for a general critical theorizing to assist in explicating the "little understood, seldom problematized, mystifying and occluding signs, practices, orientations, textures and power dynamics of society and culture that represent the phenomenon of 'scriptures'" (Wimbush 2008, 12–13; see also Wimbush 2012, 2013). In doing so, Wimbush advances his notion of scripturalization. He says,

> the orientation that I call for here has been inspired and made compelling by a shift in forms that I make from European–North American or "white" religio-cultural histories and experiences as the unacknowledged default template for critical analysis to … the histories and forms of expressiveness of dark, historically subaltern or subordinated peoples around the world. (Wimbush 2008, 4)

THE SIGNIFYING MONKEY TROPE OF HENRY LOUIS GATES JR.

One of the ways this different orientation approaches the scripturalizing task is to appropriate the African American literary theory of Henry Louis Gates Jr. that is centered on signifyin(g).[18] To "signify" has taken on sev-

---

18. See Gates 1988, 4. Gates chooses to spell the word in this manner to denote "black Signification" as opposed to "English signification." There is an entire series of oral narrative poems about the "signifying monkey" in the African American tradition. A general outline of the monkey's story goes like this: the lion claims to be king of the jungle, but everyone knows that the elephant is the real king. The monkey, fed up with the lion's roaring, decides to do something about it. He insults the lion

eral meanings, but generally it means to hint, to insinuate; it is a play on words with an understanding that meanings are fluid. It implies to put on an act, to agitate, to sound off, or, in African American culture, "to play the dozens." It is a contest in hyperbole.

In these conceptions, signifyin(g) sounds not too different from the traditional category of rhetoric known as "epideictic," a term used for a speech that puts the orator's gifts on display (*epideixis*). Yet, for Gates, to assimilate black signifyin(g) to the Greek or Eurocentric tradition of classical rhetoric is to lose the sense of a black difference. Therefore, he traces the concept to the Ifa tradition, the religious system of the Yoruba people, especially connecting the practice to Esu-Elegbara, the trickster figure of the Yoruba pantheon.[19] For Gates, "Thinking about the black concept of Signifyin(g) is a bit like stumbling unaware into a hall of mirrors: the sign itself appears to be doubled, at the very least, and (re)doubled upon ever closer examination" (1988, 44). Thus signifyin(g) is an act of re-presentation that is double-voiced. To account for this doubling, Gates relates "signifyin(g)" (or "black Signification") and "English signification" as two distinctly different forms that should be considered homonyms of each other. He states,

> In the extraordinarily complex relationship between the two hom-
> onyms, we both enact and recapitulate the received … confrontation
> between Afro-American culture and American culture. This confronta-
> tion is both political and metaphysical. We might profit … by thinking
> of the curiously ironic relationship between these signifiers as a con-
> frontation defined by the politics of semantics, semantics here defined
> as the study of the classification of changes in the signification of words,
> and more especially the relationships between theories of denotation
> and naming, as well as connotation and ambiguity. The relationship that

---

publicly and at length—his "mama" and his "grandmama, too"—and when the lion grows angry, the monkey shrugs that he is merely repeating what the elephant has been saying. Furious, the lion heads out to challenge the elephant, who impassively trounces him. There are several different endings of the story: the monkey either gets away with his deception or does not, but in any event he is a success at "signifyin(g)." Womanist biblical scholar Clarice Martin incorporates Gates's concept of signifyin(g) in her 2005 essay, which I review in ch. 5 below.

19. Esu-Elegbara is characterized by the qualities of satire, parody, irony, indeterminacy, open-endedness, and indirection. He mediates between the grammar of divination and its rhetorical structures. His African American descendant, the Signifying Monkey, embodies the ambiguities of language, wreaking havoc upon the signified.

> black "Signification" bears to the English "signification" is, paradoxically, a relation of difference inscribed within a relation of identity. That, it seems to me, is inherent in the nature of metaphorical substitution and the pun, particularly those rhetorical tropes dependent on the repetition of a word with a change denoted by a difference in sound or in a letter … and in homonymic puns…. These tropes luxuriate in the chaos of ambiguity that repetition and difference … yield in either an aural or a visual pun. (Gates 1988, 45)

Indirection, doubling, figuration, pastiche, parody, and irony, as signifyin(g)'s most salient features, are made evident when one speaker or writer repeats another's structure by a fairly exact repetition of a given narrative or rhetorical structure.[20]

When applying Gates's rhetorical suggestions to the notion of African American scripturalization, one sees the biblical narratives, then, as constructing a new language as dictated by the syntactical rules inherent in the new language. As Sze-Kar Wan notes, "if scripture is double and multivoiced, and if a canonical text achieves an excess of meaning by means of signification, the meaning of scripture must by definition be indeterminate; if it is scripture at all, it becomes scripture by being a signifier" (Wan 2008, 114). And, according to Wimbush, signifyin(g) "captures the critical mode of investigation that is more encompassing than, and therefore more different from, the various assumptions, methods, and approaches … usually associated with conventional textual interpretation and communication of meaning" (Wimbush 2008, 4). African American scripturalization generally theorized as signifyin(g) with Scriptures, therefore, "brings into focus the power relations and dynamics that are often masked in the communication of meaning" (4).

AFRICAN AMERICAN SCRIPTURALIZATION
AS SIGNIFIER OF CULTURAL MEMORY

Wimbush's proposal for the framing of African American scripturalization as signifyin(g) on Scriptures obviously depends on a cultural-historical engagement with the biblical texts. Yet I suggest that his proposal must not

---

20. See ch. 3 for an extensive illustration of the use of signifyin(g) in African American culture in providing a counternarrative of the American myth. Also, see chaps. 4 and 5 for the use of signifyin(g) in reading Revelation.

only engage historical experiences, but African American scripturalization must intentionally function as a *lieu de mémoire* (site of memory) or
as a *carrier of cultural memory*.[21]

Cultural memory can be considered as "twice-behaved behavior," a
remembering that is a product of fragmentary personal and collective
experiences communicated via technologies and media that shape even as
they transmit memory (see Hirsch and Smith 2002; Pinn 2003). Culture
and memory operate at two different levels: individual and communal.
Astrid Erll states:

> The first level of cultural memory is concerned with biological memory.
> It draws attention to the fact that no memory is ever purely individual,
> but always inherently shaped by collective contexts. From the people we
> live with and from the media we use, we acquire schemata which help us
> recall the past and encode new experience. Our memories are often trig-
> gered as well as shaped by external factors, ranging from conversation
> among friends, to books, and to places.
>
> The second level refers to the symbolic order, the media, institutions
> and practices by which social groups construct a shared past. Societ-
> ies do not remember literally; but much of what is done to reconstruct
> a shared past bears some resemblance to the processes of individual
> memory, such as the selectivity and perspectivity inherent in the cre-
> ation of versions of the past according to present knowledge and needs.
> (Erll 2010, 5)

Thus cultural memory is not necessarily about recalling past events as
accurately as possible, nor about ensuring cultural continuity—it is about
making meaningful statements about the past in a given cultural context of the present conditions. Since individuals learn their collective
memories through socialization, they are free to break out of it and offer

---

21. The concept of collective memory was first introduced by Maurice Halbwachs, who argued that people remember their past according to the needs and stimuli
of their present. He maintained that various memory communities existed within a
group and that different groups can remember the same things in different ways. See
Halbwachs 1975. The German Egyptologist Jan Assmann drew upon Halbwachs's concept of social memory (Assmann 1992). Sometimes the various versions of the past
coexist peacefully or sometimes they come into conflict as countermemories collide
with more dominant discourses. See Nora 1989. See also Wan 2008, 113: "whoever
holds the key to the collective cultural memory of a community or nation, made 'real'
in biblical exegesis, can unlock the door of power."

alternative views of the past that may later become part of this collective memory. It is important to note, therefore, that collective cultural memory need not be homogeneous, but different segments of the community can have different cultural memories, based on social locations, example, class, race/ethnicity, and/or gender locations.

In addition, each time we interpret cultural memories, they move farther from the moment of their conception and their concrete tie to historical reality because direct contact with the context is lost as time continues to move forward; and, therefore, re-presentation replaces reality (Pinn 2003, 108–9). For instance, as Anthony Pinn illustrates, the development of a North American collective cultural memory is an example of memory distortion and loss. He claims that the great potential of early North America created a sense of progress that caused memory to be dissociated from the artifacts. The selective memory of Euro-Americans and their disregard for the past resulted in a shallow self-identity and consciousness that made the denial of both African Americans and Native Americans easy (ibid.).

Cultural Memory as Resisting Oppression

Jeanette Rodriquez and Ted Fortier state that the cultural memory of oppression has two distinct characteristics: (1) the survival of a historically, politically, and socially marginalized group of people, and (2) the role of spirituality as a form of resistance (2007, 1).[22] The authors suggest that the construction of identity is "rooted in religious ideology that manifests a spirituality grounded in experience and is endemic to the continuum of self-preservation and reproduction of humanity" (2). This means that a group's religious ideology (and its rituals and myths that reflect that ideology) can be considered as tools of resistance and identity construction. Therefore, the religious ideology of an oppressed group, including the acts of ritual and mythmaking that perpetuate that ideology, is a carrier of cultural memory that fulfills a basic need of the community.

---

22. The authors present four case studies to advance their suggestions: (1) the image of Our Lady of Guadalupe and the devotion it inspires among Mexican Americans; (2) the role of recovery and secrecy and ceremony among the Yaqui Indians of Arizona; (3) the evolving narrative of Archbishop Oscar Romero of San Salvador as transmitted through the church of the poor and the martyrs; and (4) the syncretism of Catholic Tzeltal Mayans of Chiapas, Mexico.

Although African American communities have nurtured their cultural production by making sense of their cultural memories (and religious ideology) damaged during years of bondage and continued discrimination, this does not imply that there is a completely linear transmission of cultural information. African American cultural memory is hybrid, that is, split between an urge toward blackness—conceived in cultural terms—and the continued presence of European cultural ideas (Pinn 2003, 109). Therefore, pieces of cultural artifacts can be lost along the way depending upon what groups and individuals consider important or unimportant developments. As Toni Morrison writes regarding the works of black writers during slavery, such as Olaudah Equiano and Frederick Douglass,

> Over and over, the writers pull the narrative up short with a phrase such as, "But let us drop a veil over these proceedings too terrible to relate." In shaping the experience to make it palatable to those who were in a position to alleviate it, they were silent about many things and they "forgot" many other things. There was a careful selection of the instances that they would record and a careful reading of those that they chose to describe. (Morrison 1999, 301)

When African American scripturalization is considered as a carrier of cultural memory, it appears as the mnemonic art par excellence for signifyin(g) with Scriptures a complex and dynamic identity construction. This is because the memorial presence of the past takes on many forms and serves many purposes, ranging from conscious recall to unreflected reemergence, from nostalgic longing to polemical use of the past to shape the present. African American scripturalization understood as a carrier of cultural memory allows, through the engagement of the biblical texts, for the simultaneous looking (and talking) back while moving forward, reshaping identity construction and in so doing reshaping the discipline itself. The addition of the concept of cultural memory, in my opinion, enriches Wimbush's theoretical proposal for reading Scriptures undergirded by black Signification by providing a dynamic that the focus on the history of the African American experience disallows because it provides a shift from a homogeneous oppressed community to a complex and diverse community with different memories of the past. By working with cultural memory, African American scripturalization can better evince the work Scripture does in deconstructing and reconstructing identity.

MOVING FORWARD BY RECONCEPTUALIZING THE PAST:
REDESCRIBING THE KEY TASKS OF AFRICAN AMERICAN BIBLICAL
INTERPRETATION AS AFRICAN AMERICAN SCRIPTURALIZATION

This section examines the developmental stages of African American biblical interpretation from a corrective historical-critical method of the tenets
of Euro-American scholarship to the specific cultural-critical engagement
of the biblical texts through the concepts of African American scripturalization proposed above.

The first task of African American biblical interpretation focused on
uncovering the black presence in the Bible by "literally researching all
references in the Bible which refer to Egyptians, Ethiopians and Cushites
and treating the text as a reliable historical document" (Brown 2004, 21).
This was accomplished through exegetical work mainly on the Hebrew
Bible utilizing the methods of the historical-critical paradigm. Providing a
corrective lens to a predominant Euro-American historical approach that
either erased the presence of blackness from the Bible or located that presence as marginal, African American scribes unveiled references to black
people (ibid.). So, it can be said that the early stages of the enterprise signified in counterpoint to the Euro-American biblical engagement that "privileges things European to the detriment of other sociocultural orientations
and methods" (ibid.).

A chief scribe in this first-wave scripturalizing task was Charles
Buchanan Copher. Trained as an historical critic, Copher spent his academic career at Gammon Theological Seminary in Atlanta, Georgia,
teaching African American students. It was in this context that he recognized the benefits of the relationship between texts and contexts, and this
realization provided him with the impetus to examine the Scriptures for
the presence of blackness. Copher concluded, "In the veins of Hebrew-
Israelite-Judahite-Jewish peoples flowed black blood" (1991, 164).

Renouncing the negative portrayal of black-skinned peoples, he inves-
tigated specifically (1) the color of Hamites and Elamites in the Table of
Nations, (2) the modern Euro-American ethnic category of "black," (3)
ancient discussions of "race," (4) the use of color designators in ancient
Hebrew literature, and (5) modern scholarship's understanding and use of
all four (Copher 1991).

Concentrating on the terms ḥām, qēdār, šāḥar, kûš, and ḥōšek over
various time periods, he concluded that "the most probable original text
of the Hebrew was free of pejorative statements with respect to peoples

regarded as black by the original authors" (Copher 1986, 245–46). He noted that it is the Septuagint text that places the curse on Ham, Canaan's father, and not on Canaan himself. He asserted that this one text may show "a move in the … Intertestamental Period towards a curse-on-Ham position in some circles, or by a translator or scribe, even though *ham* may not necessarily at the time refer to blackness" (229). He suggested that rabbinic Judaism was responsible for a stream of thought that provided extensive and negative commentary regarding dark-skin people that has unfortunately survived the passage of time and extended into the modern era and was most detrimental during the slave era in Western civilization.

Copher's scripturalization, penned contrapuntal to the prevalent Eurocentric position, argued that blacks resisted the traditional interpretations that denigrated the descendants of Ham as cursed and instead stressed a heroic and powerful persona. His scripturalization focused on reshaping a traumatic collective cultural memory by re-presenting and therefore reconnecting the community to a glorious and honorable past. He argued that, although Euro-American scholarly exegesis refuted the Hamite curse as incredible and fallacious, the refutation was not a determined attempt to dismiss a pejorative interpretation, but was actually a result of the methodological tendency to position the academic study of the Bible as a totalizing Eurocentric production. In so doing, the scholarly agenda erased away the presence of blackness in the biblical texts; and, as a result, Africans were not considered as subjects in the biblical accounts about Cain, Ham, Canaan, or any other biblical character. The cord that connected dark-skinned people to the biblical narratives was completely severed. In other words, the Euro-American paradigm based on scientific objectivity obliterated Africa and Africans from the biblical narratives altogether (Brown 2004, 26).

Copher can be considered the first major African American scribe to employ the biblical narratives with the aim of confronting the dominant point of view that blackness in the Bible is evil and perverted and to strive, instead, to instill a sense of pride and dignity from the narratives that are considered as the Word of God for so many in that oppressed community. Copher's work was being developed in the 1970s at the same time that African American popular culture produced posters, books, and so on of black biblical characters. His work is an example of the work black liberation theology and biblical scholarship can achieve when working to instill hope and perseverance in a marginalized community.

However, Copher's contrapuntal scripturalization can be argued to have obscured the *motive* for the "othering" or marginalization of blackness in the Bible. His scripturalization evaded several important sociopolitical factors influencing the interactions of peoples and nations situated in the Mediterranean basin. A greater emphasis on the political complexity of the ancient world might have revealed that the pejorative rhetoric against Egypt, Canaan, and Ethiopia actually alluded to the presence of black power in the ancient world. Copher disregarded acknowledging the colonizing motivations of black nations in the biblical world, shying away from certain problematic biblical passages, such as Exod 1:11–16, which illustrate that the Egyptians employed oppressive policies against the "other."

Despite this critique, however, Copher's work helped to deconstruct a collective cultural memory affected by such pejorative readings as he revisited the past in order to reconstruct productive and meaningful communities of the present and future.

TRUDGING ON THE STONY ROAD: AFRICAN AMERICAN SCRIPTURALIZATION AS LIBERATORY PRAXIS

The second task of African American scripturalization is to challenge the totalizing tendency of Euro-American biblical interpretation that results in the eradication of multiple productions of meaning based on the diversity of race, ethnicity, gender, and economic locations. Cain Hope Felder's scripturalization in the late 1980s is evidence of this second task. In the introduction to *Troubling Biblical Waters: Race, Class, and Family* (1989), Felder states his overall critique and objective that his scripturalization addresses:

> The purpose of this book is to provide some sorely needed correctives regarding the Bible in relation to ancient Africa and Black people today. Despite the fact that the Bible has a favorable attitude about Blacks, post-biblical misconstruals of biblical traditions have created the impression that the Bible is primarily the foundational document of "the White Man's religion." (1989, xi)

He supports the view throughout his writings that "recent studies have helped us to recognize both a tacit cultural ideological tendency and a principle of racial exclusion ... that showed little positive regard for non-European peoples and their religious heritage" (1998, 22). Felder believes that when any one culture, race, or ethnic group is valorized above all others, there is a tendency to subvert the Bible's authority. Throughout Western history, the authority of the Bible has been predicated upon the assumption of the preeminence of European cultures. This ideology resulted in positioning African Americans, Afro-Asiatics,[23] Hispanics, and Asians as secondary or marginalized cultures. And, though European scholarship struggled to apply a universal and objective biblical interpretation, in actuality the discipline practiced a disguised particularity "without reference to the authority of the biblical authors and what they thought and did in their ancient contexts" (1998, 23).

Felder's work is among the first to explicitly respond to the call of black liberation theology for a scripturalization that addresses the sociopolitical, economic, and spiritual needs of the community based on African American culture: "the rise and proliferation of liberation theologies ... witnessed in the last two decades have come to represent profound impatience with Bible scholars who have been perceived as less than helpful in clarifying important but complex hermeneutical issues" (1989, 53).

Felder insists on an ethics of transformation that involves perceiving the biblical world through the lens of diversity that is paradigmatic for contemporary life in the United States and elsewhere (see Brown 2004, 35). He says, "people must seek to liberate themselves from the tendency to deify the Bible as *the* definitive and exclusive Word of God as if God's entire revelation only exists in the canon of biblical literature" (Felder 1989, 53). This proves to be an extremely profound statement for African American scripturalization during this pioneering stage because it foreshadows the paradigmatic shift that is currently being argued. Felder's statement reveals the importance of engaging with the biblical narrative in terms of social context and therefore implies the importance of cultural memory in approach. This is illustrated in the structuring of his framework around the idea of recontextualization, which is a "process of rediscovering some essential features of the black religious experience in Africa, including African traditional religions and doing this as one enters a new dialogue of liberation as found in the Bible" (ibid.). Felder's work begins to engage the biblical narratives in a contemporary cultural location, claiming that only by incorporating the knowledge of subjugated peoples into the discipline

23. Felder uses this term to refer to Middle Eastern ethnicity, including those living in Israel. Yet he distinguishes European Jews as Eurocentric and not Afro-Asiatic.

will a radical reorientation and reassessment of the discipline occur. I suggest that Felder is actually exhorting for the process of reforming a *cultural memory* by including essential features of the black religious experience in Africa. With the emphasis on contemporary context, Felder implies that Scripture is a carrier of cultural memory whose power emerges out of the complex interstices of recalling the past while living in the present.

Felder's liberatory stance in *Troubling Biblical Waters* argues from a position of multiculturalism as a core component of a just society that displaces the totalization he sees in Eurocentric readings. He advocates for an emancipation from a hegemonic Euro-American point of view by replacing those readings with an Afro-Asiatic centrality, in which he groups African, Asian, and Latina/o ethnicities. Yet Felder does not engage other ethnic approaches in his exegetical work. His approach remains focused on reconceptualizing the text to an Afrocentric worldview, claiming that the biblical (con)texts would be released from a predominant Eurocentric understanding by this cultural specific reassessment (1989, 53). Therefore, one can argue that his Afro-Asiatic point of departure focuses entirely on an African American engagement and does not include the variety of ethnic engagements his proposal implies.

However, Felder's contribution to African American scripturalization is significant, for his radical reorientation of the discipline responds to the cultural memory of African Americans in the scripturalization process. With Felder's work a nascent African American scripturalization is launched.

READING SCRIPTURES DARKLY: THE EARLY WORK OF VINCENT WIMBUSH

The third task of African American scripturalization is to analyze the historical engagement of the Bible by African Americans. In the essay "The Bible and African Americans," Wimbush articulates his dissatisfaction with the study of African American religious traditions, which he sees as "either a total neglect or a superficial treatment of the role of the Bible in the religious traditions of African Americans" (1991, 82). He continues: "since the Bible has from the founding of the nation served as an icon, a history of African Americans' historical readings of the Bible is likely to reflect their historical self-understandings—as Africans in America" (ibid.). He provides a working outline of five historical readings in an attempt to articulate his notion of a cultural-historical engagement of the Bible. The five different readings "correspond to different historical periods and are meant to reflect different responses to historical (socio-political-economic) situations and (collective) self-understandings" (83). The assumptions of each reading are communal, with "each 'reading' ... [emerging] out of particular life-settings, and to have been ... manifested and preserved in different types of sources—e.g., songs, sermons, testimonies, addresses" (ibid.).[24]

The time periods that the readings traverse are from the seventeenth century to the late twentieth century. The first reading responds to the strangeness of home that the Africans experienced upon arrival into the Americas. During this time period, the enslaved Africans took note of "the powerful influence of the Bible upon the Europeans' self-image, culture, and orientation" (85). Their reaction to this was one of ambivalence and caution. "On the one hand, they seemed to reject or be suspicious of any notion of 'Book Religion.' ... On the other hand, the fact that those who had enslaved them and were conquering the New World were 'Bible Christians' was not at all lost on the Africans" (ibid.).

The second reading period was a time of transformation evidenced by mass conversions of Africans to Christianity in the eighteenth century. During this period the Africans began to imitate the evangelicals in "reading" the biblical texts in light of their sociopolitical situation. They were attracted mainly to the Hebrew Bible and the aspect of bondage and liberation, "the oracles of the eighth-century prophets and their denunciations of social injustice, ... and to the New Testament texts concerning the compassion, passion, and resurrection of Jesus" (86). These biblical themes were transmitted orally and mainly expressed through song and sermon. In this oral stage, aspects of African spirituality became enmeshed with European Christianity and produced a specific religio-political sensibility expressed in a unique style that reflected and satisfactorily responded to the predicament of the enslaved Christian.

The third reading sees the establishment of canon and the beginning of an independent church movement in the nineteenth century. The access to public forums by educated Africans represents this reading. In a political environment in which Scripture waxed profusely in civic engagement, African Americans joined in with their own particular enunciation (90). In this period, public oratory is key in denounc-

---

24. I also suggest that the activities of mythmaking and the performance of rituals that are associated with the act of retelling the story are implicated in the above sources.

ing an unjust sociopolitical environment. The transmission of Scripture from private worship to public oratory is an indication of the maturity of African American Christianity as the community revealed its ability to engage with the biblical text publicly as a tool of resistance. Pamphlets and speeches written by freed African activists such as David Walker, Maria Stewart, and Frederick Douglass are examples of this period.

The fourth reading occurs in the early twentieth century, which sees the establishment of elitist group formations. These groups claim an esoteric knowledge as the basis for the reading of Scripture that corresponds to their willingness to establish themselves along the periphery of the dominant society (94). Examples of this group include the Nation of Islam.

The fifth and last reading proposed by Wimbush represented a reading of the present (1991) community; it is a fundamentalist reading that is embraced by African Americans attracted to white fundamentalist communities. Wimbush posits that the significant rise in fundamentalism among African Americans in the early 1990s signified a crisis of thinking, of security. This reading period represented the intentional attempt to interpret the Bible without respect for the historical experiences of African Americans (96).

Here Wimbush echoes the concerns of his colleagues Charles Copher and Cain Hope Felder, denouncing what he calls the "Europeanization" of the Bible that has resulted in a cultural siege and containment. "The silencing of the present with respect to the engagement of the Bible—most often signaled by the calls to 'begin with the texts,' to 'stay with the texts'—reflects the European co-optation and cultural-naturalization of the Bible and the high cost paid by all.... The scholar of the Bible ... adequately silenced, comes to represent either innocuous antiquarian practices or a type of religio-cultural foundationalism and apologetics" (Wimbush 2000b, 10, 11). Instead of beginning with the texts, Wimbush suggests we begin with the reception of the text in a contemporary context. Wimbush's early work begins to speak of the power of African American scripturalization to reflect a shared past of common (and contested) norms, conventions, and practices.[25]

---

25. See the critique of Wimbush's proposal above.

We Are Black and Comely ... and Western: Womanist Scripturalization as Caution to Community

The fourth task of African American scripturalization is to reframe the biblical narratives in a wider and more complex set of conflicts within the African American community itself. As mentioned above, this is usually the role of womanist scribes whose pens morally challenge and advocate for a just society, yet extend that challenge to their own community by cautioning the communal adherence to the oppressive elements of a capitalistic, patriarchal society. A womanist scribe is the moral compass of the community regarding the cultural negotiations that transpire within her community and also outside of her community. The role of the womanist scribe is particularly vital since many African Americans are fast moving into the center of American life and therefore are susceptible to embracing the status quo. Thus the main objective of the womanist scribe is to present the full complexity of the double-consciousness ethos of the twenty-first-century African American community. This is illustrated clearly by Cheryl Kirk-Duggan's essay "Let My People Go! Threads of Exodus in African American Narratives" (2003). Her work exemplifies the present direction of African American scripturalization as a contemporary engagement with the biblical text as proposed by Vincent Wimbush.

In her essay, Kirk-Duggan challenges the African American ideological view of the exodus narrative as a quest for liberation, arguing that the oppression-liberation paradigm does not adequately inform the African American community. She claims that it is much easier to deal with the concept of a chosen people and to cheerfully disregard matters of manifest destiny and how the vast complexities of class and diversity play out within the biblical narratives (2003, 129). She urges liberationists to be mindful not only of the two-edged nature of the texts, but also, I would suggest, of their own double-consciousness identity when examining the ambiguities and paradoxes within the Bible, for there will always be the potential for the adoption/adaptation of the oppressive elements of a capitalistic, patriarchal society. (Here she is echoing the thoughts of Anthony Pinn when he argues that African American cultural memory is split between an urge toward blackness—conceived in cultural terms—and the continued presence of European cultural ideas.) She states that "many womanist scholars question the move to use the biblical experience as a normative model for validating God's liberative acts for all oppressed peoples of the world" (128). Furthermore, "Although the warrior-God tradition ... inspired social movements of liberation and freedom, they are themselves violent and antithetical to peace and social justice" (130).

Kirk-Duggan explores Lorraine Hansberry's *Raisin in the Sun* as a contemporary biblical narrative depicting the yearning of a deprived community's aspirations of realizing the American dream and highlights the complexity of the struggle for attaining that goal as the family prepares for its exodus out of the inner city into the suburbs. Individual family members respond to the tension of liberation in different ways as they await for God to appear in the mail, for in this version of the biblical narrative God is an insurance check. It is revealed that both Walter Lee and Beneatha (whose name is a pun on "lower class"), like Aaron and Miriam, have their own selfish views about the money. We begin to ponder if the hopeful place of dreams has become a place of bondage, as Hansberry reveals to us each of the characters flaws based on their individual desires of attaining the American dream.

Alternatively, in the same essay, Kirk-Duggan examines the music of Sweet Honey in the Rock, an a cappella women's group who sings songs of protest and resistance. She hears in their songs an embodiment of the spirit of exodus. The song "More Than a Paycheck" is an indictment against the freedom to bring environmental illnesses, disease, injury, and stress upon our families in the name of money; and the "Battle for My Life" urges us to be free enough to see the problems of the human condition (139).

Kirk-Duggan reveals the awareness of ambivalence in identity construction and is an example of how the African American engagement with the biblical narratives can complicate the collective cultural memory of a group by provoking the community to be aware of its own contradictions. Her work reveals that cultural memory is not necessarily about remembering past events as accurately as possible, nor is it about ensuring cultural continuity—it is about making meaningful statements about the past in a given cultural context of the present conditions.

Conclusion

In this chapter I have discussed African American scripturalization within the framework of the cultural-critical paradigm, a reading paradigm based, first and foremost, on contemporary social location. African American scribes approach the biblical text in this manner and are connected with a global community of scribes who read similarly. The chapter illustrated that the objectives of the African American scribe are traditionally expressed by writing contrapuntal to the dominant Euro-American ethos.

This practice is greatly influenced by the dialectics of the civil rights movement and the black power movement of the 1960s in general, and black liberation theology in particular. Therefore, African American scribes are influenced by an ambiguous cultural praxis, a double-consciousness that reflects the "strangeness of home"—that is, the voicing of dissent with the oppressive elements of American society, while simultaneously embracing American society. Yet the discipline has seemingly become stagnant when, in fact, the community remains dynamic, moving forward in increasingly complex directions.

As a response to this lacuna, I suggest the renaming of the enterprise from "African American biblical hermeneutics" to "African American scripturalization" to connote the next phase in the discipline, which is the literary theorization of the enterprise as proposed by Vincent Wimbush, who takes his lead from the work of Henry Louis Gates Jr. on black Signification (or signifyin[g]). I have argued that although Wimbush advocates for the formation, deformation, and reformation of community in his use of the signifyin(g) concept, his proposal does not sufficiently reveal why or how the reconstruction of community is possible. I have also argued that emphasis on historical experience did not allow for an articulation of the complexity of identity. Therefore, I suggest that focusing on memory instead of history enables the deconstruction and reconstruction of identity. In the last section I examined the key tasks of African American scripturalization via a recap of four major scribes in the field: Charles Copher, Cain Hope Felder, Vincent Wimbush, and Cheryl Kirk-Duggan.

In the next chapter I continue the discussion on theorization and African American scripturalization. The project suggests that in order to fully derive the understanding that African American scripturalization is a praxis that addresses the complexity of African American identity, there must be a proposal for a theorization of cultural identity, in addition to a literary theorization. In the following chapter, therefore, I discuss how elements of postcolonial theory supplement the concepts of an African American scripturalization that I laid out in this chapter.

2

"Almost the Same but Not Quite Like": Postcolonial Theory through an African American Lens

It is a peculiar sensation, this double-consciousness, this sense of always looking at one's self through the eyes of others, of measuring one's soul by the tape of a world that looks on in amused contempt and pity. One ever feels his two-ness—an American, a Negro; two souls, two thoughts, two unreconciled strivings; two warring ideals in one dark body, whose dogged strength alone keeps it from being torn asunder.
— W. E. B. Du Bois, *The Souls of Black Folk*

In this chapter I discuss the development of postcolonial studies and comprehensively analyze the work of three of the major postcolonial theorists, Edward Said, Gayatri Spivak, and Homi Bhabha, through an African American lens with the aim to: (1) examine the junctions and disjunctions of postcolonial theory and African American scripturalization, and (2) discuss the merits of a fusion of postcolonial theory— particularly aspects disseminated by Homi Bhabha—and African American scripturalization for the purpose of illustrating the complexity of identity construction that is produced by the double movement of shifting away from Western constructions of the "Other" while simultaneously (and ironically) shifting toward appropriating the ideological, theological, linguistic, and textual forms of Western power.

The fusion is effective because both approaches (1) focus on the devastating aspects of neocolonialism and the lingering forms of discrimination and inequality that the system perpetuates, (2) critique Western epistemology that is based on hierarchical binary formation, and (3) utilize the concept of cultural memory in articulating the experience of officially sanctioned domination and oppression. Thus both disciplines are compatible and enhance one another. Whereas postcolonial theory contributes to African American scripturalization by resituating it out of its local context and placing it into a broader global conversation, African American scripturalization is ideally situated to reveal the (neo)imperial practices of the United States. Therefore, the supplementation of postcolonial theoretical concepts to the framework of African American scripturalization aids in producing a reading strategy that better reflects the often complicated cultural negotiations of a postenslaved community.

The Development of Postcolonial Studies

The term *postcolonial* was first used after World War II to demarcate an historical period following the dismantling of European colonies in Africa, Asia, the Caribbean, and Latin America and the ensuing reconfiguration of the various leaderships, parties, and governments that had gained their independence from colonial rule.[1] As the result of this global reconfiguration, an enormous degree of creative scholarship was produced that

---

1. It is often suggested that when the term is presented in the hyphenated form, *post-colonial*, the sense implied is of a chronological period. Robert Young refers to the economic, political, and material conditions as *postcoloniality*, a term that defines "the conditions that determine the global system in which the postcolonial nation is required to operate—one heavily weighted towards the interests of international capital and the G7 powers." In addition, it is important to note that decolonization released a variety of political and economic ideologies—Marxism, socialism, communism, capitalism, nationalism, etc. This fact can often be submerged by some who present a somewhat homogeneous understanding of *the* postcolonial condition. Also, the system of European colonialism that controlled 85 percent of the globe at the time of World War II should be differentiated between settler countries—where the colonizer settled into the occupied territory (Australia and Canada, for example)—and nonsettler countries (India, Sri Lanka, Jamaica, and Nigeria). And yet colonialism was even more diffuse and divergent than that, as, for example, the apartheid system in South Africa attests. See Young 2001, 1, 37. See also Ashcroft et al. 1989, 1–11; Shohat 1992; Bahri 1995, 63–65; Prakash 1995; Ashcroft 1996.

The knotty position of the United States attests to the fluidity in colonial power dynamics. This can be illustrated by tracing U.S. history from its British colonial roots and its simultaneous role as an "internal colonizer" to its present status as *the* world's super(neo)colonizer. The United States surely occupies an extremely ambiguous position in relation to postcolonial discourse. See Buell 1992, 411–13; Singh and Schmidt 2000, 3–72; R. King 2000, 1–20.

focused on multiple issues including political, sociological, psychological, and religious concerns of the decolonized or "third world" countries.[2]

These dynamics that erupted in the aftermath of European colonialism were, of course, reflected in the literary works that were produced within the postcolonial nations. Some of the major names of the literary critics and artists cited in a variety of postcolonial readers as influential during this period include: Frantz Fanon, C. L. R. James, Albert Memmi, Aime Cesaire, V. P. Naipaul, J. M. Coetzee, Chinua Achebe, Buchi Emecheta, Bessie Head, and Ngugi wa Thiong'o.[3] Each in his or her own way articulates the "psychological, cultural and political damage that European colonialism had inflicted on millions of people" (Sugirtharajah 2002, 16).

The critical thought of the Martinique psychiatrist and political activist Frantz Fanon, who was involved in the Algerian War of Independence, occupies a prominent position in the canon of "postcolonial" writers and critics. Fanon has been recognized by many scholars as a vital critic of the relationship between the colonizer and the colonized. His ideas have inspired and incited anticolonial liberation movements for more than four decades. *Black Skins, White Masks* and *The Wretched of the Earth* are considered "must reads" for anyone seriously interested in pursuing postcolonial studies.[4] The primary goal of these anticolonial texts is to expose the

---

2. The term *third world* was coined in 1952 by the French demographer Alfred Sauvy as an analogy to the third estate, the commoners of France before and after the French Revolution. The term implies exploitation and underdevelopment whose destiny is revolution. Demographically, the term typically refers to Africa, Asia, Latin America, and the internal colonies of the Western world, including Africa America.

3. After some initial hesitation by postcolonial critics, the work of W. E. B. Du Bois, Marcus Garvey, and the work of the Harlem Renaissance literary writers— Langston Hughes, Claude McKay, Eric Walrond, Zora Neale Hurston, and Nella Larsen, just to name a few—are now included in the list of postcolonial studies. The expansion of the canon signifies that the general emphasis of the discourse allows for a wider range of cultural investigation in the commonality of power dynamics and how those similar dynamics are negotiated differently in various cultural contexts. In particular, Du Bois's entrance as an early contributor to postcolonial studies is a further indication of the complexity and fluidity of the discourse, since his concept of double-consciousness is a pre-"postcolonial" construct articulated in 1903, thus long before European decolonization, a process that did not begin to occur in earnest until after World War ll. See Philipson 2006.

4. See Fanon 1952, 1961. Homi Bhabha cites Fanon's work rather extensively in the conceptualization of his postcolonial theory. See Bhabha 1989; 1994, 57–93. See also Gates 1991; Gibson 2003.

unsavory and debilitating processes of the colonized psyche that is produced as a result of colonialism.

According to Fanon, the strategy of European colonialism relied on instilling a sense of inherent inferiority in the natives that justified the invasion of the Europeans. Precolonial existence was presented as exotic, uncivilized, and unenlightened by the colonizer. Therefore, to a large extent, the schema of Western colonialism rested on conniving the colonized into believing that by adopting the colonizer's system, the colonized are protecting themselves against their own selves. Fanon writes in *The Wretched of the Earth*:

> Colonialism is not simply content to impose its rule upon the present and the future of a dominated country. Colonialism is not satisfied merely with holding a people in its grip and emptying the native's brain of all form and content. By a kind of perverted logic, it turns to the past of the oppressed people, and distorts, disfigures and destroys it. (Fanon 1961, 145)

In other words, the strategy of the colonizer was to trespass on and distort the colonized cultural memory so as to reconstruct a self-demonization that legitimated the colonizer's claims of European supremacy, which, in turn, justified the rape and pilfering of the "uncivilized nations."[5] Given Fanon's importance to postcolonial studies, the obituaries marking his death in 1961 were slight; the two inches of type offered by *The New York Times* and *Le Monde* inadequately describe his achievements and role. But he has remained influential in both leftist and antiracist political movements, and all of his works were translated into English in the decade following his death.

---

5. The Christian mission played a prominent role in colonial domination in that it influenced the disruption of the sacred aspect of cultural memory and the construction of self and community. The colonizer's attempt to reconstruct the colonized ancestral concept of God and humanity as ignorant and insufficient aided in the self-demonization of the colonized. The self-demonization of the colonized stifled the impulse of resistance made all the more impotent with the belief that their religious system was insufficient. See Fanon 1961.

REDEFINING POSTCOLONIAL

Despite the creative and invaluable contributions of Fanon and his con-
temporaries in exposing the oppressive schemes of colonialism, to attach
the label "postcolonial" as understood today to their work would be inappropriate. The term did not yet point to an academic discipline. It was far
more usual to refer to these critics as either "anticolonial" or "third world"
(Lazarus 2004, 2). To have called these writers postcolonial "would have
been in a sense merely to set the scene, historically speaking, for the analysis to come" (ibid.).

It was not until the late 1970s that "postcolonial" denoted a critical
practice. Led by the literary critic Edward Said at Columbia University, the
reconceptualization came about when third world literary scholars and
cultural critics refocused their lens, zooming in on the practices, experiences, and peculiarities of European colonialism.[6] This intensity resulted in
the formulation of a theoretical discipline that produced new insights and
inquiries regarding the interrelationships of literature, power, and empire
with a political commitment toward those who were formerly colonized.
After the 1970s, "postcolonial" refers to a critical system of thought aimed
at revealing and disrupting the manipulative political and cultural strategies of colonial occupation, as well as establishing the diverse ways the
colonized articulate their identity, self-worth, and political empowerment
(Quayson 2000, 25). By the 1990s, postcolonial studies had become fully
steeped in the discursive waters of literary studies, history, anthropology,
sociology, psychology, classics, medieval studies, cultural studies, religion,
and biblical and theological studies.

Presently, the critical engagement concentrates on: (1) favoring a
focus on the boundaries that exist on the cusp of imagined determinate
categories (Lazarus 2004, 4); (2) the provocation of a Western epistemology that is established on binary thinking; (3) the disavowal of homogeneity and totality; and (4) theorizing the complex dynamics of empire,
nation, transnationalism, migrancy, and hybridity with modes of cultural
production across a global field of political circumstances, including the
circumstances of those on the margins in the United States (Moore-Gilbert 2000a, 11).

---

6. In the discussion below on Edward Said I speak further of this refocused analysis of colonial discourse.

Therefore, the term *postcolonial* has morphed from a purely historical designation and transformed into a theoretical/methodological weapon wielded as protection against certain political and philosophical constructions that presume continuity between the colonial and the postcolonial periods. *Postcolonial* is now defined as a catalyst that instigates and creates opportunities for critical forces to converge together to assert their denied rights and to "rattle the center" (Sugirtharajah 2002, 13).

However, for many, the term remains a very slippery designation since it not only signifies that which succeeds the colonial, but also refers to the neocolonized. In addition, it has been suggested that the discipline's primary focus on the British Empire fails to locate itself within a larger historical framework (Bahri 1995, 61). This failure has often led to the perception of colonization as a modern phenomenon.

Deepika Bahri argues for a postcolonial analysis that transcends time, maintaining that the "placing of ancient history alongside the present, is not asking for a reduction of disparate geopolitical experiences to one generic framework, but is rather seeking a sensitivity to the relationships between the two so as to understand both in ways that relate to the here and now" (Bahri 1995, 61). Ancient Mediterranean historian Irad Malkin echoes Bahri's view when he suggests that ancient Greek practices of colonization could provide historical depth to postcolonial theory, which could then contextualize itself as firmly relevant to past millennia (Malkin 2004, 341; also see Webster 1997; Hose 1999; Sugirtharajah 2006, 67–68).

Postcolonial Biblical Criticism

While postcolonial biblical scholars may concede that the term *postcolonial* might indeed be problematic, these scholars (myself included), who are interested in revealing the intersections of cultural domination both in the ancient and contemporary worlds, acknowledge that approaching the text via a postcolonial lens with its emphasis on empire, nation, ethnicity, and migration provides a very provocative reading strategy (Byron 2009, 165–66).

In uncovering the persistent colonial manifestations evident in biblical texts, biblical scholars often rely on the works of Said, Spivak, and Bhabha, even though the biblical narratives play a marginal role in their own writings. However, as R. S. Surgirtharjah points out, the postcolonial biblical critic operates explicitly within the context of cultural domination: "Postcolonial biblical criticism makes clear that biblical studies can no longer be confined to the history of textual traditions but needs to extend its scope to include issues of domination, western expansion and its ideological manifestations as central forces in defining biblical scholarship" (2002, 74–75).[7]

The postcolonial biblical scholar must be hermeneutically suspicious that an ideological bias implicitly informs the production of meaning by traditional historical biblical scholars.[8] With this suspicion in mind, the theoretical propositions of Said, Spivak, and Bhabha are particularly compelling analytical tools.

Sugirtharajah claims that a postcolonial biblical hermeneutic explicitly identifies four codes that are embodied in the narrative: hegemonic, professional, negotiated, and oppositional.[9] The hegemonic code functions to legitimate the dominant values and ideological interests of the ruling class. It tends to embrace colonial models and patriarchal practices. The professional code is concerned with preserving, centralizing, and interpreting laws, traditions, and customs. The negotiated code is concerned with how an event or experience is interpreted to meet new theological/ideological situations. The oppositional code is the voice of the group on the margins that locates their place in the discourse in spite of the text being produced by those who have vested interests. Postcolonial biblical scholars can be said to be oppositional in that they "write back" by dismantling any "persisting colonial assumptions and ideologies" (Sugirtharajah 2005, 558–59).

Musa W. Dube's work is an illustration of the oppositional code of postcolonial biblical hermeneutics. Through a close literary reading of Matthew, particularly Matt 15:21–28, Dube spins the imperial symbolism that is threaded throughout the text, including Jesus' tendency to "exorcise" the native demons he comes in contact with on his many travels throughout foreign lands. In the Matthean pericope, Dube portrays the

---

7. I suggest that this extension in scope is especially successful when a deconstructive and poststructural methodology unlocks the text's religio-political meaning that, in turn, releases an interpretive reconstruction that addresses issues of domination and ideological manifestations that are embedded in the biblical narratives.

8. The active application of a hermeneutic of suspicion is vitally necessary even in this era of biblical studies since the early historical-critical method remains entrenched in the graduate programs of religion in American universities. Feminist, womanist, and cultural critics working within "marginal" locations all adopt a hermeneutic of suspicion.

9. Sugirtharajah borrowed and revised these terms from Stuart Hall, the British cultural critic, who applied these terms to his analysis of how televisual discourse operates. See Sugirtharajah 2002, 75; Hall 1980.

Syrophoenician woman and her daughter as types of the land in order to set up a "decolonization" of the narrative. Looking through an oppositional codal lens, Dube relates Jesus's healing of the daughter with the Western world's entrance into her homeland, Africa, under the modern guise of "progress." That is, Jesus's actions are read metaphorically as Western Christian invasion and conquest. The Syrophoenician woman symbolizes premodern, nonprogressive Africa that is incapable of providing either physical or spiritual sustenance for her own people symbolized by the (absent) daughter. Dube's reading serves to provoke and question the underlying motivation for the supposedly traditional, objective interpretation. By diligently working within the dynamics of this code, the postcolonial biblical scholar exposes a more complex meaning than that of the traditional historical biblical scholar (Dube 2000, 125–56).

Stephen D. Moore suggests that postcolonial biblical criticism should be grouped into three clusters: (1) a version of liberation or contextual hermeneutics in which he situates the prolific works of Sugirtharajah and Dube; (2) empire studies, a cluster of scholars who work mainly within the historical-critical paradigm foregrounding the Roman imperial context and its role in the formulation of New Testament texts, including Richard Horsley's several works on Jesus and Paul and empire (1997, 2003, 2006), and Warren Carter's work on Matthew and John (2001, 2008); and (3) the extrabiblical cluster that includes those scholars who have "achieved fluency in 'theory' as a kind of scholarly second language" (Moore and Segovia 2005, 9). The work of Erin Runions (2002), Tat-siong Benny Liew (1999), Yong-Sung Ahn (2006), Virginia Burrus (2007), and Stephen D. Moore (2007) are examples of biblical interpretations that utilize a poststructural methodology as these scholars read the texts through Bhabha's theoretical lens, applying the concepts of cultural hybridity to the constructions of the reader/interpreter and/or to the ancient constructions of the implied author/audience of the text (Moore and Segovia 2005, 5–10).

While the above works in the extrabiblical cluster are pioneering a postcolonial theoretical interpretation, this phase of postcolonial readings on the New Testament is not overly concerned with tweaking the hermeneutical implications/assumptions that inform the theoretical enterprise. In this initial stage, the focus seems to be more on analyzing the text through the lens of postcolonial theory, and therefore critics concentrate mainly on reconstructing an ancient context informed by this poststructural analysis. Since the emphasis is on applying the theoretical abstraction with a lesser focus on articulating cultural specificity, the end productions

are often quite similar, despite the fact that the critics range from vast geopolitical locations. To date, there have been very few attempts to comprehensively articulate the cultural elements that inform the hermeneutical
process of a specific social location in terms of a postcolonial theoretical
analysis of the New Testament.[10]

The fusion of African American scripturalization and postcolonial
theory, therefore, fulfills a lacuna in postcolonial biblical hermeneutics.
The fusion reveals that the emphasis on cultural specificity exposes the
unique ways in which a particular community negotiates domination and
subjugation and that the end result need not be universal, although con-
taining common practices and processes. African American scripturalization, therefore, is an exemplum of how postcolonial theory, when used as
a supplement, affords an opportunity for an enhanced understanding of
the work Scripture does in the construction of a specific cultural identity.

THE DOCTRINES OF THE POSTCOLONIAL TRINITY:
SAID, SPIVAK, AND BHABHA

As mentioned above, the procession of postcolonial studies as cultural critique into Western academia was led by the late Edward Said with the publication of his groundbreaking work, *Orientalism*, in 1979. In this work,
Said brilliantly targeted the Occidental (Western) conceptualization of
the Orient (East) from the middle of the eighteenth century to the present, based, to a large degree, on his personal experience as a Palestinian.
According to Said, Orientalism is a set of academic disciplines concerned
with studying the East, that is, Egypt, Palestine, Arabia, and the Asian
nations, based on a hierarchical existential difference between the West
and the East. It is a system of re-presentation that imagined the Orient as a
backward, exotic, eccentric, and despotic cultural landscape.

---

10. Sanchez (2008) offers a compelling ethno-cultural, postcolonial reading of
Revelation through the lens of Mexican religious culture. He parallels the Mexican
Virgin Guadalupe with the dragon slayer narrative in Rev 12, analyzing both as subversion of imperial myths: the dragon slayer myth as subverting Roman imperial
myths and the virgin myth as subverting a *Conquista* myth of seventeenth-century
Mexico. Moore (2001) interestingly parallels the Irish mythological context with that
of the book of Revelation illustrating a similar motif of the warrior-hero draped in
violent imagery. However, Moore does not engage in postcolonial theoretical concepts
in this reading.

Said unveiled the falsehood of these assumptions by challenging the various paradigms of thought that are accepted on individual, academic, and political levels. His work *Orientalism* revealed the Occidental tendency to identify the Orient as the "other," an identification that becomes the projection of aspects that Westerners do not choose to acknowledge in themselves. In so doing, he revealed that colonialism was not merely a military occupation, but was also a discourse of domination.

Robert Young posits, "It was Said who appeared more than anyone else to have broached the formal articulation of the political commitments and ideological critiques of the anti-colonial movements with other theoretical work, in particular that of structuralism and poststructuralism" (Young 2001, 383). And although Young acknowledges that Said's anti-colonial predecessors contributed widely to colonial discourse, he argues that Said's work, which corresponded to the development of new critical paradigms in academia, advanced the work of the anticolonial critics by his incorporation of these new theoretical concepts as the backbone of his methodology.

Specifically, Said's work is informed both by the poststructuralist Michel Foucault's analysis of discourse and power and by the Italian Marxist Antonio Gramsci's concept of cultural hegemony.[11] He appropriated Foucault's notion of power, discourse, and knowledge mainly from *The Archaeology of Knowledge* (2002), *Discipline and Punish* (1977), and "The Order of Discourse" (1982), written to understand how "the will to exercise dominant control in society and history has also discovered a way to clothe, disguise, rarefy, and wrap itself systematically in the language of truth, discipline, rationality, utilitarian value, and knowledge" (Said 1983, 216). Discourse, for Foucault, is the particular language that specialized knowledge has to conform to in order to be regarded as true (Young 2001, 365). And, although Said acknowledges the problem the Foucauldian analysis poses because of its location in a Western epistemological base that subsequently leads to political inaction, he nevertheless admits that there lies within the analysis the possibility of using the proposition as a framework for the various networks of history, power, knowledge, and society. He agrees with Foucault that the development of a discourse, a knowledge rooted and defined in a specific language or style, is an aspect

---

11. To call Michel Foucault a poststructuralist, or more accurately a structuralist who transformed into a poststructuralist, is by and large a label given by other scholars who have critiqued his work. Foucault never self-identified as a poststructuralist.

essential to the formation of any discipline and that necessary boundaries must be put in place to delimit the object of that discipline. Said's achievement in *Orientalism* is the ability to display the rhetorical power of the text based on a discourse analysis with a real world of domination and exploitation. In this way he illustrates that Orientalism as discourse is an uneven exchange between the colonizer and the colonized.

In *Orientalism*, Said complements Foucault's discourse analysis with the concept of cultural hegemony conceived by Gramsci. Cultural hegemony is the concept that everyday practices and shared beliefs provide the foundation for multiplex systems of domination. Domination is not exerted by force, but by the subtle and inclusive power of one group or class over the social, cultural, and economic institutions of a diverse culture. This facet of a "ruling ideology" is thought to be missing from Foucault's model of power. By linking Gramsci's idea of hegemony with Foucauldian thought, Said is able to argue the persistent power of colonial discourse (Kennedy 2000, 31). Thus, for Said, Orientalism as colonial discourse is an exemplum of how cultural hegemony works in society to reinforce the ruling ideology not by domination but by consent. In addition, Gramsci's concept provides the sense of an historical process by linking power with dominant interests, whereas Foucault's analysis fails to historicize the relationship between discourse and power.

SAID AND THE UNSAID: AN ORIENTALISM CRITIQUE

Edward Said's seminal work has received its fair share of critique. As the Indian historian Gyan Prakash notes, "*Orientalism* came as a breath of fresh air to many, but it also left others gasping for breath" (1995, 206; see Varisco 2007, 3). The major critique regarding Said's approach in *Orientalism* is the dependency on the Western way of knowing that formulates knowledge based on the hierarchical juxtaposition of two entities that establishes an imbalanced binary in which one half of the binary is lifted at the expense of "weighing down" the other.

In embracing Western epistemology for his colonial discourse, Said has been accused of painting a theoretical landscape that presents an incomplete and somewhat simplified worldview that fails to recognize the complexities involved in the interrelationship between cultures. Some also maintain that his thought leaves the colonized with no sense of agency or a means of resisting the colonizer (Chowdhry 2007). In response to this critique, Said adjusted his theoretical approach beginning in 1984 when he first articulated his concept of the *contrapuntal* in the article "Reflections on Exile" (see Said 2000, 173–86). The fuller development of this concept was then fleshed out in *Culture and Imperialism* in 1993. Said argued that a contrapuntal reading uncovers the presence of empire in canonical texts, and that by doing so, the resistance to empire is made possible by unveiling what has been excluded in the text:

> In practical terms, "contrapuntal reading" … means reading a text with an understanding of what is involved when an author shows, for instance, that a colonial sugar plantation is seen as important to the process of maintaining a particular style of life in England.… The point is that a contrapuntal reading must take account of both processes, that of imperialism and that of resistance to it, which can be done by extending our reading of the texts to include what was once forcibly excluded. (1993, 66–67)

Said's Worldliness Displayed: An African American Critique of Said's Contrapuntal

On close examination, Said's approach continues to rest on a Western epistemology. This is evident in *Culture and Imperialism,* in which he points out that his contrapuntal conceptualization was influenced by his deep love for Western music:

> In the counterpoint of Western classical music, various themes play off of one another, with only a provisional privilege being given to any particular one; yet in the polyphony there is concert and order, an organized interplay that derives from themes, not from a rigorous melodic or formal principle of the work. In the same way, I believe, we can read and interpret *English* novels. (1992, 59–60)

We must not overlook that the "concert and order" of which he speaks is based on a *Western musical scale* that organizes and controls the way that the "various themes play off of one another." This means that there is a common musical structure that each melody is patterned after so that the melodies can flow in harmony with one another. That pattern is structured on a Western standard. Said's contrapuntal approach, which is influenced by his training in Western classical music, continues to be framed by a Western epistemology. Therefore, I question how this contrapuntal approach plays out when the "melodic themes" of two minority communities are placed in a Western counterpoint to each other. Will not these two resistant strands be defined by a Western way of knowing?

An examination of Said's article "Reflections on American Injustice" (2001), addressed to elite Arabs who were in support of the U.S. stance on Iraq, provides us with a possible answer. This discussion reveals the limitations of his contrapuntal conceptualization when applied to two ethnic communities. In order to convince his audience that America cannot be trusted regarding its relations in the Middle East, Said presents a generalization of the African American community to illustrate the unjust practices of America. His rhetoric immediately slips into a Western discourse in his monolithic portrayal of African Americans. The following quotation from that article illustrates that his discourse is based on a totalization and is dependent on binary formation:

> one must pay close attention to an aspect of America's history mostly ignored by or unknown to educated Arabs and their ruling elites, who continue to speak of (and probably believe in) America's even-handedness. The aspect I have in mind is the contemporary treatment of the African American people, who constitute roughly 20 per cent of the population, a not insignificant number. There is the great prior fact of slavery, first of all. Just to get an idea of how deliberately buried this fact was beneath the surface of the country's official memory and culture, note that until the *1970s no program of literature and history paid the slightest attention to black culture or slavery or the achievements of the black people* [emphasis mine]. I received my entire university education between 1953 and 1963 in English and American literature, and yet all we studied was work written and done by white men, exclusively.... There were no black students when I was educated at Princeton and Harvard, no black professors, no sign at all that the entire economy of half the country was sustained for almost 200 years by slavery, nor that 50 or 60 million people were brought to the Americas in slavery. The fact wasn't worth mentioning until the civil rights movement took hold and pressed for changes in the law—until 1964 the law of the land discriminated openly against people of colour—as a result of a mass movement led by charismatic men and women....
>
> As a living monument to American injustice, therefore, we have the stark numbers of American social suffering. In relative but sometimes absolute terms, African-Americans supply the largest number of unemployed, the largest number of school drop-outs, the largest number of homeless, the largest number of illiterates, the largest number of drug addicts, the largest number of medically uninsured people, the largest

number of the poor. In short, by any of the socio-economic indices that matter, the black population of the United States, by far the richest country in recorded history, is the poorest, the most disadvantaged, the longest enduring historically in terms of oppression, discrimination and continued suppression.

I opine that Said himself resorts to the typical Western way of knowing that he denounced in *Orientalism* by maintaining a limited representation of the "other" in this article. He presents a generalized view of the African American community to the educated, middle-class Middle Easterners he addresses (a group that surely did not need Said to give them a lesson on American history and societal structure). In his own lopsided details, Said does injustice to a community as he distorts the facts, privileging those distortions for his own rhetorical spin.

Operating within a contrapuntal framework would reveal that there were, of course, academic programs that focused on black literature, as the many historically black colleges/universities can attest and where many published African American literary scholars and authors taught. Therefore, Said's statement implies that since these programs were not located in either Ivy League universities or Euro-American schools, they were invalid. Also, several African Americans had graduated from Harvard and Princeton (and other schools) long before Said's arrival in the United States. For example, W. E. B. Du Bois and Alain Locke graduated from Harvard six decades before him. And Ralph Ellison, James Baldwin, Martin Luther King Jr., and Malcolm X delivered lectures at Harvard in the 1960s, the time in which Said was in attendance. Said neglects to mention that at the time this article was written, many African Americans were firmly established in high-level academic, socioeconomic, political, and military positions in American society. Yet, for his own rhetorical spin, Said evades these facts.

Since a contrapuntal approach reveals that which is silenced or erased, then the African American community should have been presented in a much more complex manner than Said portrayed in this article. So, in answer to the question posed above, What happens when two marginalized communities are placed in counterpoint to each other? (à la Said), it seems that the groups continue to be conceived in terms of a Western epistemology that is established on a dichotomous system.

Citing, commenting on, and critiquing Said's methodological approaches both in *Orientalism* and in *Culture and Imperialism* seemingly have become a rite of initiation for cultural critics who are interested in working within a postcolonial framework. *Orientalism* especially has become a touchstone that has legitimated the work of many in the academy to such an extent that it can be said to be hegemonic in its own right. Nevertheless, in spite of the critiques and comments of countless scholars, the ideas of Said that are presented in *Orientalism* and *Culture and Imperialism* continue to be redeployed by those who are interested in embarking on, while simultaneously provoking, the field of postcolonial studies.

Pursuing the Potential of Postcolonial Theory

Two South Asian literary scholars, Gayatri Chakravorty Spivak and Homi K. Bhabha, are credited with advancing the development of postcolonial theory. In fact, Said, Spivak, and Bhabha are often referred to as the "trinity of postcolonial theory." The trio often delivered papers at the same conferences; their seminal writings continue to be reproduced together in various readers and primers on postcolonial studies; and, inevitably, they often critiqued and challenged one another's ideas. Their critique of one another is mainly based on the different theoretical models they employ to frame their abstractions. As mentioned above, Said used Foucault and Gramsci to shape his (post)colonial discourse. Although Gayatri Spivak incorporates a variety of theoretical lenses, Jacques Derrida is extremely influential in her work. She has been labeled a feminist Marxist deconstructivist (a label she would vehemently deny since she claims that "the critic must not succumb to seeking analytic totalization"; Moore-Gilbert 2000b, 451). Bhabha also has an arsenal of theoretical concepts at his disposal, but Derrida and the poststructural psychoanalyst Jacques Lacan are extremely influential in his work. While both Spivak and Bhabha admit that Said's work is groundbreaking in terms of colonial and discourse, many have suggested that both of their eclectic theoretical styles are a result of their critique of Said's totalizing tendency as presented in *Orientalism* (Moore-Gilbert 2000b, 452). As Henry Louis Gates Jr. quips, postcolonial theory mostly entails "Spivak's critique of ... Bhabha's critique of Said's critique of colonial discourse" (Gates 1991, 458).

Gayatri Chakravorty Spivak: Creating Space for the Subaltern

Like Said, Spivak also aims to unveil the worldliness that is embedded in the text. She examines the ways in which the real world is constituted by and reflected in a network of texts, from British colonial archives to U.S. foreign policies, computerized stock exchange market reports, World Bank reports on "third world" debt, British literature, and so on. She accomplishes this textual excavation primarily with the tools of deconstructive theory that she learned while a student of Paul De Man at Cornell University. Spivak's groundbreaking English translation (1974) of Jacques Derrida's *De la grammatologie* (1967) and her comprehensive preface, which covers most of the key concepts and intellectual influences of Derrida's early thought, launched Spivak's own reputation as a deconstructionist. Spivak is recognized in academia for bringing deconstructive theory to North America.

Deconstruction challenges the logocentricism or the metaphysics of presence that is so dominant in Western philosophy. In order to break down that logocentrism the deconstructive process involves a close, critical reading of texts to uncover the unperceived contradictions and tensions that undermine the unity of meaning. With deconstructive theory, there is the notion of an explosion of multiple meanings derived from the "play" that results from one meaning bringing on another, and so on. Through the unfolding of meaning, the unsaid, the unmentioned, bursts free from the confines of logocentricism, dismantling the hierarchical binary opposition by illustrating how these oppositions are contradicted by every effort to formulate and employ them.

Yet Spivak conceives deconstruction somewhat differently. She insists that the popular notion of deconstruction as apolitical and relativistic is both reductive and simplistic. According to Spivak, deconstruction unveils the political and rhetorical blind spots of the text that stabilize conventional notions of truth and reality. Therefore, Spivak's deconstructive reading reveals how the world is represented by the "first world" to the exclusion of other groups, especially the subaltern,[12] who is defined as a subordinate member of various segments of South Asian society, but particularly South Asian women (see Landry and MacLean 1996, 269–70).

---

12. Spivak's use of the term *subaltern* refers to those who are systemically silenced or erased from official history and who are not represented in the sociopolitical and economical fabric of society. The term seems to be a work in progress for Spivak. Over the years, she has so expanded on her theoretical propositions of subalternity "that even she has difficultly living up to its rigor." See Moore 2011, 20.

Importance of Poststructuralism in Spivak's Work

Although French poststructuralist theory is integral to both Said and Spivak, Said, as discussed above, relied on the fundamentals of modern academic discourse by working within the confines of binary opposition. Contrary to Said, Spivak places emphasis on dismantling the binary in order to recover the voices of the underrepresented. In order to accomplish this, she insists on a reading of ethical singularity—the conscious act of making discursive room for the subaltern that depends on a response that is mutual and responsible and is not an act of benevolence toward the subaltern.

Spivak recognizes that the discovery of a text's worldliness and the production of an ethical reading on behalf of those who have been silenced may be hampered by the elite since they often speak for the subaltern. This is explored in her work with the Subaltern Studies Group and expressed in the article "Can the Subaltern Speak? Speculations on Widow-Sacrifice" (1985). She concludes in that article that the attempt to make the subaltern a subject is in fact a reinscription of a subordinate position in society that, ironically, supports neocolonial domination, economic exploitation, and cultural erasure.

In an attempt to create space for the subaltern, Spivak deploys the term *catachresis*, originally a figure in Greek rhetoric that denotes the use of a word far removed from its signification. Spivak reuses this term in order to deflect the assumption of reinscription by suggesting that there is a strategic appropriation of elements of colonial/imperial ideology by the colonized that resists colonial/imperial domination. Thus the element of strategic essentialism is integral to her accounting of the subaltern predicament. She argues that it is often necessary to perform an essential role play where certain assumptions of the dominant cultural paradigm are proven in order to figure out how to effectively find ways to counteract domination (see Morton 2003; Ray 2009).

Deconstructing Spivak through an African American Lens

It is extremely difficult for a cultural critic residing in the United States to avoid engaging in the dynamics of race and the construction of identity. Yet I opine that Spivak maintains an extremely limited engagement in her cultural analyses. African Americanist Malini Johar Schueller argues that Spivak's constraint on race and the issues of the local unwittingly reproduces the racism of a liberal multiculturalism that effaces power relations (2009, 48). She directs our attention to statements made by Spivak to support her claims, such as: "South Asians in the United States don't share the same history of oppression with the local Blacks, the East Asians and the Hispanics, on the other hand our skins are not white, and since most of us are postcolonials, we were trained in the British way, so we can be used as affirmative-action alibis" (ibid.); and "South Asians of the post-65 migration to the United States have often been typecast as the model minority 'solution' in opposition to what Du Bois saw as the fate of African Americans—being seen as the 'problem.'" In examining these statements, Schueller argues that Spivak positions racial groups in America into a binary opposition to the third world, particularly to South Asia (ibid.).

Schueller also points out that Spivak disregards the fact that the 1965 Immigration Act was politically related to the 1964 Civil Rights Act that, in turn, was related to the contradictions of U.S. foreign policy during the Cold War (2009, 37). She also tends to downplay the short-lived Third World Movement of the 1960s led by "a coalition of African American, Native American, Asian American and Chicana/o students who combined a critique of internal racial oppression with a critique of colonization by declaring ghettoes as 'internal colonies'" (Schueller 2009, 37).

I agree somewhat with Schueller's concerns that Spivak does not perform a sustained deconstructive analysis of the racial dynamics in the United States. I also agree that Spivak fails to apply her close reading skills to the U.S. affirmative action policies that were largely established as a result of the efforts of the civil rights movement led by African American clergy that spearheaded the passing of the various laws that protected the rights of those on the periphery. As a result, Spivak's silence of this important aspect can be construed as a contradiction to her deconstructive approach. Spivak herself silences the praxis of African American activists and scholars on how they inform her own thoughts.

Homi K. Bhabha: Crossbreeding in the Interstitial Space

Homi K. Bhabha is perhaps the most viable of the three postcolonial theorists in terms of providing concepts—interstitial space, performative practice, hybridity, mimicry/mockery, and ambivalence—that are fluid enough to supplement a multicultural framework. While his writing style is notoriously dense and abstruse, sprinkled abundantly with puns, metaphors, allegories, and other rhetorical tropes, the collection of essays in *The Location of Culture* has established him as a major contributor to postcolonial theory (Bhabba 1994).

Bhabha's cultural identity as a Parsi, a Zoroastrian community that migrated from Persia to India in the eighth century and are referred to as the "Jews of the East," definitely influenced his conception of postcolonial theory. As David Huddart writes:

> Bhabha's references to his origins are hardly statements of fixed ethnic identity. A principal characteristic of Parsi identity is … its cultural/ linguistic hybridity, which accompanies an economic mobility and international experience. Bhabha's own educational background demonstrates this mobility: he first studied at the University of Bombay, before moving to the University of Oxford. His teaching career has continued this mobility, taking in the University of Sussex in the UK, before crossing the Atlantic to Chicago and then Harvard. In his work, Bhabha explores the extent to which hybridity and migrant experiences of many kinds are defining features of modern life. His work also translates art and ideas between different contexts, and sees how this translation is in fact *transnational*, and this translation is comparable to Parsi culture as Bhabha understands it. (Huddart 2007)

Bhabha employs his vast expertise in British and American literary and critical theory, especially deconstruction and the poststructural psychoanalytical work of Jacques Lacan, to launch his postcolonial analysis by way of a close reading of literary and other texts. In the collection of essays that make up *The Location of Culture*, Bhabha mends Said's colonial discourse that operates within binary formation by emphasizing the dismantling of binary opposition and thus presenting a more complex colonized identity construction.

The Interstitial Space

Bhabha states that the interrelationships between the colonizer and the colonized are negotiated in the interstitial space (also referred to interchangeably as the third space, the liminal space, the middle space, or the in-between space).[13] The interstitial space is the site in which both conflict and

---

13. The interstitial space is also synonymous with "the contact zone" that cultural critics often adduce.

mutual assimilation occur when two cultures encounter each other. Thus it is the site of identity formation, deformation, reformation, and transformation. These multiplex formations are possible because the middle space is not a space of separation that produces privilege, but a space of mutual lingering and active interaction between cultures.

Since this space prohibits any idea of a pure or uncontaminated cultural site suspended and hovering over all others, cultural identity can never be defined independently because of the continual exchange that produces mutual representation of cultural difference (Bhabha 1994, 123). Since identity is perceived as a multicultural production, marginalized cultures actively participate in the formation of identity. However, this does not imply that, approaching colonialism from the middle space, the powers at play are equal. It is simply to suggest that colonial domination never involves the simple imposition of one culture onto another, but is a constantly shifting space that creates the possibility of displacements, resistance, and subversions.

Performative Practice

Displacement, resistance, and subversion are produced by the tensions created when the dominant narration of nation (or its myth of origin) is intersected by the performative practices of the marginalized. Performative practice is that "repetitious, recursive strategy" in which the dominated group constructs a national identity differently by integrating, yet revising, the national story (Bhabha 1994, 209; see Runions 2002, 74). Therefore, the performative practice of a people on the periphery disrupts the national myth of origin and interrupts homogenization.[14]

The three main concepts of postcolonial theory that structure performative practice are mimicry, ambivalence, and especially hybridity.

Mimicry

The reproduction of the colonized as "almost the same but not quite like" is an explicit colonial gesture. Colonial discourse necessitates that the colonized mimic the colonizer by adopting the cultural habits, assumptions,

---

14. The following chapter will illustrate the performative practice of the African American community throughout various historical stages.

and values of the colonizer. It was the habit of British imperialism to select a class of interpreters within the Indian populace who would be "Indian in blood, but English in tastes, in opinions, in morals, and in intellect" (Macaulay 1957, 729). Mimicry, the exaggerated copying of the language, culture, manners, and ideas of the colonizer, is urged by colonial authority because the system needs intermediaries and collaborators in order to function. Yet, according to Bhabha, the result of this "blurred copy" of the colonizer can be quite threatening. The reason is that mimicry can never be a mere duplication, a mere imitation, because aspects of the colonized culture will always transform the colonizer's culture into something new. Therefore, the "semi-mirroring" of the colonizing culture by the colonized contain elements of mimicry *and* mockery so that mimicry is at once a difference, a resemblance, and a menace (Bhabha 1994, 123). The emulation of the colonizer is consistently undermined by a sly civility and signification. The colonizer's identity is constantly slipping away by the effects of writing, joking, and repetition (Huddart 2006, 76). Though these effects are present in any act of enunciation, they are most compelling when performed by the colonized as conscious strategies of resistance.[15] It is from the interstitial site that mimicry slips into mockery, "where the reforming, civilizing mission is threatened by the displacing gaze of its disciplinary double" (Bhabha 1994, 123).

Ambivalence

The second concept integral to Bhabha's postcolonial theory is *ambivalence*. The term developed in psychoanalysis and refers to the simultaneous attraction toward and repulsion from an object, person, or action. Ambivalence disrupts "the clear-cut authority of colonial domination because it disturbs the simple relationship between colonizer and colonized" (Ashcroft, Griffiths, and Tiffin 1998, 13). On the one hand, the ambivalence of the colonizer is represented by the exploitation and the nurturing that exists simultaneously in their relationship with the colonized. On the other hand, the colonized relationship is ambivalent because the colonized is never simply complicit with, nor resistant to, the colo-

---

15. I am informed by Spivak's strategic essentialism by my assertion here. I suggest that the mimicry of the colonized provides them with the much needed time to learn the ways of the colonizer in order to consciously rattle the nerves of colonial authority. In this way, mockery/mimicry is an act of agency.

nizer. Ambivalence describes the "fluctuating relationship between mimicry and mockery which is fundamentally unsettling for the colonizer and is, therefore, an unwelcome aspect of colonial discourse" (ibid.).

Hybridity

Hybridity is defined as a new form of cultural identity that is created in the interstitial space where the colonizer and colonized cultures make contact and is a productive "third space of enunciation from which the colonized initiates self-authentication" (Singh and Schmidt, 2000, 24). According to Bhabha, cultural hybridity that is informed by mimicry/mockery and ambivalence decenters authority from its position of power so that authority itself becomes hybridized. Hybridization is an ongoing process and is key to the disruption of homogenization and is responsible for forming a fragmented and ambivalent identity.

Generalization of Bhabha's Postcolonial Theory

As mentioned above, Bhabha's work is extremely appealing to scholars who are interested in theorizing cultural identity. However, his analysis makes him vulnerable to the charge of producing a universal postcolonial condition. One can argue that postcolonial theory on its own does not adequately articulate how a particular community negotiates empire. This can be corrected, I opine, by taking special note that once the colonizer and colonized cultures make contact in the interstitial space, a specificity in the performative practice of the colonized is produced. This is because the colonized brings to the contact zone cultural elements that are unique, although those elements may be similar to other cultures. These specific cultural artifacts are traceable and extremely viable within the colonized community after making contact in the interstitial space. In fact, it is the unique elements of a people's culture that produces the revised performative practice. Therefore, the performative practice of, say, Ghanians cannot be expected to be the same as the performative practice of Indians or Palestinians, although all three of these groups were once colonized by the British.

Yet it is the general nature of these concepts when used as a *supplement* to the study of specific communities that makes Bhabha's work so compelling. Thus his work has the potential of forming a scholarly solidarity across various fields because of its capacity to speak to a commonality in cultural negotiations across broad cultural-political spectrums, yet also allows for an articulation based on specificity that complicates that notion of generality when fused with other methods of cultural analysis.[16]

The Join: African American Identity and Bhabhaian Postcolonial Theory

I suggest that Bhabha himself gestures toward this solidarity with African American cultural critics in *The Location of Culture*. This gesture is rarely commented on, or when it is noticed, is dismissed as a mere token gesture, as Bart Moore-Gilbert apparently does (2000a, 129). The twelve chapters in *The Location of Culture* were initially individual essays that were written over a ten-year span and first published in various journals, with most of the chapters discussing the relationship between the British colonizer and the Indian colonized. The introductory and concluding chapters of *Location of Culture* form an *inclusio*. In other words, these chapters serve as bookends that bind the entire essay collection together in a cohesive whole. It is interesting to note that the discussion in these two chapters emphasizes African American identity construction, whereas the other chapters do not. For instance, the introductory chapter, "The Locations of Culture," includes the artwork of African American artist Renée Green and the literary work of Toni Morrison's *Beloved* (1987).[17] In the conclusion, Bhabha returns to *Beloved* and also brings Du Bois's *Souls of Black Folk* (1996) into the discussion. According to Kenneth Mostern, the last paragraph from *The Souls of Black Folk* is intentionally positioned as the last paragraph in *The Location of Culture* so that it is "a double in the Bhabhaian sense, and also a reflection of the nonlinearity of historical time in cultural development" (Mostern 2000, 259).

Homi Bhabha and Renee Green

Renee Green's commentary on her own work, entitled *Sites of Genealogy,* serves to supplement Bhabha's concepts in her artistic representation of an internally colonized community via the middle space. Her art is compat-

---

16. In ch. 4 I will illustrate how a specific identity construction, African American, negotiates Bhabha's concepts in a particular sociopolitical environment.

17. Bhabha also discusses the work of South African Nadine Gordimer, *My Son's Story* (1991). Again, I suggest that a reason is to fill a void in his earlier essays by bringing in the issue of race and South African apartheid.

ible to Bhabha's understanding of hybridity as she imagines her work as having "a lot to do with a kind of fluidity, a movement back and forth, not making a claim to any specific or essential way of being" (cited in Bhabha 1994, 4).[18] Bhabha cites Green here in order to demonstrate how an African American artist "reflects on the need to understand cultural differences as the production of minority identities that 'split' … in the act of being articulated into a collective body" (Bhabha 1994, 4). Writing in dialogue with Green, Bhabha states:

> Political empowerment … come[s] from posing questions of solidarity and community from the interstitial perspective. Social differences are not simply given to experience through an already authenticated cultural tradition; they are the signs of the emergence of community … that takes you "beyond" yourself in order to return, in a spirit of revision and reconstruction, to the political *conditions* of the present. (ibid.)

Green goes on to describe her architectural site-specific work as an exhibition that "takes you beyond yourself" by dismantling the binary opposition. She says, "The stairwell became a liminal space, a pathway between the upper and lower areas, each of which was annotated with plaques referring to blackness and whiteness" (cited in Bhabha 1994, 5). Bhabha again glosses Green:

> The stairwell as liminal space, in-between the designations of identity, becomes the process of symbolic interaction, the connective tissue that constructs the difference between upper and lower, black and white. The

---

18. Her comment echoes that of the "Post-Soul Aesthetic." Post-Soul Aesthetic, often referred interchangeably as New Black Aesthetic, Post-Black, Neo-Soul, and New Black, references African Americans who were born after the civil rights movement and are of the mind-set that blackness is constantly in flux and denies the notion of a fixed, ironclad black aesthetic. The "posterizing" of blackness is considered a device for clearing conceptual space and for expressing skepticism and suspicion. This space-clearing gesture is necessary in order to diverge from a common root, yet keep a trace of the common point of departure. It is a positive assertion indicating a relation to the past. It is also a negative assertion, a gesture toward the lack of any other common theme in which to unify the diversity of the present. Post-Soul Aesthetics both embraces and rejects the homogeneity of a black consciousness and tends to mock nationalism in ways that demonstrate allusion-disruption strategies. The concept was first expressed by the author and film producer Trey Ellis (1989). See Ashe 2008; P. Taylor 2008. See also Bhabha 1995.

hither and thither of the stairwell, the temporal movement and passage
that it allows, prevents identities at either end of it from settling into
primordial polarities. (5)

Here Bhabha is illustrating the similarity in the ideas of a post-soul aesthetic (see n. 18 above) and his own thoughts on cultural location. Both
Bhabha and Green define a fluid, post-soul/postcolonial condition: an
elastic, cultural, mulattoesque sense of identity.[19]

Beloved and Bhabha

Through a postcolonial analysis of Toni Morrison's *Beloved*, Bhabha finds
the space to speak about the uncanny, the unhomely, or the *unheimliche*,
a Freudian term signifying that "'presencing' begins because it captures
something of the estranging sense of the relocation of the home and the
world," the public and the private, the dominant and the subordinate, "that
is the condition of extra-territorial and cross-cultural initiations" (Bhabha
1994, 13).

    Beloved is an historical fiction based on the true life story of Margaret
Garner, a runaway slave woman who murdered her two-year-old daughter
as a means of providing freedom for her daughter when they are about to
be brought back into captivity after escaping to Ohio. The plot revolves
around the troubling psyche of Sethe, the protagonist of the story, who
lives at 124 Bluestone Road, where the spirit of the dead child haunts the
dwelling. The main characters, Sethe, Paul D, and Denver, are ex-slaves
who, now free, attempt to reclaim their individual and collective identities,
but are haunted by the unspeakable past. Told in the form of a slave narrative, it reveals the devastation of American slavery on the lives of African
Americans and the haunting of a past that informs the present and the
future. Their anxiety and repression of being declared as property causes a
fragmentation of the self and a loss of true identity. Their subjectivity can

---

    19. The cultural mulatto archetype is described as being constructed by a multi-
racial mix of cultures that can also navigate easily in the white world. The term *cultural mulatto* implies that there is no longer a need to deny or suppress any part of a
complicated and contradictory cultural baggage to please either white or black people.
The function of the cultural mulatto is to trouble blackness in ways that depart signifi-
cantly from previous—if necessary—preoccupations with struggling for political freedom or with an attempt to establish or sustain a coherent black identity. Ultimately,
however, this troubling is done in the service of black people. See Ellis 1989, 235.

only be reconciled by a "rememory and disremembering" of the trauma of their past.[20]

For Bhabha, the unhomely moment is when we take "the measure of [our] dwelling in a state of 'incredulous terror,'" the moment when our world shrinks, leaving us breathless and anxious, uncertain and afraid (1994, 13). Although Bhabha claims that the unhomely is a paradigmatic colonial and postcolonial condition, he recognizes that it also has resonance with a range of transhistorical sites, including sites of slavery/postslavery in America. Thus the haunted house on 124 Bluestone Road is unhomely, illustrating "how the recesses of the domestic space become sites for history's most intricate invasions; how the borders between home and the world become confused; where the public resides in the private" (Bhabha 1992, 141). It is in the anxiety or the disoriented state of 124 Bluestone Road that the opportunity exists to expand into something new. In this case, the unhomely haunting of 124 Bluestone Road symbolizes the cultural memory of the African American community.[21]

Bhabha is consciously selective in analyzing only certain aspects of *Beloved*, focusing primarily on the main character, Sethe, the black female ex-slave, who must come to terms with a fragmentation of self on many levels and overcome enormous obstacles regarding race, gender, class, and motherhood. For Bhabha, she is indeed *the* representation of a troubled African American identity. However, Bhabha fails to take notice of how Denver, Sethe's youngest daughter and co-dweller in the unhomely space of 124, obtains healing and reconciliation for both herself and her mother. (He also neglects to mention that the young males of the house, Denver's brothers, leave home as soon as they are of age, and what that symbolizes.) This occurs when Denver ventures out of the house and reaches out to her community of elder women, women who come together and *collectively* draw Sethe out of her haunting. The women are led by Ella, who recognizes how detrimental Beloved's reappearance is to the community, and rises to help Sethe free herself from her own haunting.

In a scene from the film,[22] the women gather with the Bible and a twig root—a symbol of Western culture in one hand, and a symbol of African

---

20. Sethe's words for "remember and forget."

21. All African Americans do not have a history of being enslaved. Some, in fact, were slave owners, making the system of slavery a very peculiar system indeed.

22. The book was made into a film in 1998.

culture in the other.[23] It is here in the middle space of Western religion and African religious tradition that Sethe steps out of 124 Bluestone Road. This is an example of the function of the in-between as Bhabha puts it:

> It is in the emergence of the interstices—the overlap and displacement of domains of difference—that the intersubjective and collective experiences of *nationness*, community interest, or cultural value are negotiated. How are subjects formed 'in-between,' or in excess of, the sum of the 'parts' of difference (usually intoned as race/class/gender, etc.)? How do strategies of representation or empowerment come to be formulated in the competing claims of communities where, despite shared histories of deprivation and discrimination, the exchange of values, meanings and priorities may not always be collaborative and dialogical, but may be profoundly antagonistic, conflictual and even incommensurable? (1994, 2)

I think that the discussion of African American culture and the inclusion of the work of the African American women Renée Green and Toni Morrison at the outset of *The Location of Culture* is intended by Bhabha to join race and gender in his discourse as a sign of solidarity with African Americans and was written to round out the discussion and address issues that the other essays do not consider.[24]

Bhabha and Du Bois

Bhabha discusses Du Bois's *Souls of Black Folk* in the last chapter of *The Location of Culture* entitled "'Race,' Time and the Revision of Modernity." According to Kenneth Mostern in his cross-reading of *The Souls of Black Folk* with *The Location of Culture*, the move from *Souls* to *Location* is a

---

23. The film includes another scene that reveals the syncretistic worship style of African Americans where Baby Shugs, Sethe's mother-in-law and the religious leader of the Ohio community, leads the shout in the bush, a form of call and response that was the style of West African religious tradition.

24. Bringing in the voice of the African American in the introduction was a logical move on Bhabha's part since he had already relocated to the United States at the time of *The Location of Culture*'s publication in 1994. And, as I argued above, it is virtually impossible for a cultural critic residing in America to not include the dynamics of race in critical analysis. Therefore, Bhabha had ample motivation to make his work more inclusive than when the essays, which were written while he was living in England, appeared in various journals in the 1980s and early 1990s.

gesture in "which identical concerns are framed and overlapping terms are juxtaposed to different theoretical networks that create new synthesis in their own periods" (2000, 280). I agree with Mostern that Du Bois's ideas are seemingly reworked by Bhabha. Certainly both scholars indulge similarly in the concepts of doubling, ambivalence, hybridity, and interdisciplinarity in their respective works. In *The Souls of Black Folk*, Du Bois presents the Negro as a double that is produced by contradiction and racial domination, a presentation that has remarkable similarities to Bhabha's notion of hybridity. According to Du Bois, this double consciousness is produced in the high educational institutions that form the human and/or racial strivings which make consciousness possible. In this sense, the production of the double, or in postcolonial lingo, the hybrid, in postslavery is inevitable, and both desirable and personally disorienting. Throughout *The Souls of Black Folk*, hybridity is the productive form of African American culture, although it may not be explicitly termed as such.

Du Bois's use of the word *striving* is similar to Bhabha's *mimicry* that constructs a postslavery identity that is based on doubling and ambivalence. For instance, Du Bois "sits with Shakespeare and he winces not" (Mostern 2000, 280). And it is the Fisk Jubilee singers in *The Souls of Black Folk* who have taken the "low" folk tradition of the slave songs and the "high" artistic traditions of European concert performance and through their mutual elaboration have caused a "newness to enter the world," in Bhabhaian phraseology (ibid.).[25]

It is my opinion that Bhabha's concept of hybridity allows us to reposition Du Bois's articulation of double-consciousness for a new generation of African Americans. I posit that Du Bois's definition must be shifted from an inner striving motivated by despair to a revised understanding of an identity construction that thrives in spite of the fragmentation for it allows us to resist as well as accept elements of the dominant ethos. It is the striving in ambivalence, the embrace and the resistance of the dominant American ethos, the ebb and flow of a fluid construction that balances a double-consciousness construct. Now in the twenty-first

---

25. Few of the Fisk Jubilee singers had any formal vocal training and most of them had either been born into slavery or were first-generation freed men and women. Patti Malone was the only member to make a profession as a concert hall singer. She went to Europe where she changed her name to Desireo Plato and continued to sing on the concert stage. See Harris et al. 1974, 38.

century the striving in double-consciousness, the dwelling in the interstices of desire and revulsion, constructs new and complex identities.

However, it is important to also emphasize that it is the striving in hybridity, the embrace as well as the resistance of the dominant American ethos, that necessitates the caution against reinscription. The fluidity of twenty-first-century African American identity may no longer be the crippling double vision of the past as defined in the time of Du Bois, but indeed has the potential of being the crippling diplopia of the future as a segment of the African American community accommodates to the oppressive elements of the status quo.

Bhabha's Generalization and African American Religio-Political Dynamics

Some argue that Bhabha collapses African American culture into a generalization. For example, Malini Johar Schueller has strongly accused him of harnessing "the particularities of African American experience and history to a generalized celebration of the postmodern (re-routed to 'contramodern') and to a critique of modernity, though the tropes of liminality, interstitiality, hybridity and ambivalence" (2009, 39). She argues that the circulation of *Beloved* and *Souls of Black Folk* in *The Location of Culture* implies that the specific must always get translated to the general in order to interpret modernity.

However, I maintain that Bhabha's attempt to disseminate the complex cultural codes of Africa America into a generalization is unsuccessful because the cultural negotiations of this community cannot be neatly repackaged without incorporating its specific performative practice, a practice in which the engagement with the Bible is an integral component. The Bible plays such a central role in African American praxis because it mimics the dominant Euro-American practice that is legitimated by the assumption that the Bible is a living reality with a present and future meaning and not simply an interplay between text and reader (see Mabee 1991, 5). Therefore, African American identity is constructed and negotiated within a particular worldview. For this reason, the specificity of the African American praxis cannot be successfully collapsed into a generalization.

The colonized communities of British India experienced a different situation. They remained saturated in their own diverse cultures and religious expressions. Since the majority of Indians practice Hinduism, a well-established multiplex of cultural mores and codes remained intact.

Despite the overwhelming presence of the colonizer's culture, the majority of the colonized did not convert to Christianity, which the British would deem necessary to achieve the construction of the ideal "mimic person."

"Signs Taken for Wonders"

I suggest that this fact can be uncovered in Bhabha's essay, "Signs Taken for Wonders: Questions of Ambivalence and Authority under a Tree outside Delhi, May 1817," which first appeared in the volume *"Race," Writing, and Difference* (Gates 1986, 163–84) and is reprinted in *The Location of Culture* (Bhabha 1994, 145–74). Bhabha writes in the opening paragraph:

> There is a scene in the cultural writings of English colonialism which repeats so insistently after the early nineteenth century—and, through that repetition, so triumphantly *inaugurates* a literature of empire—that I am bound to repeat it once more. It is the scenario, played out in the wild and wordless wastes of colonial India, Africa, the Caribbean, of the sudden, fortuitous discovery of the English book. It is, like all myths of origin, memorable for its balance between epiphany and enunciation. The discovery of the book is, at once, a moment of originality and authority. It is, as well, a process of displacement that, paradoxically, makes the presence of the book wondrous to the extent to which it is repeated, translated, misread, displaced. It is with the emblem of the English book—"signs taken for wonders"—as an insignia of colonial authority and a signifier of colonial desire and discipline, that I want to begin this chapter. (Bhabha 1994, 145–46)

The English book "memorable for its balance between epiphany and enunciation" is, of course, the Bible; and it is the biblical narratives that are the "signs taken for wonders" that are repeated, re-presented, translated, and misread. Thus the essay can be understood as an attempt by Bhabha to bring in the Bible as an "insignia of colonial authority and a signifier of colonial desire and discipline" (1994, 146). The role of the Bible functions as a "process of displacement" in the colonizing moment. This is Bhabha signifying on the Western penchant for using Scripture in order to claim a transcendent or metaphysical authenticity and authority.

The opening scene in the essay confirms this point. It relates the excitement of Indian catechist Anund Messeh as he rushes to a tree grove just outside Delhi in 1817 where several hundred "natives" are instructing themselves in the reading of the Bible conveniently translated into the Hindi language. Naturally, as a catechist, Messeh wants to ensure that the group is learning Christian doctrine correctly, especially the two key Christian rites of passage, baptism and the Sacrament or Lord's Supper. The acceptance of correct doctrine regarding these two rites are key to the conversion process and must be performed with the proper understanding in order to be a properly colonized Indian Christian.

Alas, Messeh is not very successful in fully convincing the natives of the necessity of appropriating the colonizer's sacred scripts, nor of mimicking the colonizer's rituals, especially the rite of the Lord's Supper. According to this relatively small group of Christian converts convened under the trees in New Delhi, this is because the colonizers eat cow's flesh, and this they cannot comply with, saying, "To all the other customs of Christians we are willing to conform, but not to the Sacrament, because the Europeans eat cow's flesh, and this will never do for us." To which Messeh replies, "This WORD is of God, and not of men; and when HE makes your hearts to understand, then you will PROPERLY comprehend it." They replied, "*If all our country* will receive this Sacrament, then will we" (Bhabha 1994, 148, emphasis added).

Limitations of Bhabha's Postcolonial Theory in "Signs Taken for Wonders"

The colonizer's goal in distributing the Bible in the Hindi language, in the words of Stephen Moore, is "to function as a time bomb that will eventually decimate the natives' indigenous religious culture from within" (2005, 89). Despite the desire of the British, however, it is a fact that the majority of the natives were not made "instruments of pulling down their own religion and of erecting in its ruins the standards of the Cross" (ibid.). To the contrary, they resisted this devastation precisely because they did not forsake their religious belief system/culture. Christian Indians resisted an unreflected embrace of the colonizer's book under that tree outside Delhi. This is because their cultural mores prohibited the adoption of certain aspects of the colonizer's culture. Therefore, the Indians consciously negotiated the colonizer's culture by deciding what they would and would not appropriate based on their own cultural standards and traditions. It is in this negotiation in the middle space that Bhabha suggests a newness is born and hybridization occurs: "For it is in-between the edict of Englishness and the assault of the dark unruly spaces of the earth, through an act of repetition, that the colonial text emerges uncertainly.... Consequently, the colonial presence is always ambivalent, split between its appearance as original and authoritative and its articulation as repetition and difference" (1994, 153).

However, I think that the religious aspect in the interrelationship between the British colonizer and the Indian colonized does not seem to adequately crystallize Bhabha's concepts that are said to foster a colonized identity that mimics the colonizer. In terms of religious practice, there is no widely sustained "act of repetition" or performative practice by the majority of the Indian populace that mimics the colonizer's use of Christian Scripture to legitimate the colonizer's symbolic order. In fact, Hinduism, the major religio-political system of India, was integral to the resistance/subversion of the colonizer's ideological strategy.

On the other hand, Bhabha's abstractions seemingly become more succinct, in terms of religious practice, when placed within an African American context. The performative strategy of this community is, indeed, heavily dependent on the appropriation of Western Christianity in terms of identity construction. Therefore, the appropriation of Scripture is very influential in the production of the community's performative practice as a "repetitious recursive strategy" that mimics/mocks the dominant Euro-American ethos. Therefore, I posit that the obscure concepts of postcolonial theory become very concrete when placed within an African American religious/cultural context.

One of the reasons for this crystallization is because of the peculiar predicament of the African American ancestors being denied the opportunity to "legally" integrate their cultural traditions and religio-political systems in their new home (although it was impossible to actually prevent that practice). The prohibition forced enslaved Africans to appropriate Western culture, which, according to postcolonial theory, morphed into "something new" in the interstitial space, the contact zone where cultures collide. Thus the communal transformation of enslaved Africans to African Americans was achieved by a heavy borrowing of the master's tools, particularly in terms of religious praxis and the development of an American biblical hermeneutical tradition.[26]

CONCLUSION: POSTCOLONIAL THEORY'S USEFULNESS AS A SUPPLEMENT TO AFRICAN AMERICAN SCRIPTURALIZATION

The supplementation of postcolonial theory to African American scripturalization blends smoothly in ironing out the knotty dimensions of

---

26. The following chapter provides a more detailed illustration of how African American performative practice crystallizes Bhabha's concepts.

a hybrid identity construct. Postcolonial theory makes it possible to articulate the complexity of cultural negotiation in a postslavery, post-colonized community. The reason for this is because postcolonial theory and African American scripturalization are compatible discourses sharing common goals and objectives. These include: revealing the devastating aspects of neocolonialism and the lingering forms of discrimination, inequality, and racism that the system perpetuates; breaking down the barriers of cultural hierarchy and investigating issues of representation, essentialism, and nationalism; focusing on a subversive revision of the dominant version of history; giving voice to a text muted by dominant historical referents; focusing on revealing the worldliness of the text; and both make possible an imaginative invention of self beyond the limits of historical re-presentations.

As Bhabha states, "The intervention of postcolonial or black critique is aimed at transforming the conditions of enunciation at the level of the sign … not simply setting up new symbols of identity, new 'positive images' that fuel an unreflective 'identity politics'" (1994, 354). Although Bhabha theorizes solely through the lens of Western poststructural theory and thus privileges a Western epistemology, the concepts are usable because they are flexible enough to encompass the broad political and cultural spectrums that make up the African American community.

Yet the application of postcolonial theory does not satisfactorily address the particular negotiation strategies of the African American community. African American scripturalization, however, with its focus on specificity, disables the tendency of collapsing specific cultural negotiations into a generalization that is so fluid that it disallows any notion of uniqueness and difference.

In the following chapter, I discuss how the concepts of mimicry, ambivalence, and hybridity illustrate the processes of the hermeneutical praxis of the African American community and how a hybrid identity construction is produced through the negotiation of Scripture, the texts that are responsible for constructing the American myth of origin as a sacred narration of nation.

3

THE STRANGENESS OF HOME:
AFRICAN AMERICAN IDENTITY SIGNIFIED
IN THE (POSTCOLONIAL) MIDDLE PASSAGE

In the beginning ... America was a venture in exegesis. America's meaning was implicit in its destiny, and its destiny was manifest to all who had the grace to discover its meaning. A poly-ethnic, multi-racial, openly materialistic, self-consciously individualistic people knit together in the bonds of myth, voluntarily, with a force of belief unsurpassed by any other modern society.

— Sacvan Bercovitch, *The Rites of Assent*

Five hundred years ago one man claimed to have discovered a new world
Five centuries later, "we the people" are forced to celebrate a black holocaust
How can we call a takeover a discovery?

— Public Enemy, lyrics from "Hitler Day"

Nations, like narratives, lose their origins in the myths of time and only fully realize their horizons in the mind's eye.

— Homi K. Bhabha, *Narration and Nation*

CARTOGRAPHY

This volume's journey has arrived at the methodological crossroads, the threshold where cultural specificity/praxis intertwines with generality/theory, where realities are conjured by the imagined and the implied. As stated in chapter 1, since African American scripturalization is a "flesh-and-blood" reading activity that is based on a doubling—living in the present as well as reading the past—cultural context and social location must be factors in making meaning. Therefore, a comprehensive discussion of the "strangeness of home," a term I use to signify the contextual point of departure for the work of African American scripturalization, is in order.

The term is meant to imply that the "strangeness of home" is a hybrid, deconstructive communal praxis that challenges hierarchy by illustrating how identity constructions are contradicted by every effort to construct them. The "strangeness of home" implies, therefore, that there is a need for a close, critical read of the dominant context in order to expose the contradictions evident within and to unleash the signifyin(g) that the reductive tendency of the dominant ethos seeks to suppress. In this context, there is a continuous unfolding of meanings that are derived from signifyin(g) in which one meaning brings on another. This suggests that the "strangeness of home" is a contrapuntal praxis in that it exposes the unsaid, the silenced, the unmentioned, the underside of the binary that has been subordinated in the presentation of the dominant context.

The supplementation of postcolonial theory assists in comprehending the intricate dynamics of the "strangeness of home" because of its usefulness in dismantling the confining notions of a homogeneous or fixed identity construct and replacing this fixity with a more fluid idea of identity construction by providing theoretical concepts that elucidate the complex dimensions of African American identity construction, thus assisting in revealing the suppositions/presuppositions that drive the hermeneutical process.

Cultural critics refer to what I am expressing as an act of "critical conscientization, … turning criticism upon itself in a quest for self-awareness and self-reflection" (Bailey et al. 2009, 31). According to Randall Bailey, Tat-siong Benny Liew, and Fernando Segovia,

> Such conscientization moves in two directions, by no means mutually exclusive. On the one hand, it may veer toward questions of critical identity: background and motivation. Rather than engage in criticism in an unreflective fashion, the critic pauses to ponder who s/he is as a critic, whence and why s/he does what s/he does as a critic. On the other hand, it may favor questions of critical role: procedure and objective. Instead of pursuing criticism in abstract terms, the critic halts to reflect what it is that s/he does, how and to what end s/he does s/he does as a critic. Both paths of questioning are closely interwoven: while the first type of intervention lays the ground for a circumscription of critical task, the second builds on the foundations of critical identity. (Bailey et al. 2009, 31)

The mapping of a cultural journey in this chapter is to be considered a critical conscientization. The comprehensive charting of cultural context is this cultural critic's reflection on identity, background, and motivation. In articulating the knotty dynamics that are inherent in the construction of African American identity, I aim to illustrate how and why I produce meaning in the way that I do in my scripturalization of Revelation that follows in the next chapter.

The Embodied Text: An American Biblical Hermeneutic

According to Charles Mabee, the Bible, although a product of antiquity, "is yet the bearer of our own [Americans'] deepest societal aspirations" (1991, 5). He maintains that American sociopolitical events give witness to the enormous appeal of underwriting the status quo with commonly held biblical notions (although "with remarkably little hermeneutical sophistication and wrestling with actual biblical texts"; ibid.). Mabee terms this engagement with the Bible "American biblical hermeneutics," a relational way of reading biblical texts as an interaction of text and context. Based on Mabee's analysis, then, one can argue that American Protestant theology is a reader-oriented praxis and is a self-conscious embodiment that depends on an understanding of the Bible's authoritative function that "is historical fact, rather than theological prescription" (ibid.).

In the Beginning, America Was a Venture in Biblical Exegesis

The American biblical hermeneutical tradition emerged out of the abyss in the seventeenth and eighteenth centuries. Puritan and Protestant ministers and magistrates were the first to thoroughly dip the infant colonies into the Scriptures, steeping their constituents in biblical typology in their rhetorical errand to create a theocracy underscored by a particular biblical interpretation. This hermeneutical turn was commissioned to university-trained divines as they charted a course for convincing their flocks of their blessed status as a redeemed people in sacred covenant with God and with the land, constructing their congregants as "Heirs of the Promise" and as "the children of Abraham" (Valeri and Wilson 1985, 25). Puritan sermons and speeches claimed New England as the new Jerusalem and identified their errand with that of the woman who flees into the wilderness escaping the grasp of Satan, who runs amok in Babylon, old England.[1]

This modus operandi by way of biblical allusion and imagery was implanted in the settlers during their incubation in the belly of the beast— old England—when the beast was heavily involved in its political struggles with Rome.[2] During this crisis, a Protestant historiography based largely on biblical imagery played a vital role in the construction of a new historical consciousness, and the colonists brought this new consciousness with them when they entered the wilderness of North America.

Unsurprisingly, the sermon John Cotton preached as the Puritan fleet prepared to depart from the shores of an idolatrous England was entitled, "God's Promise to His Plantation." The biblical passage was 2 Sam 7:10, "I will appoint a place for my people Israel, and I will plant them that they may dwell in a place of their own, and move no more."

John Winthrop, the first magistrate of the Massachusetts Bay Colony, poignantly reinstilled this God-given right of the Puritan occupation during their crossing. While on board the *Arabella*, Winthrop waxed reminiscent of Moses, resorting to Old Testament covenantal language in his "Modell of Christian Charitie" to convey the necessity of the interdependence required between God and the people in fulfillment of the Puritan errand. He opens his "Christian Charitie" with the following preamble: "God Almightie in his most holy and wise providence hath soe disposed of the Condicion of Mankinde, as in all times, some must be rich, some poore, some highe and eminent in power and dignitie; others meane and in subjection" (Cherry 1998, 27). He assured the Puritans that "the God of Israel is among us" and that New England was to be the "Citty upon a Hill," the new Jerusalem that was to be a beacon of light to the nations.

---

1. Ironically, in contrast to the Puritans, the homilies and hymns of the Protestants in Virginia praised the Old World as the land of milk and honey, and the New World in need of salvation, especially from Spain, Portugal, and the pope. See Zakai 1992, 94–156. The Protestants of Virginia also appropriated the *Aeneid*, the Roman myth of origin, in their identity construction. Robert Bellah writes, "just as Winthrop thought of Moses so Captain John Smith thought of Aeneas in what Howard Mumford Jones calls the 'prose Aeneid' that he composed to recount his establishment of the English Colony in Virginia." Bellah claimed that "Virgil's Aeneid even fitfully rivaled the Exodus of the Children of Israel as an archetypal story of flight into the wilderness in order to found a new city" (1992, 22).

2. Protestant European-American traditions sprang to life as a self-conscious alternative to the medieval Roman mass. See Haldeman 2007, 17.

So, even before the Puritans had set foot upon the soil of North America, they had already laid claim to the land, colonized the original inhabitants, and scripted an imagined divine social order. All of this was accomplished while hovering over the waters of the Atlantic Ocean. Winthrop's speech served as the inspiration for the policies of manifest destiny, which justifies political, cultural, and economic expansion as divine providence (see O'Sullivan 1845).

Upon occupation of the land, the practice of everyday Puritan life was expressed in a fusion of sacred-secular language, a tongue spoken not only with each other, but also spoken to the other. The cloaking of colonial life in biblical metaphor was based on the deep-seated conviction of the Puritans that revelation was situated within the dimension of history. According to Harry S. Stout (1982), if American Puritan reasoning was presented in the form of a syllogism, it would go something like this:

Major Premise: God's promises of blessing and judgment recorded in Scripture apply to professing peoples as well as to individuals

Minor Premise: New England is a professing people bound in public submission to the Word of God

Conclusion: Therefore, New England is a peculiar people of God.

According to this logic, the first-generation Puritans regarded their society as a society conformed to the Scriptures. They reverently believed that their errand would usher in a new world order and that they would be standing at its helm as cocreators with God (see further Gordis 2003, 1–12).

The State of Declension

As the Puritan colony grew and as the colonists began to prosper as merchants, apostasy, worldliness, contention, greed, so-called heresies and schisms derailed their dreams and the Puritan errand turned into an error. The second-generation Puritans steadily unraveled the weave of the covenantal life, turning instead to embrace the ideals of British socioeconomics and politics. In addition, other denominational groups, such as the Quakers, Baptists, Lutherans, and Presbyterians, began trickling into North America and thereby contributed to the Puritan demise.

However, many still presupposed that New England was the new Jerusalem, as the declension-inspired jeremiads of 1650–1690 attest.[3] The jeremiads lamented the failure of New England to measure up to its divine calling. Sermons before the General Assembly became particularly doleful as the clergy bewailed the decline of godliness among the people. They moaned over the conflicts between church members, the appearance of heretics, and violations of the Sabbath, and warned impious children. Through their woeful cries, the hand of God was discerned in natural and historical events, including crop failure, Indian wars, droughts, and epidemics (Cherry 1998, 27).

Yet, these natural occurrences provided occasion for the reuse of a biblical past for both social critique of the present as well as optimism for the future. For, although new Israel was chastised by God for its sins, its sins could never extinguish the confidence that New England stood at the center of redemptive history. The broken covenant with God could never undo the Puritan self-construct of "chosenness," as the excerpt from Michael Wigglesworth's *God's Controversy with New England (written in the time of the great drought of 1662)* illustrates:

> Consider wel & wisely what the rod
> wherewith thou art from yeer to yeer chastised
> instructeth thee, Repent & turn to God
> who wil not have his nurture be despised
> Thou still hast thee many praying saints
> of great account, and precious with the Lord,
> Who dayly power out unto him their plaints,
> and strive to please him both in deed & word
> Cheer on, sweet souls, my heart is with you all,
> and shall be with you, maugre Sathan's might:
> And wheresoère this body be a Thrall,
> still in New England shall be my delight. (Cherry 1998, 28)[4]

The demise of the errand prompted third-generation divines to transfer the concept of covenant to nation. Cotton Mather writes in 1692, "O

---

3. The rhetorical form of the jeremiad alludes to the prophet Jeremiah, who issued fierce warnings to the southern kingdom of Judah of its destruction because of its disobedience to God's ordinances.

4. First published in *Proceedings of the Massachusetts Historical Society* 12 (May 1871): 83–93.

American Jerusalem.... Put on thy beautiful Garments, O *America*, the holy City!" According to Sacvan Bercovitch, Cotton Mather's *Magnalia Christi Americana* describes the colonial venture as "a history ... to anticipate the state of the New Jerusalem" (Bercovitch 1993, 137). Bercovitch claims that Mather's *Magnalia* surpasses what the *Aeneid* accomplished for Rome—the establishment of a divine corporate identity. Mather's ecclesiastical history has the Puritan emigrants excelling over the Trojan exiles and portrays the millennium toward which the Reformation is moving as immeasurably outshining the Augustan Pax Romana.

A Sacred Narration of Nation

It is during the one hundred years of external and internal conflict of the late eighteenth century through the end of the nineteenth century (1776–1865) that an American Protestant theology is formed not as an escape from culture, but as a self-conscious embodiment of culture, propelled and sustained by Scripture. According to Mark Noll, Scripture became a gateway for the minister's social, political, or cultural convictions, which had been securely in place before he had turned to the Bible, not for the proclamation of essentially biblical messages (Noll 1982, 45).

Between the Revolutionary War and the Civil War, the "Puritans became Yankees," and the thirteen independent colonies were transformed into a nation (Noll 1982, 114–37). According to Catherine Albanese, in order for thirteen clocks to tick as one, the construction of a myth of origin was vital to the establishment of a center of power (1976, 9). She insists that the Revolutionary War was the formative event in which every subsequent generation inherited an existent set of primary sacred myths and symbols created by the founding fathers. The threat of war escalated the production of a biblically informed myth of origin as the infant republic struggled for independence and liberty for all. As the colonists fought for freedom from the tyrannical rule of the British, the imagery of an errand in the wilderness fleeing from the sharp claws of the beast (this time embodied by King George III) was once again resurrected. The victory won over Old Babylon was proof of the nation's blessed status in the eyes of God.

As "sons of the fathers," the patriots marched to a fundamental cadence that fused the past and the present together by way of a sacred myth of origin (sacred narration). A collective cultural memory formed by the events of the Revolution. The biblical narratives would serve to synchronize time, re-presenting Winthop's idea of a Puritan colony to that of a *unified country* that was to be the "light to the nations," a "city on a hill." According to Albanese, "the result was so powerful a hierophany that it became a new mythic center for themselves and for those who would come after" (1976, 9). A change had occurred in the civic faith of the colonies, which now declared themselves as the United States of America. During this time of strife, the American scriptures—the Declaration of Independence and the Constitution of the United States—were written.

This was also the time of the Great Awakening, that period in American history when it was firmly believed that God had truly visited "his glory upon his people." The day of Pentecost had come, a clear portent that America was, indeed, the beloved land of God. A converted life resulted in becoming heirs to the kingdom neither by the will of man, nor by the blood of man, but by the grace of God alone. The covenant phrases of the Bible continued to be popular throughout the century: "a city set upon a hill," "a light to the nations," the servant of the Lord," "the chosen people." These phrases continued to be integral in constructing the ethos of the nation as well as individual Euro-American identity. The writings of the literate and the speech of the illiterate were explete with biblical cadences and allusions. Daniel Webster attempted to transform early education based on the reading of his own distinctly American translation of the Bible. Bible societies were formed with the objective of placing a Bible in every household. The founding fathers continued to construct an American ethos based on ancient Mediterranean and biblical imagery. Thomas Jefferson cut and pasted his own version of the New Testament and constructed his own version of the teachings of the historical Jesus.

John Adams suggested the Greek mythic imagery of the "Judgment of Hercules" be used for the Great National Seal of the United States. Alternatively, Benjamin Franklin proposed the imagery of Moses, staff in hand, hovering over the parted Red Sea and an armed pharaoh about to be devoured by the waters while in pursuit of the Israelites. The imagery was meant to memorialize the conflict between the colonies and the British by typing the colonies as the eleven tribes of Israel seeking peace from the political bondage of Pharaoh's hardened heart. The motto, "Rebellion to Tyrants Is Obedience to God," was to run along the imagery. Finally, the founders settled on the imagery of an eagle on the obverse (the bird that represented the Roman Empire) and an Egyptian pyramid on the reverse.

After George Washington's death, twenty-one sermons lamenting his demise used 2 Sam 3:38, David's cry to Abner—"Know ye not that there is a prince and a great man fallen this day in Israel?" And, in 1832, Francis

Grey extolled George Washington as "the pillar of fire by night that led us out of bondage."

The American sacred narration of nation that is based on an appropriation of the biblical narratives is also grounded in duplicity—for, as the sons of the fathers shouted out, "Give me liberty, or give me death," they were very busy building the nation's foundation on the peculiar institution of enslavement and inequality (Noll 2006, 31–50). Yet, surprisingly, the "fathers'" prodigy turned out to include daughters and sons of many hues who narrated their own particular versions of the American myth of origin.

THE AFRICAN AMERICAN PERFORMATIVE PRACTICE: AN "ALMOST THE SAME BUT NOT QUITE" SACRED NARRATION OF NATION

America, it is to thee,
Thou boasted land of liberty,—
It is to thee I raise my song,
Thou land of blood, and crime, and wrong.
It is to thee, my native land,
From whence has issued many a band
To tear the black man from his soil,
And force him here to delve and toil. (Gates and McKay 1997, 402)

James Monroe Whitfield's contrapuntal signifyin(g) in 1853 is evidence that the United States of America is far too complex to be understood by one single version of its myth of origin. The myth of America as a biblical land of the free and home of the brave is countered by many different voices crying in the wilderness (see Tweed 1997), with the descendants of Africans perhaps crying out the loudest. Many enslaved and free Africans converted to the Baptist and Methodist faiths during the Great Awakening movement, the time when the American biblical hermeneutic tradition was in its early stages of development. Following the example of white evangelicals, the Africans began to parallel their experiences with the events narrated in the "Holy Book" (see O'Neale 1993; Wills 1997).

Perhaps the collective memory of the Africans connected with certain cultural elements and mores made manifest in the Bible—the role of Moses and his conjuring abilities, the rituals of circumcision and sacrifice, divination, the laws of purity and marriage, harvest cycles and festivals, the incantations of the prophets—just to name a few of the similar cultural elements. It is indeed possible that this perception of a shared experience with the "people of the book" thrust the Africans beyond their horizon and enabled them to identify with common religio-political elements that channeled the transference to Christianity. After all, as Charles Joyner claims, "the story of the emergence of African American Christianity is a story of the emergent African American culture as well as of residual African cultures, a story of change as well as continuity" (1995, 181–82; see also Raboteau 1980, 1995b, 2001). Mercy Amba Oduyoye seems to think this is the case: "Many Africans find that the Bible has a ring of truth about it, that its language, proverbs, and ideals of morality and justice are very close to the world they know and understand.... Africans ... locate themselves within its history, its culture, its social structures, and its obvious assumption that the divine is a reality and is involved in the created order" (1995, 35–36).

This connection to biblical context is evident in 1792, when an African minister named John Marrant "told Bostonian blacks that if they wished to see themselves presented on 'the level ... with the greatest kings on the earth,' they should 'study the holy book of God'" (Saillant 2000, 236). And in 1794 Olaudah Equiano, who claimed royal African heritage, stated, "Whenever I looked in the Bible I saw things new, and many texts were immediately applied to me with great comfort" (237).

Might one suggest then that the Bible encoded signs that assisted the African to adopt a position of self-determined legitimacy? (Long 1997, 26). In any case, the converted Africans' firm belief that they too were chosen members of the kingdom cannot be denied. By mimicking the rhetorical strategy of their Euro-American counterparts by the immersion into the biblical stories, they too created the spiritual and mental power necessary to endure their situation in life. However, their sacred narration unfolded into a mockery of the Euro-American narration. The nation's claim to be the new Israel was contradicted by the old Israel still enslaved in its midst (Raboteau 1995a, 80). So, as a countersignification to a predominant ethos legitimated by Scripture, the enslaved Africans "talked back" by mimicking the tools of Euro-American identity construction, thereby thoroughly mocking that construction. By learning to "speak" the alien tongue, the enslaved Africans were able to construct a shared cultural memory, carving out a means for a cultural-political solidarity that enabled them to resist and, therefore, exist (hooks 1994, 170).

This is why I suggest that African American culture is an exemplum of Bhabha's notion of "performative practice," that repetitious recursive strategy in which people, not necessarily unified in their beliefs or by their willingness to be represented by the national identity, take part in producing national culture differently through the integration with, or the enunciation of, the national story or identity. African American cultural praxis, then, is a specific illustration to Bhabha's general statement: "Counter-narratives of the nation that continually evoke and erase its totalizing boundaries—both actual and conceptual—disturb those ideological manoeuvres through which 'imagined communities' are given essentialist identities" (Bhabha 1990, 300).

This counternarrative (or, à la Said, "contrapuntal" narration) was enacted in the public sphere, performed in the secure space of sacred language. The enslaved Africans signified resistance and subversion in all aspects of everyday life—in the songs they sang out in the fields, in their talk when they met each other in town in the presence of whites, or when they were gathered with whites at church and special festival events, and even as they sat on their front porches or worked in their gardens. Signifyin(g) with Scripture was not performed in the dark or hidden in the shade of the bush.[5] And yet, to the naïve, the uninitiated, the cultural outsider, the signifyin(g) transcript did remain hidden, blurred, and allusive. In a way, the transcript relied on the veil, on the unacknowledged enactment in the public sphere, because its performance depended on indeterminacy and the impossibility of indictment.

"Let My People Go": The Spirituals as Musical Signification

Since the enslaved Africans were forbidden to learn how to read, they created alternative venues to produce their particular sacred narration. The spirituals were a main venue against the peculiar institution of slavery. Spirituals such as "John Saw," "Put John on de Islan," "Nobody Knows de Trouble I've Seen,"[6] and "Joshua Fought the Battle at Jericho" soothed an

---

5. See Scott 1995, 17–44. His claim is that oppressed groups resist domination by a hidden transcript that is performed away from the eyes of the dominated. This is a passive resistance that is performed in the safety of the domain of the oppressed where their true feelings regarding domination can be expressed without fear of reprisal. My statement counters that argument somewhat by claiming that resistance to domination is a very public matter in terms of African American communal life. Also, my discussion below on the oratory given by African American activists during the public African American freedom festivals of the nineteenth century will attest to this fact.

6. This song was a favorite in the Sea Islands when ill feeling and trouble erupted due to government action regarding confiscated lands on the islands. See Dett 1927, 232.

anguished soul and empowered the collective psyche by creating a safe public space to resist a bizarre ideology that justified injustice and human inequality. In fact, the spiritual "Go down Moses" was so bold in its stance of resistance that it was banned from many slave plantations.

Lawrence Levine mentions the enslaved African's creativity for survival: "The spirituals are the records of a people who found the status, the harmony, the values, and the order they needed to survive by internally creating an expanded universe, by literally willing themselves reborn" (1997, 73; see Callahan 2006, 41–46; Abbington 2000; Burnim 2000). I would make a slight "rendition" of Levine—the sacred music of the nineteenth-century African American Christian community enabled them to *maintain* an inner space of status, harmony, and value. The community's performative ability to reshape the prevailing rituals of the status quo allowed them to resist and subvert the constructed symbolic order and thus give voice against an unjust and chaotic world. The spirituals were a musical mode of African American signification that mimicked while slyly mocking Euro-American musical material as a means of resistance. This was accomplished by the community's redirection of a particular Christian hymn through indirection, wordplay, and style (in other words, signifyin[g]). According to church historian Ray Allen Billington,

> the Negroes, through their songs, were able to develop a vocabulary and means of expression that was entirely their own. This was done by sprinkling their melodies with symbols, images, and concepts borrowed from their African past and completely unknown to the whites. By developing this symbolism as a universal language among themselves, they were able to harbor and express thoughts that were not understandable to others. Their masters never realized this; instead they poked fun at the Negroes for using a jargon which apparently made little sense. The Negroes gladly endured this ridicule, knowing that by doing so they helped preserve a degree of intellectual freedom. Little did the whites realize, as they ridiculed the slaves for their "ignorance," that those slaves were enjoying the satisfaction which goes with a sense of superiority. (1969, ix)

The African American spirituals serve as an example of the subversive nature of the hybrid's mimicry. This "musical mimicking" made possible the strategic enunciation of a suitable outlet of dissent from an external, immoral, and chaotic world.

AFRICAN AMERICAN FREEDOM FESTIVALS: A DOUBLE SIGNIFICATION

African American freedom festivals of the nineteenth century also contributed to maintaining a community through a counternarrative that
reconstructed cultural memory. Public celebration speeches and the pub-
lications of literate, free blacks in the first quarter of the nineteenth century were full of biblical allusions that increasingly provoked the system
of chattel slavery. These acts of counterremembering America's sacred
narration relied on a Euro-American calendar of events, yet transformed
and reordered the civic rituals in both function and meaning. According to Genevieve Fabre, during these festivals "African Americans were
not simply performing culture, they were performing crucial social and
political acts. The feasts were used as a vehicle for re-fashioning a better
world and to wield new power" (1994, 75). According to William Gravely,
this refashioning was dependent on a dialectic framework (1995, 128–29;
see Braxton 2002, 6–12). The oratory of the freedom festivals revealed
the hybridity of the African American, who doubly memorialized African origins and reiterated the advantages of being born in America. For
instance, Absalom Jones's 1808 New Year's Day oration on the end of the
transatlantic slave trade illustrates this hybridity as his rhetoric mimics
the American mode of construction by way of "an act of transfer," by a re-
presentation of the celebration of the Jewish seder:

> Let the history of the sufferings of our brethren and of their deliverance
> descend by this means to our children, to the remotest generations. and
> when they shall ask, in time to come, saying, "what mean the lessons,
> the psalms, the prayers and the praises in the worship of this day?" Let
> us answer them by saying, the Lord, on the day of which this is the anni-
> versary, abolished the trade which dragged your fathers from their native
> country and sold them as bondmen in the United States of America.
> (Gravely 1995, 128–29)

In the spirit of 1776, Peter Williams's oratory claimed the revolutionary heritage of the republic as he made reference to the "sons of 76" whose
"inspired voice" gave humankind the "noble sentiments" of the Declaration of Independence. Williams's contemporary, George Lawrence, demonstrates the ambivalent nature of African American identity construction
in his public oratory as he, on one hand, complained: "Many are the mis-
eries of our exiled race in this land," while on the other hand, "he praised

'the land in which we live' because it gave the 'opportunity to advance the prosperity of liberty'" (Gravely 1995, 129).

Just as with the spirituals, the festivals served as a site of signifyin(g) in the African American tradition. This tradition showcased the inequality and the absurdity of the nineteenth-century national ethos. The orator's "performative strategy" served to expose a remnant of history that was intentionally omitted from the mainstream collective festival celebration and that challenged the hypocrisy embedded in the American notion of democracy, freedom, and liberty.

THE BLACK JEREMIADS

Many African American public speeches and writings in the first quarter of the nineteenth century signified with the Psalms and referenced Africa, especially Egypt and/or Ethiopia. The most quoted verse in black religious history was Ps 68:31: "Princes shall come out of Egypt, and Ethiopia shall soon stretch out her hands to God." Historians consider the public use of Egyptian/Ethiopian prophecy as the "black jeremiad," a termed coined by Wilson Moses. He defines the black jeremiad as "the constant warnings issued by blacks to whites, concerning the judgment that was to come from the sin of slavery" (Moses 1993, 30–31). The jeremiad allowed black speakers to "reinforce America's belief that it was a chosen nation by admonishing that in the matter of slavery it was not keeping the covenant" (31).

Bostonian Maria W. Stewart epitomizes the black jeremiad in her unsparing examination of both the society at large and her own community. In her 1831 pamphlet *Religion and the Pure Principles of Morality, the Slave Foundation on Which We Most Build*, addressed to the "daughters of Africa" she signals the jeremiad in the following prayer, "Do thou grant that Ethiopia may soon stretch forth her hands unto thee. And now, Lord, be pleased to grant that Satan's kingdom may be destroyed" (Logan 1999, 27–29).[7] For Stewart, in her mimicry of the rhetorical strategy of the sons of the patriots, the revolution of the daughters of Africa is also sanctioned by God. Stewart's oratory is an act of double-consciousness, signifyin(g)

---

7. See also M. Richardson 1987, 6. Here is the beginning of the womanist tradition to challenge and critique the praxis of African American leadership, roles that were mainly occupied by the men of the community.

on the words of the prophet Jeremiah and the other prophets of old in the biblical texts in relation to her contemporary context.

In her 1833 "Address Delivered at the African Masonic Hall," Stewart reclaims an honorable African past in order to dismantle the hierarchical relationship between black and white. She specifically addresses the men, whom she refers to as the "sons of Afric," when she states, "Yes, poor despised Africa was once the resort of sages and legislators of other nations, was esteemed the school for learning, and the most illustrious men in Greece flocked thither for instruction" (cited in Logan 1999, 39–40). Yet, Stewart proclaimed, gross sins "provoked the Almighty to frown thus heavily upon us, and give our glory unto others" (40). Stewart's rhetorical tendency is consistent with the role of black women being the "Jeremiahs" of their communities. She instills the sense of greatness in the past that is vital to the cultural memory of the group, yet she also brings in the sense of loss that is also the reality of the group. By recognizing the ambivalent nature of African American identity, Stewart sustains the cultural memory of the African American by both praising and warning the community. The outcome of such a rhetorical strategy would be a balanced identity construct with a hope for the future.[8]

The sociopolitical circumstances that affected nineteenth-century Africa America is the impetus for the creation of a double-consciousness that will be the hallmark of African American identity—a cultural ethos that, to this very day, is defined by ambiguity and tension. This period marks the beginning of the performative strategy of a hybrid African American community whose praxis relies on deconstructing and reconstructing cultural memory "using the master's tools."[9] Nineteenth-century Africa America sets the foundation for the "strangeness of home" as a deconstructive praxis that constructs identity in the interstitial space with

---

8. One can argue that Stewart, in adopting the prophetic tradition, is attempting to prevent a disastrous slave uprising by blaming the "sons of Afric" for their own sense of loss. This may well be the case, since around this time period the South was threatened by numerous slave revolts. In 1829 *David Walker's Appeal* was banned in the South because his particular narration of nation was considered too inflammatory in its condemnation of Euro-America. Nat Turner's rebellion in 1831 was believed by many southern slaveholders to have been influenced by Walker's writings. Also, the state of Virginia banned black ministers from preaching because of their fear of Walker's influence in inciting revolt. Stewart's jeremiads might have been aimed at dousing the fire that was beginning to burn rampantly in the South.

9. This practice is what Spivak refers to as catachresis.

such fluidity that the construction effectively responds to the complexity of American society. This is noted by James Cone: "When blacks have been optimistic about America ... they have been integrationists and have minimized their nationalist tendencies. On the other hand, despair about America ... has always been the seedbed of nationalism" (1991, 4).

African Americans and the American Biblical Hermeneutical Tradition in the Twentieth Century

Charles Mabee claims that African Americans have a complex relation to American biblical hermeneutics due to the "difficulty of transforming this experience of marginalization into a net benefit for the whole of society" (2000, 104). He proposes that there are two key points in the establishment of an African American hermeneutic: (1) The nonvengeful, nonviolent response to the experience of marginalization and the transformation of that experience into a means of blessing for all. Mabee exhorts African Americans to adopt a "live and let live" policy that characterized the ancient Israelite and the early Christians. (2) The facilitation of African American reformulation of the dominant "Euro-American" culture, with particular attention to democratic political formation, capitalistic economic structures, and the American way of life (105–7).

Mabee seemingly fails to note that the African American sacred narration has never condoned violence, but does rely on the vital element of social protest in the call for a just society. Social protest, in fact, calls for the adoption of a "live and let live" attitude. The second modification I would make to Mabee's point is that African Americans must be extremely cautious in reformulating the dominant society in that they do not succumb to reinscribing an exploitative and oppressive ethos since the danger in hybrid construction is to merely mimic the dominant ethos.

Living the Dream: Martin Luther King Jr.

Dr. Martin Luther King Jr. conveyed the African American sacred narration of nation during the civil rights era of the 1960s. King's use of biblical allusion and symbolism in his public sermons and speeches was always in conjunction with the American myth of origin that he referred to as the American Dream. His gift for articulating the dream prompted millions of people to respond to his message of equality, morality, justice, and love. His message brought thousands together as they marched together on town halls, city halls, and national halls in a nonviolent manner. Any violence that erupted was inflicted upon the marchers by Euro-Americans, not inflicted by the marchers of the movement.

King was so successful in articulating a sacred narration that many urged the opening of the biblical canon in order to include his "Letter from Birmingham Jail." The famous picture of him sitting in the Birmingham jail cell serves to visually evoke images of the trials of Peter and Paul in the Roman Empire. Arrested on Good Friday in 1963, King wrote his letter addressed to "My Dear Fellow Clergymen" in response to public criticism against him. He turned to biblical symbolism to support his claim that certain (nonviolent) forms of civil disobedience are, indeed, morally sanctioned. He says,

> I submit that an individual who breaks a law that conscience tells him is unjust, and who willingly accepts the penalty of imprisonment in order to arouse the conscience of the community over its injustice, is in reality expressing the highest respect for law.
>
> Of course, there is nothing new about his kind of civil disobedience. It was evidenced sublimely in the refusal of Shadrach, Meschach, and Abednego to obey the laws of Nebuchadnezzar, on the ground that a higher moral law was at stake. It was practiced superbly by the early Christians, who were willing to face hungry lions and the excruciating pain of chopping blocks rather than submit to certain unjust laws of the Roman Empire. (M. King 1997b, 1858–59)[10]

But the major event that conveyed King's ability to espouse the African American hermeneutical tradition was on a hot and hazy August 28, 1963, when approximately 250,000 people led by King and other civil rights leaders marched from the Washington Monument (an obelisk), past the reflecting pool (crossing the Red Sea), and gathered in front of the Lincoln Memorial (a symbol of freedom from slavery). With the audience facing west, King stood at the dais and delivered the speech that was to thrust him into eternity and memorialize him as an icon in American history. No one can deny the mystical, otherworldly quality of his "Dream" oration. Millions of Americans who have seen and heard this speech give testimony of its inspirational power. The slogans, "I Have a Dream," "Keep

---

10. King echoes the sentiment of Ben Franklin when Franklin proposed the motto of the national seal to be "Rebellion to Tyrants Is Obedience to God."

the Dream Alive," and "Remember the Dream" are recited by people all over the globe.

After an opening sentence stating that this moment would go down in history as the greatest demonstration for freedom in the history of our nation,[11] King performs his narration of nation:

> Five score years ago, a great American, in whose symbolic shadow we stand today, signed the Emancipation Proclamation. This momentous decree came as a great beacon of light of hope to millions of Negro slaves who had been seared in the flames of withering injustice. But after a hundred years, the Negro is still not free.... [T]he Negro is still sadly crippled by the manacles of segregation.... One hundred years later, the Negro still languishes in the corners of American society and finds himself an exile in his own land. (King 1997a)

King goes on to dramatize a shameful condition by alluding to the covenant theology the early Americans used as foundational to their narration. He charges that the writers of the U.S. Constitution pledged a "promissory note to which every American was to fall heir." Their note ensured that all men, black and white, would have the right to life, liberty, and the pursuit of happiness. King accuses America of not "honoring this sacred obligation" and that America "wrote the Negro a bad check." He continues on, stating the fierce urgency of the time: "now is the time to make justice a reality for all of God's children. This sweltering summer of the Negro's legitimate discontent will not pass until there is an invigorating autumn of freedom and equality." And, "the whirlwinds of revolt will continue to shake the foundations of our nation until the bright day of justice emerges. We must not allow our creative protest to degenerate into physical violence. Again and again we must rise to the majestic insights of meeting physical force with soul force" (King 1997a, 80–82).

King maintains the dream by juxtaposing two versions of the American ethos— the African American and the Euro-American. By doing so, he captures the ambivalence that informs a double-consciousness identity construction. His belief that thought, memory, and imagination transcend time and space is made evident by his use of various biblical allusions and

---

11. An event only to be surpassed approximately fifty years later on January 20, 2009, when Barack Hussein Obama, the first African American president, stood at the dais and gave his inaugural address in front of millions of citizens, the majority of which were people of color.

imagery. His ability to combine biblical allusion with political rhetoric contained the power to inspire America to rewrite itself. Martin Luther King's narration of nation in line with contemporary sociopolitical/economic crisis jettisoned him into eternity as a national icon.

WAXING METAPHORICAL IN THE POLITICAL JUNGLE

In addition to Martin Luther King Jr., the African American sacred narration is performed in the oratory of Malcolm X, Louis Farrakhan, Jeremiah Wright, and Barack Hussein Obama, all performed during watershed moments in African American history in the twentieth and twenty-first centuries.

Louis Farrakhan: The Million Man March

Thirty-two years after the March on Washington, on October 16, 1995, there was the Million Man March. This time facing the east, which is appropriate for Muslims, Louis Farrakhan[12] along with other ministers of the Nation of Islam (NOI) stood on the steps of the Capitol, the end point of the Million Man March, "in the light of the sun, offering life to a people who are dead." The march was a demonstration of unity, support, and self-sufficiency within the African American male community aimed at combating the distortion of the media in its presentation of African American men as menaces to society. Farrakhan's rhetorical strategy maintained the African American sacred narration signified by his use of key phrases and images of the myth of origin intended to invert meaning. Yet, unlike King, Farrakhan adopted an oratory maintaining NOI's nationalist ideology that echoes an apocalyptic point of view.

Capturing the style of John the Seer, the author of the book of Revelation, Farrakhan imprints esoteric, mystical, and somewhat foreboding symbolism onto his rhetorical landscape. For instance, his performative strategy unlocks and unveils secret Masonic codes that are embedded

---

12. Although Malcolm X is King's contemporary who also narrated on nation and would be the likely figure to juxtapose to King, I chose here to bypass Malcolm X and highlight Farrakhan because (1) the parallelism of Martin and Malcolm has already been thoroughly discussed, and (2) the King and Farrakhan speeches were similarly a civic ritual performed in Washington, DC.

in the architectural structure of Washington, DC, as an excerpt from his speech illustrates:

> There in the middle of this Mall is the Washington Monument, 555 feet high. But if we put a one in front of 555 feet, we get 1555, the year that our first fathers landed on the shores of Jamestown, Virginia, as slaves.
>
> In the background is the Jefferson and Lincoln Memorial, each one of these monuments is 19 feet high. Abraham Lincoln, the sixteenth president. Thomas Jefferson, the third president, and 16 and 3 make 19 again. What is so deep about this number 19? Why are we standing on the Capitol steps today? That number 19—when you have a nine you have a womb that is pregnant. And when you have a one standing by the nine, it means that there's something secret that has to be unfolded....
>
> And the first president of this land, George Washington, who was a grand master of the Masonic Order laid the foundation, the cornerstone of this capitol building where we stand. George was a slave owner. Now, the President spoke today and he wanted to heal the great divide. But I respectfully suggest to the President, you did not dig deep enough at the malady that divides Black and White in order to affect a solution to the problem....
>
> So today, whether you like it or not, God brought the idea through me and he didn't bring it through me because my heart was dark with hatred and anti-Semitism, he didn't bring it through me because my heart was dark and I'm filled with hatred for White people and for the human family of the planet. If my heart were that dark, how is the message so bright, the message so clear, the response so magnificent? (Farrakhan 1995)

While the deification of race has always been prominent in NOI mythology, it frequently overlaps with, and is partly neutralized by, a rhetoric more closely connected to the Judaic idea of a divinely "chosen" people (Kelleter 2000, 63).[13] Therefore, just as with the African American Christian ministers/politicians of the civil rights movement, members of the NOI also stake a claim in the African American tradition of signifyin(g) with Scriptures. So conspicuous, indeed, is the presence of biblical rhetoric and Christian ritual in the Black Muslim community that

---

13. Unsurprisingly, the apocalyptic visions of NOI are shared, in some form or other, by millions of white American Christians who are deeply preoccupied with eschatology. The disciples of Pat Robertson and his New World Order agenda serve as one of many examples.

many feel justified in characterizing the NOI as kind of a Reformation movement within the black church that had grown all too accommodating to American racism.

In paralleling the above two speeches with each other, the concept of African American identity as an ambivalent construct—one that rejects and embraces—is clearly evident. Martin Luther King advocating integration and Louis Farrakhan exhorting a (refined) black nationalism are both based on the splitting or fragmentation of the self that characterizes the hybridity or double-consciousness of African American identity.

To accommodate or not to accommodate—that is the prevailing predicament that African Americans must wrestle with. This challenge is best met by acknowledging the adoption of *both* positions. Therefore, it is in the middle passage where identity is constructed, deconstructed, and reconstructed. Operating "in-between" requires a negotiation based on contradictoriness—the embrace and the rejection, the mimicry and the mockery. An unconscious realization of one's hybridity can be detrimental to the psyche and to a group's collective cultural memory because the denial of ambivalence results either in an uncritical mimicry or an unproductive mockery. For example, the oppression of Sethe, the protagonist in Morrison's *Beloved*, is an illustration of a tormented psyche that had not come to grips with dealing with her own fragmentation. Once that torment was unleashed onto the community it would have upset the communal hybrid balance causing all to slip into the dismal abyss of self-loathing.

Barack Hussein Obama–Jeremiah Wright Dialogue

According to Colin Powell, Barack Obama can be seen as "a transformational figure. He is a new generation coming into the world—onto the world stage, onto the American stage" (Powell 2008). Obama as a transformational figure is made manifest in his response to the comments his now ex-pastor, Jeremiah Wright, made about America during the 2008 presidential campaign. On close examination, both Obama and Wright maintained a rhetorical strategy that was based on a double-consciousness, or fragmented, identity. Wright, in his comments at various political and social venues, had urged Americans to critically examine America's role in spreading injustice in a way that was brutally honest about American racial politics. Below is an excerpt from a sermon that was most referenced in the media:

And the United States of America government, when it came to treating her citizens of Indian descent fairly, she failed. She put them on reservations. When it came to treating her citizens of Japanese descent fairly, she failed. She put them in internment prison camps. When it came to treating her citizens of African descent fairly, America failed. She put them in chains, the government put them on slave quarters, put them on auction blocks, put them in cotton fields, put them in inferior schools, put them in substandard housing, put them in scientific experiments, put them in the lowest paying jobs, put them outside the equal protection of the law, kept them out of their racist bastions of higher education and locked them into positions of hopelessness and helplessness. The government gives them the drugs, builds bigger prisons, passes a three-strike law and then wants us to sing "God Bless America." No, no, no, not God Bless America. God damn America—that's in the Bible—for killing innocent people. God damn America, for treating our citizens as less than human. God damn America, as long as she tries to act like she is God, and she is supreme. The United States government has failed the vast majority of her citizens of African descent. (Wright 2003)

Obama's speech, "A More Perfect Union," delivered on March 18, 2008, at the National Constitution Center in Philadelphia, was given as a response to Jeremiah Wright's controversial statements about racism in America and his inflammatory remarks about Israel. Obviously, Obama did not condone the behavior of Wright, but he did place those remarks in historical context by describing some of the key events that informed Wright's views on race-related matters in America. In doing so, his speech maintained the tradition of speaking to the double-consciousness of the African American.

In his opening, he mentions the great task of the founding fathers in establishing independence and in crafting the Declaration of Independence and the Constitution. He then goes on to say,

And yet words on a parchment would not be enough to deliver slaves from bondage, or provide men and women of every color and creed their full rights and obligations as citizens of the United States. What would be needed were Americans in successive generations who were willing to do their part—through protests and struggle, on the streets and in the courts, through a civil war and civil disobedience and always at great risk—to narrow that gap between the promise of our ideals and the reality of their time. (Obama 2008)

Instead of judging white America for the ills of this country, Obama chooses to speak of solidarity and unity, integration in line with Martin Luther King:

> I believe deeply that we cannot solve the challenges of our time unless we solve them together—unless we perfect our union by understanding that we may have different stories, but we hold common hopes; that we may not look the same and we may not have come from the same place, but we all want to move in the same direction.

Later in the speech, Obama resorts to signifyin(g) with Scriptures to reconstruct the collective cultural memory through the enunciation of the African American sacred narration with entails placing the contemporary context in solidarity with the ancient context.

> In my first book, *Dreams from My Father,* I described the experience of my first service at Trinity:
> "I imagined the stories of ordinary black people merging with the stories of David and Goliath, Moses and Pharaoh, the Christians in the lion's den, Ezekiel's field of dry bones. Those stories—of survival, and freedom, and hope—became our story, my story; the blood that had spilled was our blood, the tears our tears; until this black church, on this bright day, seemed once more a vessel carrying the story of a people into future generations and into a larger world. *Our trials and triumphs became at once unique and universal, black and more than black; in chronicling our journey, the stories and songs gave us a means to reclaim memories that we didn't need to feel shame about ... memories that all people might study and cherish—and with which we could start to rebuild.* (emphasis added)

Obama then comments on the dynamism and fluidity of African American identity construction, moving away from the understanding that the identity construct is static and out of touch with the twenty-first century:

> The profound mistake of Reverend Wright's sermons is not that he spoke about racism in our society. It's that he spoke as if our society was static; as if no progress has been made; as if this country—a country that has made it possible for one of his own members to run for the highest office in the land and build a coalition of white and black, Latino and Asian, rich and poor, young and old—is still irrevocably bound to a tragic past.

While Wright's performative strategy revealed a mainstream society that was ignorant (and thus fearful) of the theological gestures of black liberation theology, the Obama-Wright episodes in 2008 contributed to exposing the double-consciousness of African American identity. The positions of Obama and Wright are very similar to the ideological focuses of King and Malcolm X in the 1960s. Both Obama and Wright's rhetorical strategies engaged the fragmentation of African American identity.

The shift in the paradigm was made evident in Denver during Obama's acceptance speech of the Democratic nomination for president. The event was held on the anniversary of the March on Washington, forty-five years to the day when Martin Luther King Jr. delivered his famous "I Have a Dream" speech on August 28, 1963. The visual imagery of stadium scenery conveyed that which serves to legitimate the Western imagination, in general, and American society, in particular: Greco-Roman civilization. Yet it was also contrapuntal in that the (flesh-and-blood) image that emerged from within the Greek temple was an African American. Obama's performative strategy did not attempt to rewrite a totally new narration of nation. Instead, he reused a narration and re-presented the American collective with a new destiny.

Several months later, this time in Washington DC, during the presidential inaugural activities on Tuesday, January 20, 2009, Obama invoked the memory of a distant past through images of and allusions to American heritage and heroes, particularly Washington, Lincoln, and King.[14] Again, the biblical allusion Obama chose for his inaugural speech (1 Cor 13:11) served to re-present the nation's narration by maintaining yet transforming a particular ethos, a transformation that must be made in light of such a memorable moment in American history:

> We remain a young nation, but in the words of Scripture, the time has come to set aside childish things. The time has come to reaffirm our enduring spirit; to choose our better history; to carry forward that precious gift, that noble idea, passed on from generation to generation: the God-given promise that all are equal, all are free and all deserve a chance to pursue their full measure of happiness....

---

14. Actually, in a sense Obama unseats Lincoln from his memorial chair in the eyes of African Americans. It is now Martin Luther King Jr. and himself who are the heroes in African American cultural memory and who have carved out a niche in the epicenter of American political power.

For we know that our patchwork heritage is a strength, not a weakness. We are a nation of Christians and Muslims, Jews and Hindus—and non-believers. We are shaped by every language and culture, drawn from every end of this Earth; and because we have tasted the bitter swill of civil war and segregation, and emerged from that dark chapter stronger and more united, we cannot help but believe that the old hatreds shall someday pass; that the lines of tribe shall soon dissolve; that as the world grows smaller, our common humanity shall reveal itself; and that America must play its role in ushering in a new era of peace. (Obama 2009)[15]

Obama's speech extended past the narrow confines of simply a white and black America. His narration included voices that have been excluded, yet had influenced the story in extremely important ways. Obama recrafted a nation's narration in line with the present situation. He upheld the African American tradition of simultaneously adopting and adapting the Euro-American hermeneutical tradition. But importantly, Obama's narration of nation provoked and challenged not only white America, but black America into realizing the potential of an American myth of origin that benefits all.

THE POSSIBILITY OF AFRICAN AMERICANS REINSCRIBING AN AMERICAN ETHOS

As the mapping above illustrates, African Americans began to carve their niche in American society when they learned the complex ability to signify on many different levels and horizons, spiraling within and beyond various dimensions of indirection and subtle allusions. They began to signify with Scripture in earnest by way of song, sermon, and speech in nineteenth-century America to denounce a society that sanctioned slavery. Although the Emancipation Proclamation and the North's victory in the apocalyptic event of the Civil War cemented the enslaved Africans' belief that they too had found favor with God, the freed slaves remained strangers in their new land. They were not invited to experience the comfort of home. So they continued to write their own invitation, narrating a nation that was "almost the same, but not quite like" the dominant myth of origin. With the writing of their own narration, the disenfranchised Negro of the early

---

15. The last two lines echo the sentiment of the Pax Romana, except the world is getting smaller in Obama's rhetoric and with Augustus the world was expanding.

twentieth-century slowly morphed into a full-blown ambivalent African American who simultaneously adopts/adapts, embraces/resists, mimics/mocks the Euro-American sacred narration, inaugurating a double-consciousness framework that is the hallmark of African American identity.

Thus there lurks in the shadow a new challenge that African Americans must confront—the potential danger of slipping into a mere embrace of the dominant narration and blindly morphing into the status quo. This is a very real danger for a community whose resistance strategy is constructed by employing the rhetorical techniques of the dominant group. By spinning the concept of the "chosen people of the new Jerusalem," will the dominant sacred narration eventually become *the* narrative for the African American community? Will the African American sacred narration eventually become nothing more than a mere reinscription of a myth of origin that underwrites exploitation and marginalization?

These are the questions that African American scribes must begin to explore and address. In order to avoid the dangers expressed above, the performative strategy of African American scribes must be extremely vigilant in maintaining the vital voice of challenging social inequality within the collective group and not accommodating to the neoconservative status quo. The strategy of the scribe must focus on the ambivalent nature of African American identity in terms of relations with the dominant ethos *and also* must begin to forewarn of the devastating slip that can so easily be made when the "oppressed " becomes the "oppressor" as a result of the shift in the paradigm.

African American scribes must effectively produce more complex readings of the biblical narratives that addresses the issues and concerns of a hybrid cultural identity. They must now begin to wrestle with the meaning of hybridity and signifyin(g) with Scriptures. How does the dynamics of signifyin(g) change and what are the possible detrimental consequences of signifyin(g) with Scriptures? Can signifyin(g) with Scriptures be used effectively within the community, as well as outside the community, in such a way that allows the community to move forward, yet never forgets the struggles of the past? These are a few of the questions that African American scribes must begin to consider.

CONCLUSION

African American scripturalization privileges the contemporary cultural matrix from which meaning is produced, rather than the ancient cultural matrices in which they emerged. Only when the contemporary cultural context is mapped out will the meaning produced be fully understood. Thus in this chapter I focused on theorizing cultural location in order to illustrate the complex dynamics of identity construction, arguing that the concepts of hybridiy, mimicry, and ambivalence were useful concepts that assisted in that illustration. I suggested, through the use of postcolonial theory, that the African American cultural matrix resides within the middle passage of continuity and discontinuity, acceptance and rejection, dream and nightmare. It is by standing on the threshold that African Americans, utilizing the community's hermeneutical tradition, challenge and subvert the dominant narration of nation. Yet I warned of the exploitation that comes with an unreflective "use of the master's tools" in relation to upward mobility in a materialistic/capitalistic society. Therefore, the African American scribe has the responsibility to pen a scripturalization that is representative of the more complex, hybrid consciousness of the twenty-first-century African American.

The next chapter is an African American scripturalization of the book of Revelation that aims to do the above. I view Revelation as an extremely problematic text that justifies the use of violence and destruction in the formation of a new symbolic order that is actually based on the adaptation and re-presentation of Roman imperial ideology. The scripturalization is written as a cautionary warning of the slipperiness of reinscription and the uncritical embrace of a prevailing ethos.

Reconceptualizing Revelation: Standard Scholarship on the Book of Revelation in Conversation with an African American Scripturalization Perspective

> To everyone who conquers and continues to do my works to the end, I will give authority over the nations, to rule them with an iron rod.
>
> — Revelation 2:26–27

Introduction

In this chapter I argue that a first step in producing a more theoretically complex reading of the book of Revelation that unravels the knottiness of cultural negotiation is the re-presentation of the general scholarly issues that are considered to be central to this text. This discussion must take place, I posit, because the standard scholarship that authorizes "the correct interpretation" of the text based on the historical-critical paradigm that continues to dominant the biblical guild must be deconstructed. If not, then the historical-critical scholarship will muffle more recent cultural perspectives. Also, by the re-presentation of the historical-critical approach of Revelation fueled by the cultural-specific hermeneutical process of the strangeness of home, I attempt to illustrate that the historical-critical approach is, indeed, a subjective enterprise.[1]

The section is structured in the African American format of *call* and *response* with the discussion of the standard scholarship on Revelation in several subsections (*call*) followed by a discussion on the scholarship from an African American scripturalization perspective (*response*).[2]

---

1. See my discussion on the juxtaposition of the historical paradigm and the cultural-critical paradigm in the first chapter.

2. In African American culture, call and response is a pattern of democratic par-

Authorship and Place of Writing

Call: The author of Revelation is considered to have been an itinerant prophet named "John" (Rev 1:1, 4, 9; 22:8).[3] He is not to be confused with John the son of Zebedee, nor the "John" who is traditionally thought to have written the Fourth Gospel or the Johannine Letters. Rather, it is hypothesized that he was a Palestinian exile who found his way to Roman provincial Asia after the fall of Jerusalem to the Romans in 70 CE.[4] He mainly wandered throughout the territory visiting and instructing the seven churches mentioned in Revelation—those in Ephesus, Smyrna, Pergamum, Thyatira, Sardis, Philadelphia, and Laodicea. His teachings seemingly made no clear distinction between Jewish and Christian prophets (10:7; 11:3–13; 16:6; 22:6); therefore one can infer that an intimate connection with the past was important for John to continue in the present and the future.[5] From the tone of his letters to the churches, he most probably expressed the value of an ascetic life and the rejection of Roman imperial culture.

Both ancient and modern critics negatively assess John's use of the Greek language. Dionysius complained that the seer's grammar was coarse and barbaric compared to the relatively sophisticated Greek of the Gospel of John.[6] The modern consensus is either that (1) the work was originally composed in a Semitic tongue and errors in grammar and syntax occurred in translation; (2) the author was careless in his use of the Greek language; or, (3) the overwhelming consensus, John "wrote in a pidginized 'ghetto Greek'" of a "diasporan Jewish community that spoke an assimilated form of the language with a strong Semitic accent."[7] As a consequence, some

---

ticipation in the discussion of civic affairs, in religious rituals, as well as in vocal and musical expression. Therefore, the format of call and response in this section should not be viewed as the response refuting aspects of the call, but should be considered more in line with presenting an alternative view that can be harmonized.

3. Although John never identifies himself as a prophet, he does describe his work as prophecy. Cf. Rev 1:3, 10, 18, 19; 22:7, 9.

4. John's extensive use of the Hebrew text and the fact that he literally translated Hebrew and Aramaic idioms into Greek supports this hypothesis.

5. This is an important point that I will fully explore below.

6. Quoted in Eusebius, *Hist. eccl.* 7.25.16–27.

7. Callahan 1985, 454. Also see S. Thompson 1985, 108. Thompson suggests that the provincials of the eastern Roman Empire spoke a creolized Greek. However, Cal-

scholars contend that John must have learned to speak and write Greek as an adult.

According to tradition, John wrote Revelation while exiled on the island of Patmos "according to the word of God and the witness of Jesus" (διὰ τὸν λόγον τοῦ θεοῦ καὶ τὴν μαρτυρίαν Ἰησοῦ) (1:9). He was deported there by the Roman governor of Asia, according to the early Christian writer Victorinus, who also claimed that Patmos was the home of a Roman penal colony. However, there is no evidence to support the view that Patmos was a Roman penal colony, although several nearby islands were used for this purpose; and usually only the elite members of Roman society were exiled. Most early Christians who were tried and found guilty were executed instead.

Response: An African American scripturalization suggests that John was a member of a group of marginalized Christians who struggled to make sense of the strangeness of home. At the time of his writing Revelation, he had been twice exiled, whether literally or metaphorically, first from Jerusalem and then from the Christian communities in Asia to the island of Patmos. John's precarious predicament in Asia was a repetition of his situation in Judea. Both geographical locations are sites for some of history's most thoroughgoing invasions. The pervasiveness of Roman subjugation made it impossible to escape from the imperial ethos and agenda. Roman hegemony was both public and private. For John, there was conflict, tension, and confusion between the borders of his homeland and the rest of the world. John was in an unhomely (*unheimliche*) state. Thus, on the island of Patmos, in a state of incredulous terror, he had taken in the full constricted measure of his dwelling, leaving him anxious, uncertain, and extremely agitated (Rev 1:17–18). His "presencing" began as he captured the sense of the estrangement from home and the world "that is the condition of extra-territorial and cross-cultural initiations" (Bhabha 1994, 13). And so, from Patmos, John started signifyin(g) on empire in cryptic, encoded, and grammatically incorrect/resistantly unorthodox language that he envisioned would result in the liberation of the Christian communities from Roman domination and the reclaiming of some power within the matrix of imperial ideology.

---

lahan counters this suggestion by claiming that John was basing his grammatical style on the LXX, and thus his solecisms were intentional.

Genre

Call: Recent work on genre argues that Revelation resists classification in one pure genre due to its complex literary structure. Scholars claim that the text should be considered as a "hybrid" text because of its high level of intertextuality that has allowed us to categorize it either as prophecy, letter, drama, liturgy, or myth (Linton 2006).[8] However, the predominant view of the literary character of Revelation is that it belongs to a type of ancient revelatory literature called *apocalypse*.[9] The word is a transliteration of the Greek noun ἀποκάλυψις (which, like its Latin synonym *revelatio*, has the basic meaning "unveiling").

An apocalypse is usually written in bizarre language that must be read correctly in order to uncover its intended meaning. The name for this literary genre has its origins in Revelation, which functions as the title (Aune 1987, 226): "The revelation of Jesus Christ, which God gave him to show his servants what must soon take place; he made it known by sending his angel to his servant John, who testified to the word of God and to the testimony of Jesus Christ, even to all that he saw" (Ἀποκάλυψις Ἰησοῦ Χριστοῦ ἣν ἔδωκεν αὐτῷ ὁ θεός δεῖξαι τοῖς δούλοις αὐτοῦ ἃ δεῖ γενέσθαι ἐν τάχει, καὶ ἐσήμανεν ἀποστείλας διὰ τοῦ ἀγγέλου αὐτοῦ τῷ δούλῳ αὐτοῦ Ἰωάννῃ, ὃς ἐμαρτύρησεν τὸν λόγον τοῦ θεοῦ καὶ τὴν μαρτυρίαν Ἰησοῦ Χριστοῦ ὅσα εἶδεν) (Rev 1:1–2). Certain Jewish groups around the Mediterranean Sea basin seem to have constructed their identities using this type of literature (4 Ezra, 2 Baruch, and the Sibylline Oracles were other apocalypses in circulation at roughly the same time as Revelation). The communities that owned these texts realized that apocalyptic visions and images reflected social realities (see Thompson 1990, 31–34). According to Leonard Thompson, the dimensions of apocalyptic language and symbolic constructions do "not operate in some realm different from other social activity. Faithful recipients of an apocalypse gain true knowledge about the cosmos, religion, the political order, local economic transac-

---

8. Linton argues that no text can be limited to a single genre, but that the Apocalypse, in particular, should be considered a text that refuses to be contained by a single category or classification.

9. J. Collins 1979, 9; Rowland 1982; Charlesworth 1983; Hellholm 1982, 1983; Aune 1986; 1987, 226–52; Mazzaferri 1989; L. Thompson 1990, 11–24; Bauckham 1993, 1–38; Malina 1995.

tions, and the nature of social life" (34).[10] The addressee communities of apocalypses were very familiar with, and very adept at, decoding the political messages embedded in esoteric imagery.

The roots of apocalyptic literature can be traced back to ancient Near Eastern culture—the Canaanite/Ugaritic combat myth, Babylonian images and symbolisms, and contact with the Persian Empire have all contributed to apocalyptic literature. After the destruction of Jerusalem by the Babylonians in 586 BCE, the Jewish prophets foreshadow many features of apocalyptic literature. Ezekiel, Zechariah, Isaiah, and Joel (all of which are either referenced or echoed in Revelation) prefigure apocalyptic sensibility, particularly a future-oriented sense of history; visions or dreams interpreted by an angel; signs that mark the end times; cosmic conflict between good and evil; defeat of God's enemies; and the final judgment (Howard-Brook and Gwyther 1999, 46–79).

Response A: Influenced by postcolonial discourse, an African American scripturalization ponders the complex dimensions of Persian-Greek-Roman contact and explores the idea that the full flowering of apocalyptic literature was a genre produced in the middle space—the contact of Persian and Hellenistic cultures between the fifth and third centuries BCE. The notion of apocalyptic text as a hybrid production is particularly relevant because it supports this project's argument that Persian culture remained viable in the memory banks of the residents in the province of Roman Asia in the first century CE.[11] The perspective takes into account that the fuel for the construction of Hellenic identity in the classical era was directly related to contact with the so-called barbarous and wholly other Persians (M. Miller 1997, 1).[12] Thus John's signifyin(g) not only points to a mosaic of images based on the hybridity of Jewish and Greco-Roman culture, but is a complex web of intermingling images and significations of past occupation as well.[13]

---

10. I would add the military order of a society to Thompson's list.

11. I make this point to counter the prevalent gesture of historical biblical critics who privilege Greek culture, and as a result silence the contribution of Eastern culture to Western civilization, including Western Christianity.

12. According to Miller, "it is a commonplace of modern scholarship that the Athenians hated and despised the Persians. Indeed, by the fifth century, the word *barbarous* usually denoted an inhabitant of the Persian Empire and connoted cowardice, weakness and effeminacy" (1997, 1). See also Root 2011.

13. See Webster 1997. In the following chapter I argue that the ritual of *proskyne-*

Cultural contact via trade, the establishment of political and military zones between Greeks and Persians in the form of satrapies, diplomatic exchange, and the infusion and diffusion of the spoils of the Persian War were some of the various formal modes in which Hellenic contact was made with the Persian Empire (Webster 1997, 89).[14] Persian contact especially influenced the residents of Asia Minor, who were directly affected by the Persian Empire.[15] The standard scholarship on Revelation attests to this fact in the letter addressed to Sardis (Rev 3:1–6). William Ramsay states:

> At the beginning of the Greek memory of history in Lydia, Sardis stood out conspicuous and alone as the capital of the great Oriental Empire with which the Greek cities and colonies were brought in contact. Their relations with it formed the one great question of foreign politics for those early Greek settlers. Everything else was secondary, or was under their own control, but in regard to Sardis they had always to be thinking of foreign wishes, foreign rights, the caprice of a foreign monarch and the convenience of foreign traders, who were too powerful to be disregarded or treated with disrespect. That ancient and deep impression the Asiatic Greeks, with their tenacious historical memory, never entirely lost.[16]

The postcolonial supplementation that this volume incorporates allows the argument to be made that the performative strategy of the eastern

---

sis, a performance that John features throughout Revelation, is a hybrid performance of Eastern royal court ritual and Greco-Roman ceremonial.

14. A variety of Greek expatriates lived in Persia including political exiles, mercenaries, physicians, metalworkers, stonemasons, etc.

15. In 499 BCE the Ionians revolted from Persian rule. The rebellion arose from the failure of the Miletus tyrant, Aristagoras, to restore several exiled elites to their land of Naxos and to add Naxos to the Persian Empire. Aristagoras, not wanting to pay the Persian price for that failure, exhorted the residents of Miletus to revolt with the cry of *isonomia,* "equality of rights." The unsuccessful revolt was responsible for sending Cyrus's successor, Darius the Great, on his mission to conquer Macedonia and the islands of the Aegean in 492 BCE. Thus the Macedonian encounter with the Eastern conception of absolute kingship occurred approximately a century before the conquests of Alexander the Great in 336–323 BCE. Cf. Herodotus, *Hist.* 28.

16. Ramsay 1904, 375–76. Also see Hemer 1986; Worth 1999. Cyrus the Great conquered Lydia and obtained control of Anatolia in 547 BCE. Sardis became a chief strategic location for Persia. Other connections to Persia are made in the allusions to Dan 7 and the Nero redivus myth mentioned in Rev 13:3, 18, and 17:10, which alludes to Nero's return from Parthia, a region in northeastern Persia.

Greeks mimicked/mocked the cultural practices of the Persian Empire, an imperial system that dominated the lands from the Indus to the Aegean Sea for approximately two hundred years.

Therefore, approaching the genre of Revelation as a production formed in the middle or the interstitial space provides the opportunity to examine the influence of Persian eschatological traditions on John's apocalyptic writing. According to Casey Starnes:

> In Persian eschatology the supreme god of order, Ahura Mazda, is countered by the god of disorder, Angra Maniyu. Their battle is ongoing in a finite time period that will end when Angra Mainyu is destroyed and order (*asha*) prevails. At the end of time, the dead are universally resurrected. The world undergoes a purging of evil which involves the living and the resurrected dead. The wicked dead are annihilated in the molten metal while the righteous souls receive a blissful existence in heaven and a new physical body on earth. Finally, Ahura Mazda comes to earth as a priest and all the righteous become immortal. Angra Mainyu returns to the darkness and the molten metal seals the gate.
>
> In the fourth century BCE, a modified version of the myth took place—a twelve-thousand-year pattern was conceived in which great events occur every three thousand years. The last period is subdivided into three millennia. Each terminates with a Saosyant (savior); each experience a decline from good to evil, with good restored at millennium's end and is concluded by the *frashokereti*, "making wonderful." (Starnes 2009, 30)

The comments above reveal a similar focus in the themes of Revelation—the battle between good and evil, the birth of a savior, resurrection from the dead, and goodness restored at the end of time.

Thus an African American scripturalization suggests that this intentionally cryptic, opaque, hybrid genre that synthesizes elements of empires be understood as a "hidden transcript" of imperial religious practices of the past and the present (Scott 1995, 137). It is by talking through the veil, invoking the memory of the community's contact with past imperial structures that the subjugated Christian communities in Asia Minor could openly signify on the Roman imperialism of the first century.

DATE

Call: Dating Revelation is a challenge and has caused an interesting scholarly debate between two major opinions. The strongest argument is for a date near the end of Domitian's reign, that is, about 96 CE. The second favors a date of 68–69 CE, soon after the end of Nero's reign. Basically, scholars are divided on the issue because of the ambiguity of the text itself, which supports both dates.[17] The majority of contemporary scholars, however, adhere to the late date in keeping with the external evidence of Irenaeus, who claims Revelation "was seen not long ago, but nearly in our generation, toward the end of the reign of Domitian" (Irenaeus, *Adv. haer.* 5.30.3). However, according to Steven Friesen, Irenaeus's statement does not inspire great confidence because the time he described as nearly in his own generation was approximately a century earlier than when he was writing (Friesen 2001, 143; Eusebius, *Hist. eccl.* 3.18.3). Irenaeus's effort to shorten the distance between himself and the author of Revelation is understandable in light of his polemical intent: he was arguing with Christian millenarian movements about the correct interpretation of Revelation. He was not writing a history of the transmission of John's Apocalypse. In addition, his dating is problematic because he accepts the apostle John as the author of both Revelation and the Gospel according to John.

Internal Evidence for a Later Dating

Adela Yarbro Collins is an important voice in the establishment of a consensus for dating Revelation at the time of Domitian's reign. She argues for a late date to support her contention that the function of the book was to caution Christians about a crisis that they did not perceive—the Christian accommodation to the imperial cult "by those who wished to flatter Domitian" (1984, 77). Yarbro Collins alters previous scholarly speculation that Revelation was written during a time of extreme persecution. For Yarbro Collins (and the majority of contemporary biblical scholars), there is no real evidence that Christians were experiencing a systemic, statewide persecution in the reign of Domitian, although there may have been instances of scattered persecutions, which is supported by mention of Antipas's martyrdom in Rev 2:13. Therefore, Yarbro Collins finds it more plausible to speak of a perceived crisis of accommodation to emperor worship.

The (re)use of the name Babylon as synonymous to Rome is a weighty internal indication of a late date of Revelation. Scholars point to several

---

17. Yarbro Collins 1984, 54–83; Robinson 2000, 221–53; A. Bell 1975; Aune 1997, lviii; L. Thompson 1990, 15; Wilson 1993; Friesen 2001, 135–51; van Kooten 2007.

depictions of Rome as Babylon in the text (14:8; 16:19; 17:5; 18:2, 10, 21) to support their claims. Apparently, in both Jewish and Christian literature, the practice of referring to Rome as Babylon did not become common until after the destruction of the Jerusalem temple by the Romans during Vespasian's reign in 70 CE.[18] Scholars argue that it would have been inappropriate to make reference to Rome as Babylon before then. Therefore, the internal evidence seems to fit best the time advocated by the earliest external evidence of Irenaeus that states that Revelation was written toward the end of the reign of Domitian (Yarbro Collins 1984, 77).

Steven Friesen also argues that a date in the late first century (or early second century) is more appropriate for Revelation because "that takes into account the aspect of domination that was the logical consequence of the destruction. Babylon provided the basic symbolic resources—destroyer of the temple and imperial oppressor" (2001, 139).

Adela Yarbro Collins's most complex argument for a late date is her discussion of Rev 17:9–14, which contains the motif of the seven kings. She argues that John reinterpreted an earlier source in 17:10 for his own purposes: "of whom five have fallen, one is living, the other has not yet come, and when he comes, he must remain only a little while" (οἱ πέντε ἔπεσαν, ὁ εἷς ἔστιν, ὁ ἄλλος οὔπω ἦλθεν, καὶ ὅταν ἔλθῃ ὀλίγον αὐτὸν δεῖ μεῖναι). From the seer's point of view, the seven kings are the Roman emperors. Yarbro Collins turns to 4 Ezra, claiming that the eagle analogy in 4 Ezra 11–12 clearly alludes to three Roman emperors, Julius Caesar, Augustus, and Tiberius. This allows her to posit in regard to Revelation the plausibility "that a selection could have been made of emperors who were especially feared or hated" (1984, 77). She thus begins her count with Caligula, omits the three emperors (Galba, Otho, and Vitellius) who did not rule long enough to be feared, and picks up the count again with Vespasian and Titus. Domitian would, therefore, be the sixth emperor "who is" (1984, 64).[19]

---

18. The Jewish apocalyptic texts 2 Baruch and 4 Ezra were both written in the late first century and both refer to Rome as Babylon. See Friesen 2001, 138.

19. However, this suggestion appears far too complicated, which is an indication of a frank manipulation of facts in order to support a claim. This is especially true when a straightforward count of Julius Caesar, Augustus, Tiberius, Caligula, and Claudius shows the sixth, the one who is, to be Nero and would therefore support an earlier date.

Yarbro Collins places Rev 13:3 in line with her argument, claiming that the "eighth" king in chapter 17 refers to Nero returned from death to life: "One of his heads seemed to have received a death-blow, but its mortal wound had been healed. In amazement the whole earth followed the beast" (καὶ μίαν ἐκ τῶν κεφαλῶν αὐτοῦ ὡς ἐσφαγμένην εἰς θάνατον, καὶ ἡ πληγὴ τοῦ θανάτου αὐτοῦ ἐθεραπεύθη. Καὶ ἐθαυμάσθη ὅλη ἡ γῆ ὀπίσω τοῦ θηρίου) (1984, 59). The death blow makes reference to the Nero redivivus or redux myth, in which it was believed that Nero (who committed suicide in 68 CE), would be restored to life and rule again. Shortly after his death there was widespread belief that Nero did not actually die, but ran off to the East and would soon return leading the Parthian army (Persians) to reestablish Julio-Claudian imperial rule in Asia and the other lands surrounding the Mediterranean basin. Here Yarbro Collins turns to the Sibylline Oracles, another contemporary work that incorporates the legend of Nero as God's adversary in the final struggle. These oracles are suggested to have been written in Egypt between 70 and 130 CE. Yarbro Collins suggests that John reused this legend to fit his particular rhetorical strategy. So Yarbro Collins's argument is that the mention of Nero in the text does not necessarily mean that the text was written soon after his demise.

In her analysis, however, Yarbro Collins fails to include 13:18, which also implies a tradition about Nero: "This calls for wisdom: let anyone with understanding calculate the number of the beast, for it is the number of a person. Its number is six hundred sixty-six" (Ὧδε ἡ σοφία ἐστίν. ὁ ἔχων νοῦν ψηφισάτω τὸν ἀριθμὸν τοῦ θηρίου, ἀριθμὸς γὰρ ἀνθρώπου ἐστίν, καὶ ὁ ἀριθμὸς αὐτοῦ ἑξακόσιοι ἑξήκοντα ἕξ). The verse refers to a gematria, a puzzle game that substitutes numbers for letters. When totaling *Neron Caesar,* a direct transliteration into Hebrew from the Greek, the letters total 666, which John claims is the number of the beast. This claim is supported by Suetonius, who cites that a very popular numbers puzzle game that focused on Nero was played during Nero's life. Thus Rev 13:18 better supports the argument that the text was written during or soon after Nero's reign.[20]

---

20. There are a variety of opinions regarding the allusion in chap. 17. For instance, David Barr suggests that the wounded head implies Julius Caesar instead of Nero because his death led to fears that the republic was headed back into chaos (1998, 127–28). Jean Kim turns away from the issue of dating in this essay to a more compelling postcolonial analysis, considering "the possibility that the metaphorical figure, 'the whore,' in Revelation 17 might have had something to do with the a colonized woman's life in a (de)colonizing context" (1999, 62). Also see Rossing 1999; Davidson

Yarbro Collins analyzes the internal evidence of Revelation to establish her argument for a late dating of the text during the reign of Domitian. Although her analysis of the internal evidence is very compelling, her identification of the seven kings seems to be a bit too manipulated to support the suggestion of a date during the reign of Domitian.

Some scholars are of the opinion that the seven kings motif does not help determine the latest possible date for the composition of the text. For instance, Friesen contends that the apocalyptic method of 4 Ezra suggests that an enumeration of consecutive emperors for Revelation 17 is neither necessary nor advisable (Friesen 2001, 141). The important point is that the seven heads/kings identify Rome as the opponent and indicate that the end of Roman hegemony is near. The only significant emperor is the one who will return (Nero), but the text makes no effort to tell us which head he might be. The practice of using special numbers for groups and the multivalent imagery of Revelation 17 are bound to confuse attempts to identify the seven rulers. Friesen disagrees with Yarbro Collins that the king "who is" will help in deducing the date of Revelation (ibid.).

Internal Evidence for an Early Dating

Albert A. Bell and George H. van Kooten are among those who argue for a date of 68–69 CE for the book of Revelation based on the chaotic events of the "Year of the Four Emperors," the period of unrest and civil war that followed Nero's death (van Kooten 2007; A. Bell 1975, 93). Bell maintains that a date in the period immediately following Nero's death in June of 68 is indicated by the book itself and confirmed by outside sources, especially by the Roman historians of the early second century, Tacitus, Suetonius, and Plutarch. However, Bell's speculation falls short because he argues unconvincingly that the return of Nero would have been expected only immediately after Nero's death when the facts of Nero's demise were not yet widely known. The fifth book of the Sibylline Oracles, written in the early second century CE, which tells of Nero's future return, disproves Bell's contention (see Friesen 2001, 246 n. 17).

George van Kooten claims that the bearing of the tumultuous setting of 68 CE on Revelation has been underestimated because the external

___

2008. Davidson explores the usage of the term *Babylon* in Rastafarian liberation discourse as distinct from the exodus motif normally associated with liberation theology.

evidence of Irenaeus has unduly influenced the dating. He also examines the centrality of the allusions to Nero as one of the heads of the seven-headed beast in the seven king motifs found in Revelation 17 to propose a precise date for the composition of Revelation. Unlike Yarbro Collins, van Kooten conducts his count of the emperors in strict chronological order. He contends that whether the count begins with Julius Caesar or Augustus, the order points to a logical understanding that the text is referring to a time period of 68–69. Otho is the king referred to as "the one who is coming but remains only a little while" in 17:10, which implies that Revelation was written during the (short) reign of Vitellius, who ruled immediately after Otho (Robinson 2000, 221–53).[21]

Leonard Thompson argues that the author of Revelation does not provide much of a clue about the particular time in which he is writing. Thompson posits that the seer's references to Rome are so veiled that it is difficult to be certain that the book was written at any specific time during the Roman Empire and that chapter 17, "which elaborates on the seven-headed beast (Rev. 13:1) by specific reference to emperors past, present, and future, gives no certain information about the precise time of the writing" (1990, 13). Nonetheless, Thompson takes the position of a late date for Revelation because it allows him to discredit the diabolical picture of the Flavian Domitian painted by the Roman historians Pliny, Tacitus, and Suetonius, who wrote during the reign of Trajan and the Antonine emperors. These historians portrayed Domitian as debased, evil, and barbarous, one who forced citizens to participate in the imperial cult and worship him as their "Lord and God." Thompson's analysis posits an alternative vision of Domitian. He opines that the historians in Domitian's court never mentioned Domitian demanding to be referred to as "Lord and God," nor do any of the inscriptions, coins, and medallions from the Domitianic era

---

21. Robinson, another proponent of the earlier date, examines the unity of 11:1–13 to argue that the text was composed prior to 70 CE since this unit implies that the temple was still standing at the time Revelation was written. His suggestion is based on 11:1–2, where John is commanded to "measure the temple of God and the altar and those who worship there" (11:1), "but do not measure there the court outside the temple" (11:2a). He also claims that the text (11:13) refers to an earthquake that shook the temple, not to the Roman attack during the Jewish Revolt. There is also external evidence that supports a date of 41–54 CE in the reign of Claudius, mainly by Epiphanius, a contemporary of Jerome, whose source remains unknown. Robinson suggests that Epiphanius might have meant Nero, not his uncle Claudius, since Nero's other name was Claudius.

make any reference to him being considered as such. Relying on this evidence, Thompson suggests that the post-Domitian historians do not accurately portray the political realities of Domitian's reign. For Thompson, there is simply no concrete evidence that Domitian was worshiped as a god nor that he was a mad, tyrannical ruler. He was a product of character assassination by the Antoine emperors.

David Aune takes the middle road in the debate over the date of Revelation and suggests that both an early and a later date can be discerned in the internal evidence. He claims that both views contain aspects of the correct solution since it appears that the final redaction of Revelation occurred at the end of Domitian's reign or, more likely, in the early stage of Trajan's rulership. He also suggests an early redaction written perhaps a generation before the final edition and based on both oral and written apocalyptic material that reaches back into the 60s, if not somewhat earlier (1997, lviii).[22]

Response A: Cultural memory. While the dating of Revelation in the first century CE is important for establishing the setting, I would argue for a broader historical context for Revelation. The prevalent themes of war, displacement, dislocation, domination, and subjugation were, unfortunately, revolving events that occurred throughout the history of the Mediterranean Sea basin, including the province of Asia. Instead of focusing on speculations that are often contrived by complex calculations and overt manipulations, an African American scripturalization acknowledges that the internal evidence may indeed point to various times of composition. By approaching the text in this manner, we can bring together those debating the date of Revelation to suggest that the different periods that are implied in the text are redactions that afford an opportunity to discern the layers of the text in terms of cultural memory and communal development. This will allow for the text to be continued to be read in its literary completeness. Reading Revelation in this manner is credible because of the perspective's recognition of the vital role of text in the formation, deformation, and reformation of identity at both group and individual

---

22. Although source criticism of Revelation was the analysis of choice in the early heyday of biblical scholarship (ca. 1825–1925), scholars today mainly analyze the text as a literary whole. However, scholars do acknowledge that the text was redacted over time as they discern layers of text, as well as interpolations and dislocations. Elisabeth Schüssler Fiorenza (1998, 101–8) has suggested that the text was perhaps redacted by an apocalyptic school (as opposed to a Johannine school of the Fourth Gospel).

level. One can suggest, then, that the redaction of Revelation is an act of forging links of time that, in turn, is both an act of memory making and a recontextualization that involves the immediacy of the text, as well as looking through the text in time.

Response B: Intertextuality. Approaching the text in relation to cultural memory impels a reconsideration of the book's intertextuality. Intertextuality is the study of the way in which one signifying practice is transposed onto another, and thus is very similar to the concept of scripturalization. Julia Kristeva referred to intertextuality in terms of two axes: a *horizontal axis* connecting the author and reader of a text, and a *vertical axis* that connects the text to other texts written over time (Kristeva 1980, 69). Both the text itself and the reading of the text depend on prior codes, and by connecting these two axes the codes are shared. She claims that "every text is from the outset under the jurisdiction of other discourses which impose a universe on it" (ibid; see also Culler 1981, 105). She argues that rather than confining our attention to the structure of a text, we should study how the structure came into being. For Kristeva, this necessitates placing the text within the totality of previous texts of which it is a transformation.

Revelation scholars ponder the rhetorical gains for the author's nuanced re-presentation of other texts to his audience since he merely alludes to other texts, including the Hebrew Scriptures and local legends and myths. Did John use these texts with little interest in their original significance, or did he "honor the original meaning and intent of those texts"? With what integrity did John use the Hebrew Scriptures? Did "Scripture become servant to John's ideological interests and political agenda" or vice versa? (deSilva 2009, 150). The concept of cultural memory coupled with Kristeva's definition of intertextuality creates the possibility for an interesting and compelling examination of these issues.

An African American scripturalization suggests that John's signifyin(g), that is, his indirection and allusion, is shaped and directed by past significations that lend their power to the new shaping (deSilva 2009, 150). If the books of Isaiah, Ezekiel, Joel, Zechariah, Daniel, and Psalms (the main texts to which John alludes) inspired actions in their original context, then they remain recognizable as inspired material in the new context of Revelation. This suggests the importance of texts in persuading a community to action by invoking connections to the past. The author's re-presenting the ancient city of Babylon as synonymous to the Roman imperial system, for instance, serves to illustrate that recycling is in thorough dialogue with the author's rhetorical strategy.

The approach of reading Revelation's intertextuality by way of signifyin(g) produces a viable lens to examine the possibilities of how the author's reuse of (con)text functioned in the construction of a Christian identity. The internal evidence already suggests that several layers of historical narrative exist within the text, from at least the time of Nero in 68 CE to Domitian in 96 CE. The incorporation of the idea of cultural memory in contemplating Revelation may indeed be an intriguing response to the major scholarly debate over the date of Revelation in particular and the analysis of Revelation in general.

RHETORICAL STRATEGY

Call: It is through his oratorical arsenal that John unveils his perspective on the nature of evil, the role of the church in the in-between times, the method in which God conquers this world, the conflicted nature of humanity, the critique of humanity's self-deification, the new liberation of God's people from Pharaoh, and the urgent need for a messianic repair of a fractured cosmos (Resseguie 2009, 18). Although rhetorical criticism has been applied to the study of other New Testament letters and speeches, rhetorical critics have mainly passed over Revelation. This is due to the distance between the literary genre and the material in which classical rhetorical theory was developed—"rational speeches delivered in political, civic, or juristic settings" (deSilva 2009, 15).[23] John's style of delivery is surely not to be found in any classical rhetorical handbook, and so the books provide a very limited "framework for exploring how John (1) constructs and deconstructs credibility (appeals to *ethos*); (2) engages the feelings of the hearers (appeals to *pathos*); and (3) formulates arguments leading the audience toward the decision that the author favors (appeals to *logos*)" (2009, 17). Due to his unique rhetorical style, it is necessary to pay close attention to his narrative strategy, including his extremely nuanced use of intertextuality.

Elisabeth Schüssler Fiorenza is credited with pioneering the application of a rhetorical analysis to the book of Revelation. Her work serves as a prototype for investigating "how arguments are constructed and how

---

23. The classical rhetorician uses the ancient rhetorical handbooks on rhetorical practice dating from the fourth century BCE (Aristotle's *Art of Rhetoric*) through the late first century CE (Quintilian's *Institutio Oratoria*) as tools for analyzing the persuasive power of the text.

power is inscribed" in Revelation, as well as "how interpretive discourse affects the social formation of which it is a part" (1991, 21). According to Schüssler Fiorenza, a "critical rhetorical analysis of Revelation seeks to trace its ideological practices and persuasive goals and to identify the literary means by which they are achieved" (1991, 22; 2007, 130–48). Thus, analyzing John's usage of metaphors and similes, verbal threads, chiasms, *inclusios*, two-step progressions, indirection, and other literary devices is vital to discerning his signification on empire. In addition, the topographical, architectural, and temporal settings are not to be considered as mere backdrops against which the story unfolds, but are understood as being steeped with meaning to orient the readers/hearers to a familiar yet strange story about home.

According to David deSilva, hearing the text in this way will afford the opportunity to see the counterintuitive ways in which John problematizes peaceful coexistence and prosperity within the surrounding society. It will also allow a glimpse of the way in which "he normalizes marginalization, poverty, even the experience of violent death" (deSilva 2009, 30). Discerning the alternative understandings of the cultural landscape will make it possible to recover the other voices that John the seer's rhetoric suppresses.

Response: Mindful that in this project I argue that John's signifyin(g) reinscribes imperial practices and processes, the discernment of alternative understandings will assist in recovering John's own "imperial voice" as well.[24] That is, an African American scripturalization highlights that John's venomous rhetoric is directed not only against the Roman Empire and the local elites, but also against a significant number of Christian "hybrids" who are participating in the social, religious, and economic practices of their society.[25] Throughout the letters to the seven churches in chapters 2–3, John demands that the congregants insulate themselves from partaking in any cultic activity that involved worshiping idols. The eating of food that was sacrificed to idols signified to John cultic practices that worshiped false gods. His rhetoric was intent on denouncing cultic activity that wor-

---

24. By "imperial voice" I refer to John's mimicry of imperial practice and process.

25. According to some scholars, participation in the imperial cult was necessary in order for local elites to maintain their wealth and limited power, as well as for the merchants and artisans whose guilds depended on the existence of the state cult in the provinces. See Stam 1978; Garnsey and Saller 1987; L. Thompson 1990; Kraybill 1996; Duff 2001; Harland 2000, 2003.

shiped any deity other than Jesus Christ, and because so many scholars contend that the religio-political system of the imperial cult was an important part of the context in which John's book was written, it is plausible to posit that denouncing the participation in imperial cult practices was a primary purpose for John's isolation policy. John attempted to achieve this by drawing sharp contrasts and creating exclusive boundaries between the Christian communities and the larger society that accommodated idol worship (Carter 2009; deSilva 1992).

This is evident in his message to the churches in Pergamum (2:12–17) and Thyatira (2:18–29). According to John, these two cities are infested with false teachings that beguile the church to accommodate cultic practices that are counterproductive to his particular version of Christianity. In the letter to Pergamum, the teaching of Balaam is equated with the cultic practices of the Nicolaitans, which may have consisted of eating food sacrificed to the emperor (Aune 1997, 148).[26] Some also speculate that John is referring to the Nicolaitans in his message to Thyatira, for they too are accused of eating foods sacrificed to idols by the instigation of the prophetess whom John referred to as Jezebel. It is this immersion in cult practices that evoked the fierce messages to the churches. John simply cannot reconcile the idea that Christians can participate in Greco-Roman civic ritual/religion and also believe in the one true God. For John, there is absolutely no room for assimilation, no middle space of hybridity between the two poles of God and the lamb, on the one hand, and the dragon and the beast, on the other, who function as "counterfeit counterparts" (Aune 1983, 5; Moore 2006, 115–18). God and the lamb will utterly destroy at the appropriate time all those who participate in imperial cultic practices.

An African American scripturalization views John's isolation policy as unrealistic, ineffective, and detrimental. The drawing of strict boundaries between an ascetic or exclusive community and the rest of society results in a communal formation that is fixed, biased, and seemingly homogeneous. The community establishes an "us" versus "them" mentality, authorities police the community constantly, and harsh policies are put in place against any who do not adhere to the severe restrictions. John's signifyin(g) technique that attempted to create a "pure" Christian

---

26. Although little is known about the Nicolaitans, Irenaeus links them with Nicolaus of Antioch, one of the seven mentioned in Acts 6.

community turned on those in his own community that he considered "impure." By linking the Nicolaitans to the "evil" characters in the Scriptures, that is, Balaam and Jezebel, John slanders members of the Christian community with their own sacred texts.[27] He constructs their marginalization by spreading propaganda against them and hopes to gain an alliance with the congregations.

John's signifyin(g) appears to mimic the slanderous tactics of character assassination that were used by imperial propagandists in terms of labeling, confronting, and conquering their opponents. Ironically, John's fierce and violent signifyin(g) is turned against those in his own community in his attempt to totally segregate the Christian communities from the practices and processes of empire.

THE LETTERS TO THE CHURCHES OF PHILADEPHIA AND LAODICEA

One of the areas in the text where John's metaphorical usage exposes his "imperial voice" is in the messages to Philadelphia (3:7–13) and Laodicea (3:14–22). When juxtaposing the letters to the "poor" Philadelphians and the "rich" Laodiceans, an African American scripturalization unveils the disturbing imagery that John's metaphors convey in the exhortation formula addressed to both of these congregations (3:12 and 21, respectively). These verses, which begin with "To the one who conquers" (Ο νικῶν), function as words of encouragement and commendation that are specifically tailored to each church as the incentive for overcoming a particular impeachment. However, on a contrapuntal reading, based on an approach that is hermeneutically suspicious of John's unacknowledged ambivalence and undeclared hybridity, one can discern an "imperial transcript" tucked slyly within these two exhortation formulas (Friesen 2006).[28]

Traditionally, the letter to Philadelphia is read as a message of "brotherly love" from the glorified Christ. This church, though poor and powerless, is enduring in strength in Christ, who provides confidence to this small community (deSilva 2009, 184). The message does not instill

---

27. Balaam was slain because he was held responsible for Israel's idolatry (Num 31:8, 16), and Jezebel's corpse was torn to shreds by dogs because of her worship of the god Baal (1 Kgs 21:23–24; 2 Kgs 9:30–37).

28. Friesen reviews references to synagogues of Satan in Rev 2–3 in connection with John's blended irony, slander, and sarcasm in the messages to the seven churches. He does not, however, approach the text through the lens of hybridity.

any sense of fear or shame that is characteristic of several other messages, particularly to the church in Thyatira. The author does not condemn but rather condones this church throughout. The Philadelphian church is, for the most part, patronized by biblical scholars as an outstanding display of obedience in the face of extreme suffering, especially in 3:12, which symbolically compares the Philadelphian "conqueror" to a "pillar," which, in the traditional sense of the word, is representative of an outstanding figure in a society. The Philadelphian exhortation formula states: "If you conquer, I will make you a pillar in the temple of my God; you will never go out of it. I will write on you the name of my God, and the name of the city of my God, the new Jerusalem that comes down from my God out of heaven, and my own new name" (Ὁ νικῶν ποιήσω αὐτὸν στῦλον ἐν τῷ ναῷ τοῦ θεοῦ μου καὶ ἔξω οὐ μὴ ἐξέλθῃ ἔτι καὶ γράψω ἐπ' αὐτὸν τὸ ὄνομα τοῦ θεοῦ μου καὶ τὸ ὄνομα τῆς πόλεως τοῦ θεοῦ μου, τῆς καινῆς Ἰερουσαλήμ ἡ καταβαίνουσα ἐκ τοῦ οὐρανοῦ ἀπὸ τοῦ θεοῦ μου, καὶ τὸ ὄνομά μου τὸ καινόν).

However, an African American scripturalization questions if there is an alternative imagery that is conjured. The imagery of the Philadelphian as a "pillar" contains within its range of meanings architectural column structures sculpted in the form of human bodies that support the temple structure on their heads and shoulders. In Greco-Roman architecture two varieties of columns are sculpted in human form to support an entablature, the atlantes and the caryatids. In the atlantes, the statues of men take the place of the shafts, and in the caryatids the shafts are replaced by women figures. The atlantes were employed in the cella of the gigantic temple of Zeus at Agrigentum, while the most famous caryatids can be found at the Erechtheum in Athens. In addition, people who were subjected to the Persian Empire were often depicted in high relief sculptures, primarily as throne bearers. For instance, the statue of Darius that was situated at the entrance to the great gate at Susa depicts twenty-four subjects in Egyptian style on the rectangular base of the statue. Above each carved subject was each one's name in hieroglyphics. They are kneeling, hands above their head, palms up, supporting not only the royal throne but the land of the empire (Briant 2002, 174).

Likewise, the allusion to the Philadelphian conquerors as "pillars" in Rev 3:12 can connote the laborious, heavy burdens that the (slave or subjected) figure is forced to bear in providing the foundation and stability of the temple structure (the house of God) and, by extension, the polis. John's Christ utters that these poor souls will never leave the temple of *his* God (not *their* God, which would at least imply some sort of equality in status); therefore, they are forever bonded to this torturous activity. In addition, John's Christ will inscribe on the body of the poor Philadelphian a new name. Traditionally, the inscription of a new name functioned as a signifier of change in an individual (Gen 17:5, 17; 32:27–28; 41:45; Dan 1:7; Mark 3:17; John 1:42). However, the receiving of a new name can also connote enslavement. Among the ancients, branding or tattooing was nearly always a sign of punishment and degradation. Slaves were often branded, which signified that they were owned property (Glancy 2006, 88–89; Aune 1998, 458).[29] In addition, the branding, or sealing, on the forehead with letters signified that the slave was a captured runaway, the opposite sense of a conqueror (Jones 1987, 140).[30]

These images of marked, laboring bodies that visually represent the oppressive system of slavery do not appear to be eradicated in the new Jerusalem.[31] Rather, the new world order envisioned in 3:12 appears to be maintained and sustained by human labor. The Philadelphian "who conquers" will simply experience a change in the master/slave dynamic. The imagery that John presents is not that of liberation, but is in fact reenslavement to a new master in a new power structure. Indeed, Christ's message to the community uncovers an inversion or reinscription of the system of slavery in Asia Minor.

To the contrary, the vision of power and authority that is conjured in the exhortation formula to the Laodiceans in 3:21 implies that the rich Laodicean conqueror will fare quite differently than the poor Philadelphian in 3:12: "To the one who conquers I will give a place with me on my throne, just as I myself conquered and sat down with my Father on his throne" (Ὁ νικῶν δώσω αὐτῷ καθίσαι μετ' ἐμοῦ ἐν τῷ θρόνῳ μου, ὡς κἀγὼ ἐνίκησα καὶ ἐκάθισα μετὰ τοῦ πατρός μου ἐν τῷ θρόνῳ αὐτοῦ). The Laodicean who conquers will be permitted to share the throne of the Father and Jesus Christ. This permission is quite perplexing as the glorified Christ publicly and explicitly rejects the Laodiceans' claim to honor and glory. Indeed, his

---

29. There is documentary evidence from the Egyptian Jewish colony at Elephantine that indicates that slaves were marked on the arm with Aramaic letters. In addition, in many ancient Near Eastern religions, tattoos had a religious significance involving dedication to a deity, a custom that also implies ownership.

30. The practice of branding as a mark of punishment was first handed down by the Persians to the Greeks, who passed it on to the Romans.

31. See Rev 22:3, "His slaves [οἱ δοῦλοι] shall worship him."

opinion is of such a quality that it cannot be overturned by any riposte on the congregation's part. They are entirely stripped of the public image they think to project, exposing their "naked" state (ἡ αἰσχύνη τῆς γυμνότητός σου) to view (3:18b). There is absolutely "no word of commendation, not even about 'a few,' to help them save face" (deSilva 2009, 190). Yet, after having been put to shame and being urged to purchase refined gold from Christ, the Laodicean "who conquers" will be able to invite Christ in to dine with her/him and will sit equally with Christ on the throne of God and be given divine power, honor, and wealth. This is quite a contrary image of the faithful yet poor Philadelphian conqueror, who is forced to bear the weight of the new Jerusalem on her/his shoulders.

These two passages support the suggestion that the sociopolitical hierarchical structure of Roman Asia provides the background of John's visions of an alternative symbolic universe. The social images in the message to the community in Philadelphia and to the condemned citizens of Laodicea seem to be a mere inversion or reinscription of Greco-Roman societal stratification. Indeed, one can suggest that the imagined outcome for both congregants is based on the reality of their actual social, economic, and financial status in society. Therefore, one can also suggest that John's rhetoric mimics the "imperial voice" of empire.

THE ROMAN IMPERIAL CULT CONTEXT

Call: The immediate context of the book of Revelation is the Roman imperial cult. John's ferocious attack against the practice of emperor worship in provincial Asia is evident throughout the entire book, especially in the thirteenth chapter. As mentioned above, the beast coming out of the sea with seven heads and ten diadems on its horns is symbolic of Rome and the Roman emperors as they cross the sea in their quest of invasion (13:1–2). The second beast that rose out of the earth mentioned in 13:11–16 likely refers to the local priesthood. Scholars connect the making of an image of the beast in 13:12 to the local priesthood that is responsible for the daily operation of the imperial cult in the provinces, while 13:16–17 connects the economy of Asia with imperial cultic practices.

Background

After Octavian's (Augustus's) victory over Cleopatra and Antony at Actium in 29 BCE, Roman court rhetoricians, poets, artisans, and architects began the fabrication of an imperial ideology and ethos that was central to the Roman understanding of the world and their role in it.[32] This ideology was expressed in imagery that portrayed Augustus as both conqueror and political savior who put an end to war and brought order to all things. He was conceived as the usher of the golden age, the herald of the Pax Romana. As Pliny writes:

> The boundless grandeur of the Roman Peace, which displays in turn not men only with their different lands and tribes, but also mountains and peaks soaring into the clouds, their offspring and also their plants. May this gift of the gods last, I pray forever! So truly do they seem to have given to the human race the Romans as it were a second sun. (*Nat.* 28.3)

The new age was seen as the fulfillment of prophecy, included heaven as well as earth, was universal, was enacted through official celebrations, and considered Augustus as the son of god (Howard-Brook and Gwyther 1999, 115). By the end of Augustus's reign, a myth of origin was created and a single integrated system of images had fully evolved into a "superculture" that combined the best traditions of both Greek and Roman culture, Greek aesthetics with Roman propriety and *virtus* (Galinsky 2005, 10–28).

Since the emperor rarely visited the provinces and the provincials rarely traveled to Rome, the emperor's genius was made manifest through a variety of ways—statues, inscriptions, coins, feasts, and games. Yet, most importantly, the manifestation of the emperor's presence was literally dependent on the flesh and blood of the local priests of the *poleis*. During festive processions the images of the imperial family were carried either by the council of elders or by the *sebastophoroi* (imperial officials), who were escorted by military honor guards and proceeded by flute players and trumpeters. The "honor" to make manifest the emperor's image permitted the local priests to maintain a wide range of civic offices and duties. Since the context in which they operated was religio-political, the local priesthood was responsible not only for the rituals of sacrifice, burning incense, singing hymns, and initiating festivals and games, but also political negotiations, administration of the financial centers, trade negotiations, economic expansion, the enforcement of laws, the collection of taxes, and of

---

32. Adler 2003, 41–53, 147–57; Chisholm and Ferguson 1981; Millar 1997, 2002; Goodman 1997, 123–33; Galinsky 1998, 90–127; Dench 2005, 1–36; Barchiesi 2005; Mattingly 2011.

course the waging of war. These were all channels of power made available to the local priests and other administrators (62). These provincial responsibilities were avenues that led to Rome. The son of a provincial priest could move up the social ladder and gain equestrian status, and the priest's grandson could claim senatorial and perhaps consular status (L. Thompson 1990, 161). Therefore, the local elites embraced the imperial cult because the cult established hierarchical positions of power within the provincial populace.

Arguably, the most impressive provincial official was the *archiereus*, the chief priest, who presided over the provincial assembly of Asia that comprised over one hundred delegates from various cities. The prestige of a city being bestowed the honor of *neokoros* (temple warden) of the imperial cult that allowed the city to maintain "an imperial temple flamed the rivalry and competitive spirit among the cities of Asia" (L. Thompson 1990, 160; cf. Friesen 1993, 76–89). As S. R. F. Price notes, "the reasons for the long-term vitality of this fluid and elaborate system of cults lie in its capacity to exploit the competitive values of the urban élite" (1984, 62; Ando 2000, 131–74). It appears that the seven cities mentioned in the book of Revelation were very caught up in the exploitation encouraged by the competitiveness of the cult. Pergamum, Smyrna, Ephesus (where a third temple was built), Sardis, Philadelphia, and Laodicea were all cities that had hosted the provincial assembly at one time or other. The cities became leaders in erecting statutes, temples, and altars in honor of the emperors, each city seemingly outdoing the others for imperial favor (Price 1984, 102).

It would be a mistake to assume that this religio-political setting first occurred with the Roman occupation of Asia. To the contrary, it was the way of life in western Anatolia for generations. The provincial residents of Roman Asia were members of a society that contained well-established sets of institutions, practices, and a common language from which they constructed the cosmos and their place in it long before the Romans crossed the sea into their territory (see Isager 1990; Woolf 1994; Kallet-Marx 1995, 97–124).

Immediately prior to the Roman occupation, the ancient people of the cities made sense of their world through the practices of the local Hellenistic cult, a praxis that worshiped the ruler or hero as divine. The court ceremony of the local Attalid dynasty, which ruled the region from their monarchial base at Pergamum just prior to the Roman incursion, appointed priests for their cult as soon as they assumed royal office. Festivals and athletic contexts celebrated the divinity of these living kings.

Temples and altars were constructed in their honor and sacrifices were dedicated to them. Attalus III, the last king, had his statute placed in the temple of Asclepius and incense was burned to him every day on Zeus's altar. Similar to the imperial cult, these ritual acts also contributed immensely to the formulation of the populace's understanding of their relationship to their kings, rulers, and tyrants, and also with one another.

As in the Roman provinces, the acropolis, the city's fortified high ground, was delineated as the sacred space of the city where the political, financial, military, and economic systems were headquartered. Since public space was also sacred space, the temple grounds and the pathways throughout the city were crucial in the construction of identity. For instance, the route of a procession passed along sacred and civic monuments memoralizing important events or acts of beneficence from prominent citizens of the city. These images served as visual markers in which the legends and myths transcended the everyday life of the provincials impressing upon them a certain group identity.

When the Roman Empire seized control of the province of Asia, the residents of the region did not abandon their religio-political system. Instead, they recontextualized aspects of the Hellenistic ruler cults by overlaying the local cults with Roman imperial imagery (Zanker 1988, 297–334).

Response: As mentioned above, an African American scripturalization that is fused with postcolonial discourse perceives that contact with the Persian Empire influenced the construction of imperial ideology in Asia Minor. The Persian Empire, as the largest international empire of the time, had constructed an imperial ethos that affected the region for approximately two centuries before the Hellenistic rulers came into power.[33] In particular, Darius I, the "Great King" (or King of kings), had imposed the idea of the unbounded nature of his authority over territories and populations (Briant 2002, 213; Lincoln 2007, 33–49). Persian inscriptions and sculptures carved on tomb facades, palace walls, Egyptian stelae, and the statute of Darius at Susa all reconstruct to some extent the Persian idealized image of the world. The imperial images at Susa attest to the royal desire to depict tribes, peoples, and tongues conquered by the Persians as being united in harmonious cooperation with the empire. In this palace

---

33. Goldstone and Haldon 2010; Wiesehöfer 2010; Finley 1978; Wallace and Harris 1996; Lampela 1998.

imagery, the far corners of the Persian Empire are recognized, including the city of Sardis, which was considered a major strategic site for the Persians in Asia Minor. In fact, the Persian Royal Road began at Persepolis and ended at Sardis.

Lily Ross Taylor in 1927 argued for the existence of a Persian ruler cult. This assumption, however, is now largely dismissed by New Testament scholars, who mainly follow the thought of S. R. F. Price, who reasons that because there were no actual cults of the Persian king or his governors in the Greek cities, including Anatolia, there was no adaptation of Persian court ceremony (1984, 26). As Price notes, "the Persian monarchy was highly developed and posed major problems for the cities, but cults would have been inappropriate. Persian rule was resented or rejected rather than accommodated within the city" (ibid.).

However, Taylor had argued quite convincingly that the Persian kings were indeed worshiped. The Persian kings were the successors of a long line of Eastern kingships—Egyptian, Babylonian, and Assyrian. The Egyptian rulers were considered gods, while the Assyrians and Neo-Babylonian kings, although not considered as deities per se but rather as shepherds or stewards of the local gods of their lands, were nevertheless considered to be divinely appointed and divinely empowered (Taylor 1927, 53–54).

The Persian kings were heirs to the majesty and unlimited power that had characterized the sovereigns of the East (Taylor 1927, 53–56). This majesty and power are demonstrated by Persian royal ritual. Taylor particularly highlights *proskynesis*, the act of prostrating or subordinating oneself before the king. This performance took on various forms: a bow at the waist, laying prostrate on the floor, or extending a kiss to the image of the king at the banquet table. (The king purportedly never sat down to eat with his nobles. Instead, the courtiers set up a special table for the king's spirit and placed on it offerings of food and drink.)

Alexander the Great, directly influenced by Persian court ceremony, incorporated the ritual of *proskynesis* into Macedonian court ceremony. The practice was an important aspect of worship in relation to the Hellenistic rulers and Roman imperial culture. This is substantiated by Phillip Alexander and Loveday Alexander in their discussion of the Jewish perspective on Eastern kingship:

From Palestine the Jewish image of the Oriental monarch was transmitted westwards to the Greek-speaking Diaspora, through translations of the books of Esther and Daniel. There it met and readily merged with similar Greek ideas of Oriental monarchy. These went back ultimately to Herodotus and the struggle between "democratic" Athens and "absolutist" Persia.... This polemic began, by all accounts, as early as the time of Alexander the Great who took over many of the trappings of the Persian court, and who required *proskunēsis*.... It echoed down the centuries of Greek and, indeed, of Roman, political life, at least to the time of Diocletian, who, when he introduced new elaborate ceremonial into the Roman court was accused by some of "Persianizing." (Alexander and Alexander 2007, 101–2; see Aune 1983)[34]

In addition, Taylor points to the worship of the dead kings at the royal tombs at Pasargadae as being very similar to the cults of the dead heroes of the Hellenistic cults. Regular sacrifices were performed to the dead kings that always culminated in a meal of bread, meat, and wine shared by all. Cyrus, the founder of the Achaemenid Empire who established Pasargadae as his capital, received the greatest honor. His lavish tomb was surrounded day and night by magi who made the daily offerings, plus the monthly sacrifice of a horse. The offerings were supplied by the living king at the time.

Lastly, Taylor argued that the evidence for worshiping the essence of the living king and the existence of a cult of the dead hero is in accord with the Avesta, the sacred texts of Zoroastrianism. According to the Avesta, the Persians believed that for every person there existed a spirit called the *fravashi*, the immortal double of the soul that existed in every human being. The *fravashi* of the just—including those who are dead, those who are now alive, and those who are still to be born—will receive worship (1927, 56). She claimed that at the time of the Achaemenids, the *fravashi* closely resembled the concepts of the Greek *daimones* and the Roman *Genii*. Before the king in solemn processions was borne an altar with a fire burning upon it that symbolized the king's power. This act accords with the idea of the *hvareno*, the king's glory that is described in the Avesta as a flame. Yet the Persian king is never equated to the supreme god, Ahura Mazda, to whom the kings attribute their thrones, or to Mithra, who was added to the Persian pantheon in later times. Taking these three points into consideration, Taylor argued for the existence of a Persian ruler cult.

---

34. Aune mentions specifically that Caligula, Nero, and Domitian required *proskynesis* (1983, 16–17).

An African American scripturalization perspective considers the transference of ritual, for instance, the performance of *proskynesis*, from one imperial setting to another as an excellent example of the role of ritual in the mediation of cultural memory and identity construction. The ability to transfer rituals from one political system to another illustrates their fluidity to adapt to various sociopolitical changes while maintaining communal continuity. Ritual performance can play a role like this only when it comes from within a system that is defined and deployed in ways that interlock with how tradition and change are viewed (C. Bell 1997, 136). One can argue that ritual performance in the ancient Mediterranean world was a production formed in the interstitial space where cultures converge. The rituals of the Persian court that were integrated in the Hellenistic local ruler cults and subsequently in the Roman imperial cult were vital mediums in which imperial narratives "almost the same but not quite like" previous narrations legitimated the complex web of power in western Anatolia for generations. Throughout various historical stages, then, ritual performance has functioned to anchor an imperial worldview by providing the continuity necessary for an ideological script that must constantly be retold or re-presented in light of the inevitable ebb and flow of time.

Conclusion

In this chapter I suggested that a vital first step in producing a reading of the book of Revelation that exposes the intricacy of a hybrid identity construction is the re-presentation of the general scholarly issues that are considered to be central to this text. I argued that the deconstruction of the standard scholarship must take place because the historical-critical paradigm would "overshadow" the African American scripturalization perspective. Thus, in a call-and-response format, I placed the historical paradigm in conversation with an African American scripturalization perspective whereby I showed how the perspective allowed for a broader analysis of the text. I attempted to do this by explicitly illustrating that the scribe's context influences the analysis.. I argue that, although historical biblical critics do not explicitly state or lay out their hermeneutical process, their presuppositions drive their interpretations. By the re-presentation of the historical-critical approach to the book of Revelation framed by the "strangeness of home" approach, I attempted to unveil that the supposedly objective historical-critical approach can, indeed, be argued to be a camouflaged subjective enterprise.[35]

Now that the historical biblical scholarship has been deconstructed and re-presented, in the following chapter I am free to propose a broader and more theoretically complex reading of Revelation through an African American scripturalization supplemented by postcolonial theory. I examine the ritual performances in the heavenly throne room in chapters 4 and 5, as well as the snippets of various throne room scenes scattered throughout Revelation, to illustrate that John the Seer's counternarration is actually a mere reinscription of imperial ideology.

---

35. See discussion on the juxtaposition of the historical paradigm and the cultural critical paradigm in the first chapter.

Signifyin(g) a Heavenly Empire:
An African American Scripturalization of the
Heavenly Throne Room Scenes in Revelation

I have been in Sorrow's kitchen and licked out all the pots. Then I have
stood on the peaky mountain wrapped in rainbows, with a harp and
sword in my hands.
> — Zora Neale Hurston, *Dust Tracks on the Road*

The monkey laid up in the tree and he thought up a scheme
And thought he'd try one of his fantastic dreams.
> — Henry Louis Gates Jr., *The Signifying Monkey*

Introduction

In this chapter I examine images of imperial ritual in the heavenly throne
room scenes in the book of Revelation through the lens of an African
American scripturalization supplemented by postcolonial theory, especially as conceptualized by Homi Bhabha. The purpose of this scripturalization is to unveil the complex cultural negotiations involved in the
construction of a Christian identity. The scripting will propose that John
the Seer's signifyin(g) on empire demonstrates that he is well aware of
the oppressive nature of Roman imperialism on the lives of Christians in
the province of Asia. This is made clear by his fierce, nonaccommodating stance toward participation in the imperial cult, a ritualistic religio-
political system that justifies an imperialistic worldview. Yet, ironically,
John reinscribes imperial processes and practices. Seemingly, no matter
how determined the seer is to disconnect from the cultural manipulations
of empire, his hybridity disallows him. John's colonized construction as
"almost the same but not quite like" has resulted in the production of a
resistance strategy that is a blurred copy of the hegemonic tactics of the
Roman Empire.

John's signifyin(g) on empire utilizes various cultural apparatuses—sacred script, ritual, myth, and historical narrative.[1] An important aspect of his signifyin(g) strategy relies on connecting the past with the present and the future. Thus the images he conjures both allude to and signify on the various power structures of the ancient past, including Babylon and Persia, as well as the axis of power in his own day, the Roman Empire of the first century.[2] Key to this scripturalization, then, is that systems of domination in the past, particularly the Persian Empire as the largest international empire in the ancient world, remained vivid in the collective memory banks of the people of provincial Asia through the retelling of history, the making of myths, the maintaining of archaeological structures, and especially through the performance of ritual acts (Alcock 2001, 323–51).[3] Therefore, one can suggest that the imagery and allusions the seer presented in his signify(ing) on Rome tapped into a cultural memory that evoked identification, imagination, resistance, and desire, all elements that aid in identity construction (L. Thompson 1998, 35).[4]

---

1. Scripture for the seer would be the "Old Testament," especially Daniel, Ezekiel, Isaiah, and Zechariah. These writings are used by John for the purpose of "remembering" Judea when under the rule of Babylon and Persia in the past, and to signify on Rome in the present.

2. Although Babylon is explicitly referenced in Revelation and is interpreted as referring to the Roman Empire (Rev 17–18), there is minimal explicit reference to the Persian Empire. However, I suggest it is conceivable that John's signifyin(g) invoked the memory of Persian occupation. Persia dominated western Asia for over two hundred years (550–330 BCE) and traces of that occupation remained in the first century CE. Lily Ross Taylor claimed that "the Roman Empire grew up at a time when Rome was in close contact with the life and thought of the East. The world ruler, who now came into being at Rome, had an ancient tradition which still lived on in the kingdoms of Egypt and of western Asia" (1931, 1–4). Also see Briant 2002.

3. Alcock claims it is a well-established fact that the eastern provinces of the Roman Empire had been obsessed with their ancient past. To this day, many of the modern city names in Turkey are first recorded under their Hittite names, such as Sinop and Adana, reflecting the continuity with the ancient Anatolian past. See also Elsner 2001; van Dommelen 1998.

4. Thompson reads Revelation as being in reciprocal relations with other social, political, psychological, historical, literary, and religious structures and contexts: "To read Revelation with understanding, one eye must be on the large circle of revelatory texts, the other on the specific language and themes in John's book; with that dual vision, readers can better understand how John uses a common stock of motifs and images to communicate his distinctive message" (1998, 35). See also Aune 1997, cxxi. Many scholars have argued that John adapted and incorporated ancient Near Eastern

In this chapter, however, I propose that John's signifyin(g) is a contradiction because he seemed to have simply re-presented and reenacted imperial policy/propaganda to establish a future Christian empire called the new Jerusalem. The seer's numerous allusions that entailed violent disruption and displacement served to invoke in his audience the remembrance of the region's long history of occupation by various dynasties that rose, flourished, declined, and then collapsed in continual succession, like the seasonal rhythms of nature. His signifyin(g) remained fixed on the persistent cycles of war, conquest, and revolt, paralleled by cycles of worship, ritual, and mythmaking. How could John, who was so *against* empire, mimic empire?

An African American scripturalization of the book of Revelation insists that domination is not simply a system of military control, but a systematic cultural penetration that subjugates psychologically as well as intellectually. Therefore, a possible answer to how or why John mimics the ideological assumptions and methods of constructing empire is that it is due, to a certain degree, to his being a member of a society that embraced participation in the cultic rituals of empire. Imperial cult ritual performance caused participants to connect with imperial ideological codes that, in turn, modified their behavior. In addition, I suggest that John's denial of his own ambivalent, hybrid construction, his repression or nonrealization of his own fragmentation, his own double-consciousness, may be the cause for his contradictory stance toward empire.

As mentioned in chapters 1 and 3, cultural memory is of central importance to the notion of African American scripturalization because past events are inscribed in community consciousness that continue to be meaningful in the present and future. Scribes, being carriers of memory, deconstruct and reconstruct cultural memory in the act of producing meaning. Those who neglect the ambivalent nature of marginalized hybridity—the desire as well as the resistance, the mimicry and the mockery—become susceptible to failing to holistically respond to the complex dimensions of the dominant ethos in the construction of identity. I propose that this is the inherent danger in John's signifyin(g) with images that transmitted a continuous cycle of violence, disruption, murder, and mayhem, adaptations of imperial practices of the past and present. John's individual identity—as

---

and Greco-Roman myths about chaos and the divine warrior. See Yarbro Collins 2001; van Henten 2006.

well as his collective community's identity—had long been constructed by negotiating cycles of imperial power. One power decreased while another increased, most often by simply reconfiguring (not dismantling) the systemic structures of the previous power. Thus the seer's script of a future Christian empire, the new Jerusalem, was simply a recycled imperialism.

In this chapter I examine select images in the heavenly throne room scenes in the book of Revelation, particularly in chapters 4 and 5—the throne room itself, the twenty-four elders, the ritual act of *proskynesis*, the lamb/lion imagery, and the hymns of praise—through the lens of an African American scripturalization to illustrate how these images reflect an imperial ideology that affected the construction of a marginalized identity. It is by way of an analysis of the throne room scenes that I illustrate that John's signifyin(g) reinscribed an imperial ethos. I suggest that this recycling of imperial ideology was partly due to his being a member of a society whose communal identity had long been constructed by ritual/ceremonial performances that imposed a cosmological order that mystified political domination and shaped cultural dispositions.

This manner of identity construction had become insidiously embedded in the memory banks of John and his community. By the time of the Roman occupation, the peoples of the Mediterranean had been thoroughly molded to adjust to Roman imperial procedures and processes that were similar to the practices of conquerors of the past, albeit with alterations—different faces may have stared down at the populace from the statues and the idols carried by the local elites and the priests, but overall, similar media strategies were used in the presentation of power.

Throughout the ages, the people living in the Mediterranean experienced "the strangeness of home." In other words, they had to navigate the subtle, seductive power of political narrations and myth of origins. They were required to negotiate the narrations of the dominant power structure, as well as participate in the civic rituals that reconstructed and refortified the myths.

John the Seer challenged the Roman Empire via a hermeneutical tradition that had for centuries been used by apocalyptic communities to "talk back to empire." In line with the tradition he upheld, John's signifyin(g) exposed the oppressiveness and destructiveness concealed within his re-presentation of an imperial narration.[5]

---

5. Allen Brent incorporates the concept of "contra-culture" (Brent's terminology)

However, the scenes described by John as occurring in the heavenly throne room are mere replications of provincial Asia's religio-political reality. In a "magnificent concatenation of sights, sounds and odors" (Aune 1983, 7), John in his unhomely state carved an open door through which he simply thrust the images and ceremonial rituals of a diabolical earthly court up into the heavenly sphere.[6] Thus John's signifyin(g) strategy that was so heavily dependent on the mirroring of images and ritual performances that connoted imperial domination down through the ages backfired, and therefore his anti-imperial rhetoric is a contradiction. It failed because John's mocking mimicked the *very process of re-presentation* that the various power systems in the ancient Mediterranean world employed to construct a sacralization of sociopolitical structures and systems.

RECENT AFRICAN AMERICAN READINGS OF THE BOOK OF REVELATION

This African American scripturalization of Revelation presents an alternative reading of the text as presented by the few African American biblical scholars who work on the book of Revelation.[7] These scholars typically frame the text through the lens of liberation theology, which positions the

---

to his reading of the imperial cult in Revelation that is expressed in imagery that creates a frame of reference that is a mirror image of the Greco-Roman culture and is a reconstruction of social reality that finds status and self-esteem that the dominant culture denies them (1999, 15, 164–209). Stephen D. Moore provides a compelling postcolonial reading with the help of Gayatri Spivak's resuscitation of the Classical Greek term *catachresis* to suggest that John's transfer of imperial cult images to the heavenly realm should be understood as the colonized strategic reuse of the colonizer's rhetorical methods with the aim of flipping those methods back onto the colonizer. Moore's analysis complicates Brent's proposal by pointing out that with reappropriation there are consequences because the "most fundamental instance of catachresis in Revelation … is its redeployment of the term 'empire' (*basileia*) itself" (2006, 106).

6. Aune argues against the major view that John's description of the heavenly ceremonial in the throne room of God reflects early Christian liturgical practice (1983, 7). Instead, he claims that it "bears such a striking resemblance to the ceremonial of the imperial court and cult that the latter can only be a parody of the former" (5). He claims that the throne scene is a pastiche of images and conceptions drawn from Israelite Jewish kingship and traditions and ideologies from Hellenistic kingship traditions and from the Roman imperial cult.

7. For example, Blount 2005a. Blount notes that because so few African Americans interpret Revelation, the use of popular material such as hymns and sermons becomes extremely critical. Blount has also written a full commentary on Revelation

mainstream African American Christian community as (America's) sacrificial lamb and the faithful witness of Jesus Christ.[8] They extract from Revelation a message of endurance from oppression in the hope of liberation that is achieved in the advent of the new Jerusalem (Rev 21). African American biblical scholars typically shy away from pondering the use of John's violent and bloodthirsty images as replicating an oppressive sociopolitical ethos because it would be counterproductive to their emancipatory approach. Yet by not wrestling with this text and coming to some sort of terms with what it means to embrace John the Seer's visions of a virulent, bloodthirsty deity and a warrior Jesus, scholars risk guiding the community to accept the idea of violence and deprivation (as long as it is not enacted against them).[9] Discussed below are two readings of Revelation by two African American biblical scholars, Brian Blount and Clarice Martin.

Can I Get a Witness? Reading Revelation through African American Culture

Brian Blount's reading of Revelation through the lens of the black church religious tradition exemplifies African American biblical hermeneutics (2005a, 40).[10] His analysis is grounded in a cultural hermeneutical approach that is based on the sufferings and struggles of African Americans in the midst of oppressive assimilation. He sees the ethical role of the black church as nonviolent resistance and patient witness to Jesus Christ as Lord and Savior (41).[11] Listing the "magnificent seven" mainstream denominations as the "spiritual cover" for 80 percent of the African

---

(2009a). The commentary is a traditional historical-critical approach to the text with a hint of the influence of an African American context.

8. See discussion below of Blount 2005a.

9. For example, Callahan (2009) takes the position that John challenges contemporary readers to escape the impending destruction of global imperialism. However, he does not critique the violent manner in which John envisions the establishment of a new world order.

10. I am intentionally using the term *African American biblical hermeneutics* here to connote a discipline undergirded primarily by black liberation theology and thus framing the text in terms of a homogeneous oppressed community as opposed to African American scripturalization, the renaming that signifies a more complex notion of identity.

11. Blount openly acknowledges the difficulty presented in applying an African American biblical hermeneutical lens to this text because of its violent nature.

American Christian population, Blount maintains that these denominations are responsible for the shaping of a collective community that resists
oppression.[12] He states: "When at its best, the Black Church has developed
forms of praxis geared toward addressing the terror and dread of objecti-
fication through the nurturing of socio-politically and economically vital
and vibrant Americans, who exercise all the rights and responsibilities
endemic to full citizenship" (41).

Blount then provides the essential discussion necessary for a cultural
reading with his treatment of the context in which the black church developed during the years of slavery in America—African Americans were
punished for unauthorized worship services. Blount understands that
"the very act of worship was an expression of political defiance" (ibid.).
He claims:

> At every critical stage in its existence, the Black Church has preoccu-
> pied itself with the task of finding a way to respond appropriately to the
> racially charged context that conceived it and gave it birth. Of all the
> traits that might be used to describe the Black Church, then, the one
> that might be considered its most enduring, constant, and characteristic
> would be its drive toward the uplift and thus liberation of its people. (42)

In this statement, Blount aligns himself with the major black liberation
theologians agreeing that African Americans are to be active agents of
God in bringing about an end to their oppression.

Interestingly, Blount claims that this agency operates from the same
synergy that "the first-century apocalyptic writers believed was the connection between their efforts and God's" (44).[13] Yet this apocalyptic agency
is not to be confused with a violent resistance. Basing his claims on his
modification of Adela Yarbro Collins's idea of synergy, Blount proposes
that the seer's apocalyptic agency is not a passive acceptance of suffering,
but a call to active, nonviolent resistance to Rome's claim of lordship over

---

12. The denominations listed: African Methodist Episcopal Church; African
Methodist Episcopal Zion Church; Christian Methodist Episcopal Church; National
Baptist Convention, USA; National Baptist Convention of America, Inc.; Progressive
National Baptist Convention; and the Church of God in Christ.

13. Here Blount is adapting Adela Yarbo Collins's synergistic proposal that suggests that the believer's suffering brings about the confidence that the suffering is
actually in some way promoting God's own revolutionary cause. See Yarbro Collins
1977, 243.

humanity (see Yarbro Collins 1977, 243). He then brings the contemporary and ancient context into solidarity by noting that the resistant ideology of John the Seer based on nonviolent apocalyptic agency is similar to the active mission of the black church—Christians are called to witness to Jesus Christ. After fully fleshing out this argument, Blount proceeds to read Revelation through this interpretive framework.[14] He examines specific texts of Revelation that promote active witness in their relation to the black church. For instance, Blount sees the slaughtered in Rev 6:9–11 as nonviolent resisters who provoke the action of Jesus Christ. Similarly, Blount claims that the African American images of lynched relatives also provoke action, knowing full well that more suffering might come as a result (Blount 2005a, 53). He observes the supposed "weakness" of the Lamb as the "homeopathic cure" (79–80). Following Theophus Smith's work in *Conjuring Culture*, Blount is compelled to pick up the conjure concept of the homeopathic cure. "In effecting a 'cure,' the conjuror takes an obvious negative and reconstitutes it into something positive and efficacious" (79). The John in Revelation transfigures "a slaughtered Lamb into a conquering Lion without surrendering either its homicide or its helplessness"; this is a homeopathic act (ibid.). John creates an antidote by capturing a small "dose of violence [the disease], the slaughter of the Lamb, and homeopathically reconfigures it into the one weapon capable of tearing violence apart" (80). By the same notion, Blount argues, the tactic of Martin Luther King was to similarly use the homeopathic method by deploying a small amount of civil disorder, which resulted in the unleashing of much violence in return. Locally and internationally, individuals were horrified at the eruption of such violence and thus initiated action for a cure. As Blount explains, "At the very moment their oppressors executed their violence against them, the moment of their symbolic 'slaughter,' their battle was won" (83). Therefore, Blount examines the image of the lamb as a model for Christian behavior, as a suffering and resurrected sacrifice.

In the final chapter, Blount claims that the hymns in Revelation are analogous to the gospel, blues, and rap in African American culture. This comparison allows him to make the argument that the hymns in Revela-

---

14. Blount reproduces this reading framework in both 2009a and 2005b. However, in the latter he shifts his methodological framework to reading Revelation in the context of the slave narratives (spirituals, autobiographies, oral histories, interviews, sermons, etc.).

tion are a "celebration of confrontational resistance" (107). From the early hymns of the slaves to gospel to blues to rap, black music has continually looked to the past in order to promote resistance in the present (109). He claims that African American hymns, in particular, should be heard as coded calls to champion God's cause and the cause of transformative liberation. He suggests a similar meaning in understanding the function of the hymns in Revelation.

"Polishing the Unclouded Mirror: A Womanist Reading of Revelation 18:13"

In an essay, womanist interpreter Clarice Martin examines the way in which Rev 18:11–13, with its reference to "slaves and human lives," functions as a "mirror" or "looking glass" for African American history (2005, 83). She demonstrates how this contemporary cultural framework sheds new light on understanding the "rhetorical and ideological functions of *Revelation* 18:13 in its first-century socio-historical and rhetorical context" (ibid.). Her methodology is based on four assumptions: (1) all interpretations are relative; (2) her specific reading lens is womanist; (3) therefore she reads Revelation from within an extended African community that is based on activism; and (4) her method deals with John's critique of slavery in the first century. Martin stresses that although John the Seer's reference to "slaves and human lives" in 18:13 does not mirror precisely the slave system of early America, nevertheless the Greco-Roman system of slavery does prompt her to compare it with that peculiar institution of the South, which influences her reading of the ancient historical context. The work of Orlando Patterson is useful to Martin in examining the similarities between the ancient and contemporary systems of slavery (Patterson 1982, 58). In particular, Martin concentrates on Patterson's articulation of the master-slave relationship and the concept of the natal alienation of the slave, that is, the slave as socially dead, in order to suggest that since antiquity the slave was thought to be "defectively souled" (Martin 2005, 89).

To support her position that the seer's rhetorical strategy in 18:13 is indeed subversive, Martin turns to Henry Louis Gates's notion of the signifying monkey trope to demonstrate how the enslaved African used the "inside meaning of words" to subvert the oppressor's arrogant assumptions of privilege by applying the signifyin(g) practice to the seer's rhetoric. Thus Martin suggests that John signifies on Rome by "using language in indirect and covert ways to critique the larger hegemonic, imperial power of what he deems to be the 'evil empire,' including all power arrangements arising from the subjugation of human beings in slavery" (Martin 2005, 96).

Critique of Blount and Martin from an African American Scripturalization Perspective

While having to address the trauma of racism and social inequality is, unfortunately, an element of African American life, past and present, and that Blount and Martin do remarkably well, their readings do not address identity complexity.

Although Blount's work is a vital attempt to read with a community a text that has traditionally been avoided, by failing to acknowledge or address the multiplex social locations of African Americans, his work does not accurately reflect the complexity of identity construction. In particular, he does not acknowledge that there is a segment of the community that has steadily strengthened both in numbers and influence in various positions in the sociopolitical and economic arena and thus are challenged with different sets of issues and concerns and are in potential danger of adhering to the oppressive tactics of the status quo. One can suggest that Blount's reading valorizes the morphing of the sacrificed lamb (that is representative of the African American community) into a roaring lion without explaining the danger of the "homeopathic cure" mutating into a full-blown transformation that reinscribes the oppressive aspects of the dominant society.

Like Blount, Martin provides a compelling reading of Revelation based on an African American context. However, as she tilts her mirror, the refracted images that she chooses to set her sight on are the images of oppressed slaves. She does not cast her eye on the other images that illumine her mirror, fragmented images that envision the possibility of the oppressed emerging as the oppressor. Therefore, I question whether her reading adequately "mirrors" the African American community of the twenty-first century by fixating her gaze on enslavement. Like Blount, Martin's reading does not offer alternative visions of identity construction that reflect the evolving economic, social, and political influence of the community and with it the potential danger of reinscribing the exploitive nature of the American ethos, as the present African American scripturalization on Revelation proposes.

The Heavenly Throne Room as a Mirror of an Imperial Setting

The scene opens in chapter 4 glistening in bright jewels that are created from the minerals of the earth accenting the one seated on the throne in heaven. The one seated is described as a shining vision of jasper and carnelian; the throne itself is lit up like an emerald rainbow (4:3). Although throughout his text John presents the primary task of God as punishing past breaches of divine law and rewarding the righteous (11:18; 14:7; 16:7; 18:8; 19:2, 11; 20:12, 13), the one seated on the throne in 4:2–3 appears to not have any agency whatsoever. This one does not speak, does not move, does not breathe—it simply is there; its presence is central, yet not proactive. By contrast, the occupants surrounding the throne—the twenty-four elders, each sitting on his own throne (4:4) and worshiping the one as cued by the four living creatures (4:6–11); the angel who serves as John's guide in the heavens and, of course, John, himself—all breathe, speak, move, and even sing, yet the one seated on the throne appears ... lifeless. The vision the author conjures is that of an impassive, yet impressive, statue decorated with magnificent jewels sitting on an equally marvelous throne chair, similar to what one would find in an imperial court structure (Aune 1983, 9).

John's description of the heavenly throne room was possibly modeled on the descriptions of throne rooms in the ancient world—splendorous sacred spaces where rulers presided over official ceremonies, held council, granted audiences, received homage, awarded high honors and offices, and performed other official functions. The intentionally marvelous nature of the throne room transmitted the values and beliefs regarding social and political identities in the form of direct experience, which, in turn, prompted the enactment of a certain performance. The point of such awe and wonder was to dazzle and overwhelm visitors and dignitaries with the magnificence, luxury and might of the sovereign.

David Aune contends that there is very little common knowledge of Roman ceremonial court in the first and second centuries. However, John's throne room images are so vivid that surely the author and his audience were knowledgeable somehow of the splendor of an earthly ceremonial court (1983, 6). The residents of the provinces, especially the local priests and elites, were certainly exposed to the *adventas* of the emperor into the provincial cities with his court in attendance. Surely the daily administration of the civic duties and rituals performed by the local priests/elites exposed the average resident to some aspects of ceremonial ritual. They would have been aware that the role of the Roman emperor, similar to his predecessors, was the dispensation of justice through the reading of petitions, hearing cases orally, and receiving embassies from various cities (roles that were enacted by the local priests/elites in the emperor's absence). Therefore, it is plausible that firsthand exposure to imperial court practices was experienced by provincial residents over the years (ibid.).

In addition, the residents of Asia would have been made aware of Persian ceremonial court rituals through the passing down of communal memories, oral traditions, theater performances, historical narratives, iconography, coins, inscriptions, myths/legends, and the reconceptualization of the Hellenistic rulers and the Roman emperors. We know this is true since there is literary evidence that the Persian king and his court migrated periodically between various royal residences (Briant 2002, 256). The king relocated with not only members of his close family, household, and courtiers, but also various administrators. It was a massive production with specialized personnel erecting a mobile royal palace that rivaled the splendor of the court in Persepolis, reproducing to the last detail the private apartments of the palace (ibid.).[15] Lucetta Mowry states:

> The Seer's setting of the scene recalls the familiar conception of the splendor of the royal courts as they existed in fact and in fanciful elaboration in folk lore and story of the Orient generally. An understanding of the setting of the throne room scene takes us back ultimately, therefore, to the royal palace of Thebes and Memphis or Babylon and Assur, of Persepolis and Parsargadae, of Alexandria and Antioch. From extant remains and from glowing descriptions of ancient authors about the throne rooms of such palaces recent investigators have contributed to our knowledge of the magnificence of the thrones that stood therein, of the ceremonial occasions that were celebrated in such chambers and of the significance of kingship in general in the ancient Near East. From the days of Darius on the glorious pageantry of the king and his court are evident in the remains of royal buildings ... and in the monuments of imperial art depicting the veneration given to the king by his subjects. (1952, 76)

---

15. Alexander the Great copied the model of the Persian portable royal tent. He sat on a gold seat surrounded by his personal guard, which included Persian bodyguards.

In all of these various ways, the residents of Asia would have absorbed the images of the ritual performance/ceremony of the imperial court.

Signs and Wonders in the Throne Room

John's depiction of seeing flashes of lightning and hearing rumblings and peals of thunder in 4:5 is reminiscent of the visual and auditory ploys that were manipulated in imperial cult practices. Contrived wonders were not unusual in the ancient world, and the simulation of thunder and lightning were popular special effects (Scherrer 1984, 599–610, 605). That John is referring to some kind of mechanical device that simulates lightning is plausible especially when it is recognized how important the symbolism of thunder and lightning is in connection with the Roman emperors (ibid.). Thunder and lightning were associated with the Roman god Jupiter, symbolizing his authority and divinity and have been imitated by the emperors. Suetonius reports that Octavian's father "dreamt that his son appeared to him in the guise more majestic than that of mortal man, with the thunderbolt, scepter and insignia of Jupiter Optimus Maximus" (Suetonius, *Gaius* 52). Also, Gaius Caligula often "exhibited himself with a golden beard, holding in his hand a thunderbolt, a trident or a caduceus, emblems of the gods" (ibid.).

There is evidence in the ancient world of magicians simulating thunder and lightning. The sound of thunder could be produced by rolling stones down wooden planks onto plates of brass. Another device was created that mimicked the sound of thunder on the theatrical stage. Dio Cassius writes that Gaius Caligula had a thunder and lightning device: "he had a contrivance by which he gave answering peals when it thundered and sent return flashes when it lightened. Likewise, whenever a bolt fell, he would in turn hurl a javelin at a rock" (59.26.7). There are also numerous references by Domitian's court poet Martial to both Jupiter and Domitian as Thunderer (*Epigrams* 8.39; 9.3, 11, 91). Scherrer argues that the use of mechanical devices in the imperial cult is plausible since there is literary evidence that many of the Caesars enjoyed employing the latest technology and gadgetry so as to keep the populace in awe of their might. Suetonius writes of Nero's *Domus Aurea* as having revolving doors and "dining rooms with fretted ceilings of ivory, whose panels could turn and shower down flowers and were fitted with pipes for sprinkling guests with perfume" (*Nero* 31.2). In light of all this, John's visions in 4:5 might have been influenced by the special effects activity that supported imperial power.

The Twenty-Four Elders

Although scholars offer diverse explanations about the identity of the twenty-four elders who sit on their own thrones that surround the one sitting (4:4),[16] I posit that their presence is similar to the inner advisory circle of the Roman emperor and that their roles are similar to that of the local priests of the imperial cult. They are described as: (1) being dressed in white robes wearing golden crowns (4:4b); (2) prostrating themselves before God in worship (4:10a; 5:14b; 7:11; 11:16; 19:4) and throwing down their golden crowns as part of the heavenly liturgy (4:8–11; 5:11–14; 7:11–12; 19:1–8); (3) singing hymns of praise to God (4:11; 5:9–10; 11:17–18); (4) carrying harps and censers of incense; and (5) speaking to John (5:5; 7:13), with one elder acting as the *senior interpres* (7:14–17) (Aune 1997, 288).

The wearing of white robes was the appropriate ritual apparel in Greek worship. White was the sacred color among the ancients and was regarded as pleasing to the gods. The insignia of many imperial priests in the East was a gold crown adorned with the emperor's likeness. In particular, an edict of Antiochus III commanded the high priestesses of Laodicea to wear a golden crown bearing a likeness of the queen (Fishwick 1991, 515).[17] The emperor was customarily presented with gold crowns by the senate and provincial cities on various civic occasions, such as victories and anniversaries. The presentation of gold crowns to a sovereign was a ceremony inherited by the Romans from the traditions of the Hellenistic kings, who, in turn, inherited it from the Persians (Aune 1983, 6).[18] Thus the image of the elders casting their golden crowns before God's throne may also point to the emperor's being presented with gold crowns by the senate on special occasions as part of the ritual act of *proskynesis*.

---

16. There have been many explanations purposed regarding the identity of the twenty-four elders varying from leaders of the twenty-four Jewish priestly courses of the Second Temple period; the twenty-four divisions of musicians descended from Levi; the sum of the twelve sons of Israel and the twelve apostles; and figures from astral mythology, such as the twenty-four Babylonian star-gods of the zodiac.

17. The ancient Persians wore a high and erect royal tiara encircled with a diadem.

18. The scene of the twenty-four elders throwing down their crowns before the throne becomes comprehensible only in light of the ceremonial traditions of Hellenistic and Roman ruler worship.

Ritual Performance of *Proskynesis*

The ritual of *proskynesis* (obeisance) is mentioned eight times in Revelation (1:17; 4:10b; 5:8; 7:11; 11:16; 19:4, 10a; and 22:8b). Indeed, the act performed by John himself serves to bind the entire text together, serving as bookends, so to speak, with 1:17a as *inclusio* A and 22:8b as *inclusio* B. In 1:17a it is the act of obeisance performed by John on the island of Patmos that opens the narrative: "when I saw him, I fell at his feet as though dead" (Καὶ ὅτε εἶδον αὐτόν, ἔπεσα πρὸς τοὺς πόδας αὐτοῦ ὡς νεκρός); and it is the (aborted) act of obeisance that closes the text in 22:8b: "and when I heard and saw them, I fell down to worship at the feet of the angel who showed them to me" (καὶ ὅτε ἤκουσα καὶ ἔβλεψα, ἔπεσα προσκυνῆσαι ἔμπροσθεν τῶν ποδῶν τοῦ ἀγγέλου τοῦ δεικνύοντός μοι ταῦτα).

Here in 22:8b John prepares to prostrate himself (inappropriately) before the angel who guided him to the new Jerusalem (and seemingly has returned him back to Patmos). He is prevented from performing the rite by the angel, because this act of obeisance is misdirected.[19] The angel informs John that he and "his comrades, the prophets and all who keep the words of this book," are on equal standing with the angel. Instead, the angel exhorts John to "worship God" in 22:9b. These verses reveal that John has come very close to not being in that number when the saints come marching into the new Jerusalem. He demonstrated in this act that, after all has been said and done, he continued to accommodate to the civic ritual practice of willingly subordinating oneself to someone other than God. It is this misguided, willful subordination to one other than God that set John off on his rant in the first place and was the reason for which he wrote. Ironically, John himself has not learned the lesson.

The rite of obeisance is transported into the heavenly realm starting at 4:10a and continues to appear throughout the various throne room scenes in the text, implying the importance of this rite. In chapter 4 the elders are programmed to fall down as though dead before the throne whenever the four creatures give praise and glory to the one seated on the throne (4:9). Thus 4:10a says: "the twenty-four elders fall before the one who is seated on the throne and worship the one who lives forever and ever" (πεσοῦνται οἱ εἴκοσι τέσσαρες πρεσβύτεροι ἐνώπιον τοῦ καθημένου ἐπὶ τοῦ θρόνου καὶ προσκυνήσουσιν τῷ ζῶντι εἰς τοὺς αἰῶνας τῶν αἰώνων). In 5:8

---

19. He is also prevented from performing the rite before an angel in 19:10.

the four living creatures are displaced by the "lamb standing as if it had been slaughtered" (ἀρνίον ἑστηκὸς ὡς ἐσφαγμένον) (5:6) who now prompts the subordination of the twenty-four elders *and* the four creatures. In 5:14, the last verse of the chapter, it is simply the twenty-four elders who perform *proskynesis*.

The other scenes where the act of subordination occur are: 7:11, in which it is performed by the numerous angels that surround the throne, in addition to the twenty-four elders and the four living creatures; 11:16, which simply mentions the twenty-four elders prostrating before the throne; and 19:4, where it is the twenty-four elders and four living creatures who fall down as though dead before God.

That the act is mentioned consistently in the throne room scenes throughout the text suggests that the people of the eastern provinces were accustomed to performing the ritual. This ritual, as discussed above, was assimilated into the Roman system either as a result of direct contact with the Persians or by intermediate contact with Alexander the Great and the Hellenistic kings, among whom it became a widely practiced ritual performance in the royal ceremonial courts.

For instance, Plutarch has a Persian *chiliarch*, the head of the king's personal guard, explain to Themistocles, who wishes an audience with the king:

> among many fair customs, this is the fairest of all, to honour the King, and to pay obeisance [*proskynesis*] to him as the image of that god [*eikona theou*] who is the preserver of all things. If, then, thou approvest our practice and wilt pay obeisance, it is in thy power to behold and address the King; but if thou art otherwise minded, it will be needful for thee to employ messengers to him in thy stead, for it is not a custom of this country that the King give ear to a man who has not paid him obeisance. (Plutarch, *Themistocles* 27.3)

If the subject was forbidden an audience or refused to perform the act of obeisance, then the chiliarch would take the subject's petition in to the king.

In addition, Dio Cassius gives an account of the *proskynesis* of Tiridates I before the emperor Nero in 66 CE, and there is also evidence that the Roman senators performed *proskynesis* (accompanied by hymns and acclamations) before the empty throne of the living emperor Gaius. The practice may have also been performed before the empty throne of Julius Caesar at the end of the Roman Republic (Aune 1983, 13–14).

HYMNS

The hymns in 4:6–8, 11; 5:9–10, 12, 13, sung by the twenty-four elders and the four creatures, are similar to the hymns sung to the Roman emperor by both the Roman Senate and the imperial choir of Asia, initially a voluntary organization created to praise Augustus, but which eventually became an elitist institution funded by the entire province of Asia whose members performed on imperial occasions (Fishwick 1991, 569). Hymns were integral features in ancient religions and were usually reserved for the gods. When they were directed to humans, the implication was that they were equal to the gods. Lysander was the first Greek whom the cities honored as a god; they erected altars and made sacrifices to him "as to a god"; he was also the first to whom songs of triumph were sung. Antony's eulogy to Julius Caesar consisted of a hymn that identified Caesar as a god in heaven. Songs of praise were addressed to Antony, along with the offering of incense, a ritual that suggests, according to Lily Ross Taylor, that "like every conqueror of the East, Antony was hailed as divine" (1931, 108). Hymns of praise, however, were not reserved for emperors alone, but were also a constant feature of the public life and activities of provincial governors. Just like the emperors, governors were acclaimed whenever they entered and left a city, when they appeared at the theaters, or when they drove through the streets.

THE LAMB/LION IMAGERY IN REVELATION 5

As discussed above, Blount's interpretation of the sacrificial lamb (2005a) is a conservative approach influenced by a mainstream African American Christian lens constructed on suffering in the midst of oppressive assimilation. In his excursus on the lion and the lamb, this time in a full-length commentary directed toward a more general audience (2009a, 116–17), he continues the line of thought he had articulated in *Can I Get a Witness*. Blount claims that John's witnessing lamb is hardly a vulnerable figure. Rather, he is a conquering lion, armed with the fullness of God's power, who deposes the dragon by taking up the sword of God's word and meeting Satan's forces on the field of apocalyptic battle (19:11–16).

Blount argues that the lamb reveals the lion, just as the lion reveals the lamb. The weak lamb does not subvert the powerful lion; the lamb's weakness, its slaughter, is precisely the way the lion works out its power. According to Blount, whenever hearers/readers *see* the lamb in the remainder of the narrative, the staging of the character in Revelation 5 prompts them to *hear* the footsteps of a roaring lion. Blount's lion conquers, however, not by tearing its prey into pieces, but by nonviolent resistance similar to that of the civil rights movement led by Martin Luther King Jr. In King's very capable hands, the movement succeeded in maintaining a peaceable, nonviolent protest that was nevertheless a will-to-power (2009a, 116–17). Blount claims that the observer of King's nonviolent resistance could not deny that he was a "lion" for justice and equality. Therefore Blount posits that the reader of Revelation should consider that same force of nonviolent power in the lamb (117).

This provocative reading of the lamb/lion imagery does not seem to satisfactorily address the bloody, violent, destructive images and events that are endlessly recycled throughout Revelation and that begin to occur immediately after the lamb's metamorphosis in chapter 5. To suggest that the lamb, whose final metamorphosis in 19:11 is that of a warrior on a white horse whose robe is dipped in the blood of his victims, does not support Blount's argument that the lamb is an exemplum of a nonviolent resister.

RITUAL PERFORMANCE IN REVELATION AS PRELUDE TO WAR

The act of *proskynesis* and the hymns of praise are central in the heavenly throne room scenes and are important actions that are integral to the narrative. John strategically positioned the rituals as preliminary performances of war and conquest. For instance, immediately after the worship scenes in chapters 4 and 5, the seven seals are opened and the four riders on their horses are unleashed in 6:1–8, with each rider wreaking havoc in his own unique style: conquering, economical gouging, murdering, raping. Revelation 6:9–10 narrates the opening of the fifth seal by the trickster lion/lamb that exposes the suffering souls under the altar who cry out to the Lord asking how long will this go on before he judges and avenges their blood (which causes us to pause and question what is really going on here, because isn't the unleashing of the four horsemen supposed to be an act of retribution?). Verse 11 provides the response: put on this white robe and be patient, rest a little longer, until both the number of your fellow servants and their brethren suffer just like you. The verse implies that conquest, economic exploitation, disease, and murder are elements that construct the inevitable way of the cosmos that the populace must somehow come to grasp with and endure. Verse 16 details the ferociousness of the lion/lamb, as not only the kings of the earth, the commanders, the mighty and the rich, but also the poor, the slaves, and freedmen beg the mountains to fall upon them and hide them from the face of the one sitting on the throne and the wrath of the lamb.

In 7:11 the rites of *proskynesis* and praise are performed by the angels, elders, and four living creatures; these rites are followed by additional acts of worship in 7:12–17 by those who have come out of the great tribulation and are now before the throne of God and serve God day and night in the temple. Immediately after these scenes, chapters 8–10 detail another series of chaos and mayhem: plagues enacted against the earth, the sky, the sea, and humankind. Likewise, following the ritual performances in 11:16–18, which only feature the twenty-four elders falling from their thrones before God, John details a battle ensuing in heaven in chapter 12 that is to be continued on earth in chapter 13. In 14:1 we find the 144,000 who have God's name written on their foreheads, standing with the lamb on Mount Zion preparing for battle against the beast. As expected, a heavenly throne room scene is nearby in 14:2–5. In 15:1–8 there occurs yet another throne scene, with chapter 16 detailing the destruction caused by the pouring of the bowls. Finally, 19:1–6 describes a throne room scene that comes immediately before the coming of the warrior Christ in 19:11.

An African American scripturalization posits that Revelation is a text that is structured on the interrelationship between war and worship and that the acts in the heavenly throne room scene should be considered as preparation rituals for war (discussed further below). These ritualistic acts are initiated as a result of the authority given to the lamb (5:7). Verse 8a, "when he had taken the scroll, the four living creatures and the twenty-four elders fell before the lamb" (Καὶ ὅτε ἔλαβεν τὸ βιβλίον, τὰ τέσσαρα ζῷα καὶ οἱ εἴκοσι τέσσαρες πρεσβύτεροι ἔπεσαν ἐνώπιον τοῦ ἀρνίου), details the act of subordination as a response to the transference of absolute power to the lamb and its shape shifting into a roaring carnivorous lion preparing to devour its prey. Just like the Roman emperors who claim to have been delegated divine power by the Roman god Jupiter, so too the lamb has been delegated power by God. Therefore, by turning John's signifyin(g) technique on its head, one can suggest that the actions of the sacrificed lamb mimic the actions of the beast in Revelation 13 whose mortal wound had been healed and is an allusion to the Roman emperor Nero. Although intended to be a counterimage of the beast, John's lamb actually exhibits the identical mode of behavior as the beast. The lamb is a lion in sheep's clothing—a shape-shifter whose final form will be that of a warrior God who sits on a white horse and judges and makes war in righteousness (19:11).

The pattern of the ritual performances in the heavenly throne room scenes followed immediately by episodes detailing war and destruction is so consistent in John's narrative that it is plausible to argue that ritual performance was obviously a necessary enactment connected with the waging of war and conquest. This discernment, in line with the argument of this section, leads one to conclude that this pattern reflects the actual activity in John's imperial world.

Conclusion

The purpose for analyzing select images of imperial ritual in the heavenly throne room scenes in the book of Revelation was to illustrate that John's imagined power center of the new world order, his new Jerusalem, was actually based on a very real and concrete experience in which ritual practices played heavily in constructing and undergirding the ideological framework of the colonized, a framework that replicated the colonizer. I chose to examine these performances to demonstrate that ritual is multidimensional. Not only is ritual an expression and confirmation of beliefs, a means of transcending and redeeming mundane reality, but it is also a process of social interaction and a means of control. Ritual is not only a cultural construct but also a form of cognition that constructs models of reality and paradigms of behavior (see C. Bell 1992). John's visions of the ritual acts in the heavenly throne room that mimicked the means used to undergird an imperial ideology proved that John was not really as isolated or nonconforming to an imperial ethos as he so passionately proclaimed. Therefore, ritual plays a vital role in maintaining societal praxis. This is certainly because ritual can be the greatest receptacle or carrier of the cultural memory of a community. For this reason, ritual has long been considered more effective than coercive force in securing people's assent to a particular order.

Similar to the African American community, the cultural memory banks of the people in the Roman province of Asia, a people who had experienced their own particular version of the "strangeness of home," were partly formed from having to negotiate shifts in their religio-political milieu. In order to control a people effectively, there must be links to the past, but these links must be malleable and contain flexibility. If not, the links will break because of the rigidness, causing the system to fall. These links to the past were produced by mythmaking, ritual performances, and the retelling of historical events. All of these cultural mediums had to remain readily accessible for the "powers that (presently) be" to manipulate because they can never afford to completing dismantle previous images and symbolisms that instill the sense of a universalizing history.

As mentioned in the previous chapter, the Roman imperial cult was grafted onto previous religio-political systems. Thus one can argue that the cultural memory of the people of the province of Asia was informed by an extremely complex web of interlocking ritual systems as a result of constant sociopolitical disruption (Lincoln 1989, 3). In order for the Roman Empire to control such a region effectively, it was necessary that there be continuity with the region's past. Therefore, the imperial modus operandi was to carefully reconstruct a new world order that did not unravel a people's long-standing conception of the cosmos or their role in it. The region's deities and the ritual practices associated with them were integrated into the Roman system as reconceptualizations that reflected the power now in charge, yet did not overly disrupt or radically alter the cultural memory of their subjects. Thus the subjected people's myths, rituals, legends, and historical narratives that influenced the construction of identity had to remain readily accessible in order to be reused by the dominant power. The subtle manipulation of images succeeded by universalizing a people's history without explicitly saying, "That's the way it is."

And so, in apparent continuity with this tactic, John merely displaces or reverses images of reality as heavenly images without dismantling the hierarchical binary formation these images have embodied for centuries as a result of various foreign occupation and consistent marginalization. Therefore, in John's visions, the exploitative sociopolitical tactics of empire are transferred into yet another symbolic order sustained by ritual performance. His use of ritual in the heavenly throne room scenes did not reconstruct the religio-political reason for the performances, which was the preparation for war. Instead of reconceptualizing the performances as preliminary acts for establishing the nonviolent, peaceful, and holistic transformation of the old world into the new Jerusalem, John maintains the status quo and imagines a new world order founded on violence and bloodshed. Alas, although his signifyin(g) on empire attempts to salvage a group's cultural identity damaged during years of foreign occupation, his cultural hybridity prevents him from disconnecting from the imperial ethos that influences his identity construction.

CONCLUSION

Research is formalized curiosity. It is poking and prying with a purpose.
— Zora Neale Hurston

This African American scripturalization of the book of Revelation supplemented by postcolonial theory presents a shift in the ideological point of departure that typically defines African American biblical scholarship—liberation theology. I wrote this scripturalization of Revelation with the understanding that there is a need in the twenty-first century for African American scribes to better respond to the diverse identity constructions within the community. As mentioned earlier, this is not to suggest that this scripturalization argued for a postliberation or postracial sentiment, that the two great beasts of American society—racism and sexism—were no longer threats to a holistic and affirming society. What I argued in this volume is that African American biblical scribes must increasingly highlight, expose, and address the potential vulnerability to the more subtle ways of the beasts by addressing a fuller scope of African American identity, especially in terms of the complexity of cultural hybridity. Thus this African American scripturalization of Revelation sought to unveil the intricate nature of John's marginalized identity construction and to expose how his rhetoric of resistance, which on first glance appears to mock the hegemonic, imperialistic ideology of the Roman Empire, actually mimics Rome's sociopolitical agenda. The purpose of illustrating John's contradictory nature is to argue that it is imperative for a marginalized community to be aware of the possibility of reinscribing the oppressive elements of their own contemporary society. This reinscription, I argue, is inevitable if marginalized members of the community are unconscious of their ambivalent identity construction and are unaware of the subliminal messages that are conveyed in cultural media, including civic ritual, that aid in identity construction.

As a step in broadening the framework, in chapter 1 I discussed Vincent Wimbush's proposal based on Henry Louis Gates's African American literary theory of signifyin(g) to assist in the theorization of African American scripturalization. I suggested that African American scripturalization must engage not only in the *historical* experiences of African Americans, but also in the *cultural memory* of a community. I argued that cultural memory is not necessarily about remembering past events as accurately as possible, nor is it about ensuring cultural continuity—it is about making meaningful statements about the past in a given cultural context of the present conditions. Since collective memories are learned through socialization, individuals retain the freedom to offer alternative views of the past that may later become part of this collective memory. Each time we interpret cultural memories, we move farther from the concrete tie to historical reality, and representation replaces reality. Since our memory of the past ranges from conscious recall to unreflective reemergence, from nostalgic longing for what is lost to polemical use of the past to reshape the present, the incorporation of cultural memory into Wimbush's proposal supports his contention that signifyin(g) makes possible the deformation and reformation of community. I concluded the chapter with an examination of the works of four African American scribes for the purpose of illustrating the diversity of approaches ranging from a corrective historiography that mainly incorporates the tools of historical criticism to a contemporary contextual analysis of the biblical narratives.

In chapter 2 I suggested that in addition to theorizing African American scripturalization, there must also be discussion of the theorization of cultural identity, a theorization that is fluid and flexible enough to adequately enunciate the various dimensions of identity construction. Thus I proposed the supplementation of postcolonial theory. I aimed to provide a comprehensive discussion on: (1) the junctions and disjunctions of postcolonial studies and African American studies, illustrated by way of a critique of the postcolonial theorists Said, Spivak, and Bhabha, through an African American lens; and (2) the merits of fusing aspects of postcolonial theory—particularly as disseminated by Bhabha—to African American scripturalization in order to better articulate the construction of identity that is produced by the double movement of shifting away from Western constructions of the Other while simultaneously shifting toward appropriating the ideological, theological, linguistic, and textual forms of Western power. Bhabha's articulation of the interstitial or "in-between" space is helpful in articulating the clash of Euro-American and African American cultures as he defines the interstitial space as the site of negotiation, the site of identity formation, deformation, and transformation. For Bhabha, this clash produces a cultural hybridity that is a multicultural production, and therefore marginalized cultures actively participate in the formation of identity. The concepts of mimicry/mockery and ambivalence assist in enunciating this notion. I argued that what makes Bhabha's work so compelling for African American scripturalization is that his general conceptions are quite useful to a specific cultural production. I concluded that the supplementation of postcolonial theory to African American scripturalization blended smoothly in ironing out the knotty dimensions of a double-consciousness identity construct as both disciplines are interested in: (1) attempting to explore issues of re-presentation, essentialism, and nationalism; (2) providing alternative enunciations of the myth of origin; (3) critiquing how the West uses the concept of the Other and vice versa in the construction of identity; and (4) with reference to womanists and postcolonial feminists, critiquing patriarchy as it aligns with the imperial agenda, including white feminist ideology.

In chapter 3 I argued that a comprehensive mapping of identity construction represents a lacuna in the interesting work of contextual biblical scholars who strive to theorize a production of meaning based on social location because there is often the assumption that the meaning produced is fully comprehended by the scholar's audience, which include readers from various social locations. The oversimplification in articulating identity constructs in their work can lead to an essentialist or homogeneous categorization. A comprehensive discussion of the "strangeness of home," the term I use to signify the contextual point of departure for the work of African American scripturalization, was made for the purpose of illustrating that a close, critical examination of context is necessary in order to unleash the signifyin(g) that the reductive tendency of reading (con)text seeks to suppress. I insisted that the African American context produces a hybrid, deconstructive praxis in which there is a constant unfolding of meaning and identifications. Thus the signifyin(g) tradition of the African American community exposes the silenced, the unsaid, the unmentioned, the underside of the binary that has been subordinated in the presentation of the dominant context. I maintained that postcolonial theory assists in comprehending the dynamics of the "strangeness of home" because of its usefulness in (1) dismantling the confining notions of a homogeneous and fixed identity construct, replacing these general notions with the more compelling idea of fluidity of construction; and (2) providing theoretical concepts that adequately elucidate the complex dimensions of African American identity construction and thus assist in revealing the suppositions/presuppositions that drive the African American hermeneutical process.

In this chapter I illustrated how the concepts of mimicry, ambivalence, and hybridity drive the processes of the hermeneutical tradition of the African American community and how identity construction is accomplished through the negotiation of the Scriptures, the set of texts that are responsible for constructing the American myth of origin as a sacred narration of nation. I suggested that the African American hermeneutical tradition resides within the middle passage of continuity and discontinuity, acceptance and rejection, dream and nightmare. It is by standing on the threshold that African Americans, being influenced by the hermeneutical tradition, challenge and subvert the dominant narration of nation. Yet, like a prophetess, I also sought to provoke the African American community to be *cautiously aware of its own adherence* to the oppressive elements of the American ethos in its cultural negotiations. I warned of the exploitation that comes with an unreflective "use of the master's tools."

In chapter 4 I examined the book of Revelation in general, through the lens of African American scripturalization supplemented by Bhabha's postcolonial theory. The purpose of this chapter was to show how the underlying framework of African American scripturalization has the ability to produces a refreshed approach to the historical biblical scholarship on Revelation. The scripting proposed that the seer's signifyin(g) on empire demonstrated that he was well aware of the oppressive nature of Roman imperialism on the lives of Christians in the province of Asia. This was made clear by his fierce, nonaccommodating stance toward participation in the imperial cult. Yet, ironically, John reinscribed imperial processes and practices. Seemingly, no matter how determined he was to disconnect from the religio-political manipulations of empire, his hybridity disallowed him. Ironically, John's colonized construction as "almost the same but not quite like" had resulted in the production of a resistance strategy that was a blurred copy of the hegemonic tactics of empire that entail violent disruption and displacement. The images he conjured both alluded to and signified on the various power structures of the ancient past, including Babylon and Persia, as well as the axis of power in his day, the Roman Empire. I argued that Persian domination, as the first international empire in the ancient world, remained vivid in the collective memory banks of the people of provincial Asia through the retelling of history, the making of myths, and especially the performance of ritual acts. Therefore, the imagery and allusions the seer presented in his signifyin(g) on Rome tapped into a cultural memory that evoked identification, imagination, resistance, and desire, all elements that aided in identity construction.

The main section of the chapter was structured in the African American format of *call and response,* with the discussion of the standard scholarship on Revelation in several subsections (*call*) followed by a supplemented discussion on the scholarship from the perspective of an African American scripturalization (*response*). I maintained that the first step in producing a more theoretically complex African American scripturalization of Revelation was to re-present the general scholarly issues that are considered to be central to this text. This step had to be done because the standard scholarship that authorizes a "valid" interpretation, according to the historical-critical paradigm, must be deconstructed. I insisted that if this was not done, the "voice" of historical biblical criticism would muffle the new perspective.

After discussing Brian Blount and Clarice Martin's readings of Revelation through a liberative hermeneutical lens, I presented a reading of Revelation through an African American scripturalization perspective in chapter 5. Through the examination of the throne room scenes in Revelation, I proposed that John's signifyin(g) on empire was a contradiction: he simply reconfigured and reenacted imperial ritual in the establishment of the new Jerusalem. I suggested that his signifyin(g) remained fixed on the persistent cycles of war, conquest, and revolt, paralleled by cycles of worship, ritual, and mythmaking. I questioned, therefore, how John, who was so against empire, could mimic empire. In line with postcolonial discourse, I insisted that domination is not simply a system of military control, but a systematic cultural penetration that subjugates psychologically and intellectually. Therefore, John's mimicry of the ideological assumptions and methods of constructing empire was due, to a certain degree, to his being a member of a society that embraced the participation in the cultic rituals of empire, causing him to connect with imperial ideological codes that, in turn, modified his behavior. I demonstrated that John's new Jerusalem as replication of an old imperial order was influenced by a barrage of imperial images that was part of everyday life in Asia Minor.

In this volume I sounded the trumpet for the reconceptualizing of African American biblical hermeneutics, a discipline mainly framed by black liberation theology, to a more theoretically complex enterprise referred to as African American scripturalization as a response to new challenges. This humble attempt to approach Revelation via a theoretically sophisticated hermeneutical lens was to provide an example of such a reconceptualization. I produced it to reveal the possibility of a refreshed approach that makes it possible to articulate the more complex dynamics and fluid dimensions of African American identity that a liberation framework does not permit.

BIBLIOGRAPHY

Abbington, James. 2000. Biblical Themes in the R. Nathaniel Dett Collection: *Religious Folk-Songs of the Negro (1927)*. Pages 281–96 in *African Americans and the Bible: Sacred Texts and Social Textures*. Edited by Vincent L. Wimbush. New York: Continuum.

Adler, Eve. 2003. *Vergil's Empire: Political Thought in the Aeneid*. New York: Rowman & Littlefield.

Ahn, Yong-Sung. 2006. *The Reign of God and Rome in Luke's Passion Narrative: An East Asian Global Perspective*. BibInt 80. Leiden: Brill.

Albanese, Catherine. 1976. *Sons of the Fathers: The Civil Religion of the American Revolution*. Philadelphia: Temple University Press.

Alcock, Susan E. 2001. The Reconfiguration of Memory in the Eastern Roman Empire. Pages 323–51 in *Empires: Perspectives from Archaeology and History*. Edited by Susan E. Alcock et.al. Cambridge: Cambridge University Press.

Alcock, Susan E., Terence N. D'Altroy, Kathleen D. Morrison, Carla M. Sinopoli, eds. 2001. *Empires: Perspectives from Archaeology and History*. Cambridge: Cambridge University Press.

Alexander, Philip, and Loveday Alexander. 2007. The Image of the Oriental Monarch in the Third Book of Maccabees. Pages 92–109 in *Jewish Perspectives on Hellenistic Rulers*. Edited by Tessa Rajak, Sarah Pearce, James Aitken, and Jennifer Dines. Berkeley: University of California Press.

Ando, Clifford. 2000. *Imperial Ideology and Provincial Loyalty in the Roman Empire*. Berkeley: University of California Press.

Ashcroft, Bill. 1996. On the Hyphen in Post-Colonial. *New Literature Review* 32:23–32.

Ashcroft, Bill, Gareth Griffiths, and Helen Tiffin, eds. 1989. *The Empire Writes Back: Theory and Practice in Post-Colonial Literatures*. London: Routledge.

———. 1998. *Key Concepts in Post-colonial Studies*. London: Routledge.

Ashe, Bertram D. 2008. Theorizing the Post-Soul Aesthetic: An Introduction. *African American Review* 41:609–23.

Assmann, Jan. 1992. *Das kulturelle Gedächtnis: Schrift, Erinnerung und politische Identität in frühen Hochkulturen.* Munich: Beck.

Aune, David E. 1983. The Influence of Roman Imperial Court Ceremonial on the Apocalypse of John. *BR* 28:5–26.

———. 1986. The Apocalypse of John and the Problem of Genre. *Semeia* 36:65–96.

———. 1987. *The New Testament in Its Literary Environment.* Philadelphia: Westminster.

———. 1997. *Revelation 1–5.* WBC 52A. Dallas: Word.

———. 1998. *Revelation 6–16.* WBC 52B. Nashville: Nelson.

Bahri, Deepika. 1995. Once More with Feeling: What Is Postcolonialism? *Ariel* (Calgary) 26, no. 1:51–82.

Bailey, Randall C. 1998. The Danger of Ignoring One's Own Cultural Bias in Interpreting the Text. Pages 66–90 in *The Postcolonial Bible.* Edited by R. S. Surgirtharajah. Sheffield: Sheffield Academic.

———. 2000. Academic Biblical Interpretation among African Americans in the United States. Pages 696–711 in *African Americans and the Bible: Sacred Texts and Social Textures.* Edited by Vincent L. Wimbush. New York: Continuum.

———, ed. 2003. *Yet with a Steady Beat: Contemporary U.S. Afrocentric Biblical Interpretation.* SemeiaSt 42. Atlanta: Society of Biblical Literature.

———. 2010. My Journey into Afrocentric Biblical Interpretation. Page 20 in *The Africana Bible: Reading Israel's Scriptures from Africa and the African Diaspora.* Edited by Hugh R. Page Jr. Minneapolis: Fortress.

Bailey, Randall C., Tat-siong Benny Liew, and Fernando F. Segovia, eds. 2009. *They Were All Together in One Place? Toward Minority Biblical Criticism.* SemeiaSt 57. Atlanta: Society of Biblical Literature.

Barchiesi, Alessandro. 2005. Learned Eyes: Poets, Viewers, Image Makers. Pages 281–305 in *The Cambridge Companion to the Age of Augustus.* Edited by Karl Galinsky. Cambridge: Cambridge University Press.

Barr, David L. 1998. *Tales of the End: A Narrative Commentary on the Book of Revelation.* Sonoma, CA: Polebridge.

———, ed. 2006. *The Reality of Apocalypse: Rhetoric and Politics in the Book of Revelation.* SymS 39. Atlanta: Society of Biblical Literature.

Bauckham, Richard. 1993. *The Climax of Prophecy: Studies on the Book of Revelation.* Edinburgh: T&T Clark.

Bell, Albert A. 1975. The Date of John's Apocalypse: The Evidence of Some Roman Historians Reconsidered. *NTS* 25:93–102.

Bell, Catherine. 1992. *Ritual Theory, Ritual Practice*. New York: Oxford University Press.

———. 1997. *Ritual: Perspectives and Dimensions*. Oxford: Oxford University Press.

Bellah, Robert N. 1967. Civil Religion in America. *Daedalus* 96:1–21.

———. 1988. The Kingdom of God in America: Language of Faith, Language of Nation, Language of Empire. Pages 41–61 in *Religion and the Public Good: A Bicentennial Forum*. Edited by William Lee Miller, Robert N. Bellah, and Martin E. Marty. Macon, GA: Mercer University Press.

———. 1992. *The Broken Covenant: American Civil Religion in Time of Trial*. 2nd ed. Chicago: University of Chicago Press.

Bercovitch, Sacvan. 1993. *The Rites of Assent: Transformations in the Symbolic Construction of America*. London: Routledge.

Bernal, Martin. 1987. *The Fabrication of Ancient Greece, 1785–1985*. Vol. 1 of *Black Athena: The Afroasiatic Roots of Classical Civilization*. New Brunswick, NJ: Rutgers University Press.

Bhabha, Homi K. 1987. What Does the Black Man Want? *New Formations* 1:118–30.

———. 1989. Remembering Fanon: Self, Psyche, and the Colonial Condition. Pages 131–50 in *Remaking History*. Edited by Barbara Kruger and Phil Mariani. Seattle: Bay.

———, ed. 1990. *Nation and Narration*. New York: Routledge.

———. 1992. The World and the Home. *Social Text* 31/32:141–53.

———. 1994. *The Location of Culture*. London: Routledge.

———. 1995. Homi Bhabha on the New Black Intellectual. *Artforum* 34, no. 2:16–17, 114, 116.

Billington, Ray Allen. 1969. Foreword. Pages vii–x in *Negro Slave Songs in the United States* by Miles Mark Fisher. Repr., New York: Citadel.

Blount, Brian K. 1995. *Cultural Interpretation: Reorienting New Testament Criticism*. Minneapolis: Fortress.

———. 2005a. *Can I Get a Witness? Reading Revelation through African American Culture*. Louisville: Westminster John Knox.

———. 2005b. The Witness of Active Resistance: The Ethics of Revelation in African American Perspective. Pages 28–46 in *From Every People and Nation: The Book of Revelation in Intercultural Perspective*. Edited by David Rhoads. Minneapolis: Fortress.

———. 2009a. *Revelation: A Commentary.* New Testament Library. Louisville: Westminster John Knox.

———, ed. 2009b. *True to Our Native Land: An African American New Testament Commentary.* Minneapolis: Fortress.

Boer, Roland. 2001. *Last Stop before Antarctica: The Bible and Postcolonialism in Australia.* Sheffield: Sheffield Academic.

———, ed. 2002. *Vanishing Mediator? The Presence/Absence of the Bible in Postcolonialism. Semeia* 88. Atlanta: Society of Biblical Literature.

Bowman, Alan, and Peter Garnsey, eds. 1996. *The Augustan Empire.* Cambridge: Cambridge University Press.

Boyce, Mary. 1984. On the Antiquity of Zoroastrian Apocalyptic. *BSOAS* 47:57–75.

Braxton, Brad. 2002. *No Longer Slaves: Galatians and the African American Experience.* Collegeville, MN: Liturgical Press.

Brent, Allen. 1999. *The Imperial Cult and the Development of Church Order: Concepts and Images of Authority in Paganism and Early Christianity before the Age of Cyprian.* Leiden: Brill.

Briant, Pierre. 2002. *From Cyrus to Alexander: A History of the Persian Empire.* Translated by Peter T. Daniels. Winona Lake, IN: Eisenbrauns.

Brown, Michael Joseph. 2004. *Blackening of the Bible: The Aims of African American Biblical Scholarship.* Harrisburg, PA: Trinity Press International.

Brunt, P. A. 1990. *Roman Imperial Themes.* Oxford: Clarendon.

Buell, Lawrence. 1992. American Literary Emergence as a Post-Colonial Phenomenon. *American Literary History* 4, no. 3:411–42.

Burnim, Mellonee. 2000. Biblical Inspiration, Cultural Affirmation: The African American Gift of Song. Pages 603–15 in *African Americans and the Bible: Sacred Texts and Social Textures.* Edited by Vincent L. Wimbush. New York: Continuum.

Burrus, Virginia. 2007. The Gospel of Luke and the Acts of the Apostles. Pages 133–56 in *A Postcolonial Commentary on the New Testament Writings.* Edited by Fernando F. Segovia and R. S. Sugirtharajah. London: T&T Clark.

Byron, Gay L. 2009. Ancient Ethiopia and the New Testament: Ethnic (Con)texts and Racialized (Sub)texts. Pages 161–90 in Bailey, Liew, and Segovia 2009.

Callahan, Allan Dwight. 1985. The Language of the Apocalypse. *HTR* 88:453–70.

———. 2006. *The Talking Book: African Americans and the Bible.* New Haven: Yale University Press.

———. 2009. Babylon Boycott: The Book of Revelation. *Int* 63:48–54.

Cannon, Katie Geneva. 1985. The Emergence of Black Feminist Consciousness. Pages 30–40 in *Feminist Interpretation of the Bible.* Edited by Letty Russell. Philadelphia: Westminster.

———. 1988. *Black Womanist Ethics.* AARAS 60. Atlanta: Scholars Press.

———. 1995. *Kate's Canon: Womanism and the Soul of the Black Community.* New York: Continuum.

Carmichael, Stokely, and Charles Hamilton. 1967. *Black Power: The Politics of Liberation in America.* New York: Random House.

Carter, Warren. 2009. Accommodating "Jezebel" and Withdrawing John: Negotiating Empire in Revelation Then and Now. *Int* 63:32–47.

Charlesworth, James H., ed. 1983. *Apocalyptic Literature and Testaments.* Vol. 1 of *The Old Testament Pseudepigrapha.* Garden City, NY: Doubleday.

Cherry, Conrad. 1998. *God's New Israel: Religious Interpretations of American Destiny.* Chapel Hill: University of North Carolina Press.

Chisholm, Kitty, and John Ferguson, eds. 1981. *Rome: The Augustan Age. A Sourcebook.* New York: Oxford University Press.

Chow, Rey. 2002. *The Protestant Ethnic and the Spirit of Capitalism.* New York: Columbia University Press.

Chowdhry, Geeta. 2007. Edward Said and Contrapuntal Reading: Implications for Critical Interventions in International Relations. *Millennium—Journal of International Studies* 36:101–16.

Clay, Elonda. 2010. A Black Theology of Liberation or Legitimation? A Postcolonial Response to Cone's *Black Theology and Black Power* at Forty. *Black Theology: An International Journal* 8:307–26.

Coleman, Will. 2000. *Tribal Talk: Black Theology, Hermeneutics and African American Ways of "Telling the Story."* University Park: Pennsylvania State University Press.

Collins, John J. 1979. Towards the Morphology of a Genre: An Introduction. *Semeia* 14:1–5.

Collins, Patricia Hill. 1990. *Black Feminist Thought: Knowledge, Consciousness, and the Politics of Empowerment.* London: HarperCollins.

Cone, James H. 1986. *Speaking the Truth: Ecumenism, Liberation, and Black Theology.* Grand Rapids: Eerdmans.

———. 1987. *A Black Theology of Liberation.* Maryknoll, NY: Orbis.

———. 1991. *Martin and Malcolm and America: A Dream or a Nightmare.* Maryknoll, NY: Orbis.

Copher, Charles. 1986. Three Thousand Years of Biblical Interpretation with Reference to Black Peoples. *JITC* 13:225–46.

———. 1991. The Black Presence in the Old Testament. Pages 146–64 in *Stony the Road We Trod: African American Biblical Interpretation.* Edited by Cain Hope Felder. Minneapolis: Fortress.

Cucinella, Catherine, and Renee R. Curry. 2001. Exiled at Home: Daughters of the Dust and the Many Post-Colonial Conditions. *MELUS* 26, no. 4:197–221.

Culler, Jonathan. 1981. *The Pursuit of Signs: Semiotics, Literature, Deconstruction.* London: Routledge & Kegan Paul.

Davidson, Steed. 2008. Leave Babylon: The Trope of Babylon in Rastafarian Discourse. *Black Theology: An International Journal* 6:46–60.

Dench, Emma. 2005. *Romulus's Asylum: Roman Identities from the Age of Alexander to the Age of Hadrian.* Oxford: Oxford University Press.

Derrida, Jacques. 1974. *Of Grammatology.* Translated by Gayatri Chakravorty Spivak. Baltimore: Johns Hopkins University Press.

deSilva, David A. 1992. The Revelation of John: A Case Study in Apocalyptic Propaganda and the Maintenance of Sectarian Identity. *Sociological Analysis* 53:375–95.

———. 2009. *Seeing Things John's Way: The Rhetoric of the Book of Revelation.* Louisville: Westminster John Knox.

Dett, R. Nathaniel, ed. 1927. *Religious Folk Songs of the Negro as Sung at Hampton Institute.* Hampton, VA: Hampton Institute Press.

Dio Cassius. 1924. *Roman History.* Translated by Earnest Cary. LCL. Cambridge: Harvard University Press.

Djedje, Jacqueline Cogdell. 2008. Signifying in Nineteenth-Century African American Religious Music. Pages 134–44 in *Theorizing Scriptures: New Critical Orientations to a Cultural Phenomenon.* Edited by Vincent L. Wimbush. New Brunswick, NJ: Rutgers University Press.

Dommelen, Peter van. 1998. Punic Persistence: Colonialism and Cultural Identities in Roman Sardinia. Pages 25–48 in *Cultural Identity in the Roman Empire.* Edited by Ray Laurence and Joanne Berry. London: Routledge.

Donaldson, Laura E., ed. 1998. *Postcolonialism and Scriptural Reading.* Semeia 75. Atlanta: Society of Biblical Literature.

Dube, Musa W. 2000. *Postcolonial Feminist Interpretation of the Bible.* St. Louis: Chalice.

Du Bois, W. E. B. 1996. *The Souls of Black Folk.* Repr., New York: Penguin Classics.

Duff, Paul B. 2001. *Who Rides the Beast? Prophetic Rivalry and the Rhetoric of Crisis in the Churches of the Apocalypse.* New York: Oxford University Press.

Ellis, Trey. 1989. The New Black Aesthetic. *Callaloo* 38:233–43.

Elsner, Jaś. 2001. Describing Self in the Language of the Other: Pseudo(?) Lucian at the Temple of Hierapolis. Pages 123–53 in *Being Greek under Rome: Cultural Identity, the Second Sophistic and the Development of Empire.* Edited by Simon Goldhill. Cambridge: Cambridge University Press.

Erll, Astrid, and Ansgar Nünning, eds. 2010. *A Companion to Cultural Memory Studies.* Berlin: de Gruyter.

Eusebius. 1999. *The Church History.* Translated by Paul L. Maier. Grand Rapids: Kregel.

Fabre, Genevieve. 1994. African American Commemorative Celebrations. Pages 72–91 in *History and Memory in African-American Culture.* Edited by Genevieve Fabre and Robert O'Meally. New York: Oxford University Press.

Fabre, Genevieve, and Robert O'Meally, eds. 1994. *History and Memory in African-American Culture.* New York: Oxford University Press.

Fairbanks, James David. 1981. The Priestly Functions of the Presidency: A Discussion of the Literature on Civil Religion and Its Implications for the Study of Presidential Leadership. *Presidential Studies Quarterly* 11:214–32.

Fanon, Frantz. 1952. *Black Skin, White Masks.* Translated by Richard Philcox. New York: Grove.

———. 1961. *The Wretched of the Earth.* Translated by Richard Philcox. New York: Grove.

———. 1967. *A Dying Colonialism.* Translated by Richard Philcox. New York: Grove City.

Farrakhan, Louis. 1995. Speech on October 16. http://www.africawithin.com/mmm/excerpts.htm.

Felder, Cain Hope. 1989. *Troubling Biblical Waters: Race, Class, and Family.* Bishop Henry McNeal Turner Studies in North American Black Religion 3. Maryknoll, NY: Orbis.

———, ed. 1991. *Stony the Road We Trod: African American Biblical Interpretation.* Minneapolis: Fortress.

———. 1998. Beyond Eurocentric Biblical Interpretation: Reshaping Racial and Cultural Lenses. *JITC* 26, no. 1:17–32.

Ferguson, Russell, Martha Gever, Trinh T. Minh-ha, and Cornel West, eds. 1999. *Out There: Marginalization and Contemporary Cultures.* Repr., Cambridge: MIT Press.

Finley, Moses I. 1978. Empire in the Greco-Roman World. *Greece and Rome* 25:1–15.

Fishwick, Duncan. 1978. The Development of Provincial Ruler Worship in the Western Roman Empire. *Aufstieg und Niedergang der römischen Welt* 16.2:1201–53. Part 2, *Principat,* 16.2. Edited by Wolfgang Haase. New York: de Gruyter.

———. 1991. *The Imperial Cult in the Latin West.* Vol. 2, part 1. Leiden: Brill.

Foucault, Michel. 1977. *Discipline and Punish: The Birth of Prison.* Translated by Alan Sheridan. New York: Random House.

———. 1982. The Order of Discourse. Pages 51–76 in *Untying the Text: A Post-Structuralist Reader.* Edited by Robert J. C. Young. London: Routledge & Kegan Paul.

———. 2002. *The Archaeology of Knowledge.* Translated by A. M. Sheridan Smith. London: Routledge.

Friesen, Steven J. 1993. *Twice Neokoros: Ephesus, Asia and the Cult of the Flavian Imperial Family.* Leiden: Brill.

———. 2001. *Imperial Cults and the Apocalypse of John: Reading Revelation in the Ruins.* New York: Oxford University Press.

———. 2006. Sarcasm in Revelation 2–3: Churches, Christians, True Jews, and Satanic Synagogues. Pages 127–46 in *The Reality of Apocalypse: Rhetoric and Politics in the Book of Revelation.* Edited by David L. Barr. SymS 39. Atlanta: Society of Biblical Literature.

Fulop, Timothy E., and Albert J. Raboteau, eds. 1997. *African-American Religion: Interpretive Essays in History and Culture.* New York: Routledge.

Gadamer, Hans-Georg. 2003. *Truth and Method.* New York: Continuum.

Gafney, Wilda C. M. 2006. A Black Feminist Approach to Biblical Studies. *Encounter* 67:391–403.

Galinsky, Karl. 1998. *Augustan Culture.* Princeton: Princeton University Press.

———, ed. 2005. *The Cambridge Companion to the Age of Augustus.* Cambridge: Cambridge University Press.

Garnsey, Peter, and Richard Saller. 1987. *The Roman Empire: Economy, Society and Culture.* Berkeley: University of California Press.

Gates, Henry Louis, Jr., ed. 1986. *"Race," Writing, and Difference.* Chicago: University of Chicago Press.

———. 1988. *The Signifying Monkey: A Theory of Afro-American Literary Criticism.* New York: Oxford University Press.

———. 1991. Critical Fanonism. *Critical Inquiry* 17:457–70.

Gates, Henry Louis, Jr., and Nellie Y. McCay. 2003. *The Norton Anthology of African American Literature.* New York: Norton.

Gibson, Nigel C. 2003. *Fanon: The Postcolonial Imagination.* Cambridge: Polity.

Glancy, Jennifer A. 2006. *Slavery in Early Christianity.* Minneapolis: Fortress.

Glaude, Eddie S., Jr. 2000. *Exodus! Religion, Race, and Nation in Early Nineteenth-Century Black America.* Chicago: University of Chicago Press.

Goldhill, Simon, ed. 2001. *Being Greek under Rome: Cultural Identity, the Second Sophistic and the Development of Empire.* Cambridge: Cambridge University Press.

Goldstone, Jack A., and John F. Haldon. 2010. Ancient States, Empires and Exploitation: Problems and Perspectives. Pages 3–29 in *The Dynamics of Ancient Empire: State Power from Assyria to Byzantium.* Edited by Ian Morris and Walter Scheidel. Oxford: Oxford University Press.

Goodman, Martin. 1997. *The Roman World: 44 B.C.–A.D. 180.* London: Routledge.

Gordimer, Nadine. 1991. *My Son's Story.* New York: Penguin.

Gordis, Lisa M. 2003. *Opening Scripture: Bible Reading and Interpretive Authority in Puritan New England.* Chicago: University of Chicago Press.

Grant, Jacquelyn. 1989. *White Women's Christ and Black Women's Jesus: Feminist Theology and Womanist Response.* Atlanta: Scholars Press.

Gravely, William B. 1995. The Dialectic of Double-Consciousness in Black American Freedom Celebrations, 1808–1863. Pages 123–38 in *Religion and American Culture.* Edited by David G. Hackett. New York: Routledge.

Grether, Gertrude. 1946. Livia and the Roman Imperial Cult. *American Journal of Philology* 67:222–52.

Gundaker, Grey. 2008. Scriptures Beyond Script. Pages 155–66 in *Theorizing Scriptures: New Critical Orientations to a Cultural Phenomenon.*

Edited by Vincent L. Wimbush. New Brunswick, NJ: Rutgers University Press.

Hackett, David G., ed. 1995. *Religion and American Culture: A Reader.* New York: Routledge.

Halbwachs, Maurice. 1975. *Les cadres sociaux de la mémoire.* Repr., New York: Arno.

Haldeman, Scott. 2007. *Towards Liturgies that Reconcile: Race and Ritual among African American and European-American Protestants.* Burlington, VT: Ashgate.

Hall, Stuart. 1980. Encoding/Decoding. Pages 107–16 in *Culture, Media, Language: Working Papers in Cultural Studies, 1972–79.* Edited by Stuart Hall, Dorothy Hobson, Andrew Lowe, and Paul Willis. London: Hutchinson.

Harland, Philip. 2000. Honouring the Emperor or Assailing the Beast: Participation in Civic Life among Associations (Jewish, Christian and Other) in Asia Minor and the Apocalypse of John. *JSNT* 77:99–121.

———. 2003. Imperial Cults within Local Cultural Life: Associations in Roman Asia. *Ancient History Bulletin* 17:85–107.

Harris, Middleton A., Morris Levitt, Roger Furman, and Ernest Smith. 1974. *The Black Book.* New York: Random House.

Hatch, Nathan O., and Mark A. Noll, eds. 1982. *The Bible in America: Essays in Cultural History.* New York: Oxford University Press.

Hellholm, David. 1982. The Problem of Apocalyptic Genre and the Apocalypse of John. Pages 157–98 in *Society of Biblical Literature 1982 Seminar Papers.* Edited by K. H. Richards. Chico, CA: Scholars Press.

———, ed. 1983. *Apocalypticism in the Ancient Mediterranean World and the Near East.* Tübingen: Mohr Siebeck.

Hemer, Colin J. 1986. *The Letters to the Seven Churches in Their Local Setting.* Sheffield: JSOT Press.

Henten, Jan Willem van. 2006. Dragon Myth and Imperial Ideology in Revelation 12–13. Pages 181–203 in *The Reality of Apocalypse: Rhetoric and Politics in the Book of Revelation.* Edited by David L. Barr. SymS 39. Atlanta: Society of Biblical Literature.

Herodotus. 2007. *The Landmark Herodotus: The Histories.* Translated by Andrea L. Purvis. Edited by Robert B. Strassler. New York: Pantheon.

Hirsch, Marianne, and Valerie Smith. 2002. Feminism and Cultural Memory: An Introduction. *Signs: Journal of Women in Culture and Society* 28:1–19.

hooks, bell. 1994. *Teaching to Transgress: Education as the Practice of Freedom.* London: Routledge.

Horsley, Richard A. 1997. *Paul and Empire: Religion and Power in Roman Imperial Society.* Bloomsbury: T&T Clark.

———. 2003. *Jesus and Empire: The Kingdom of God and the New World Order.* Minneapolis: Augsburg.

———, ed. 2006. *Paul and the Roman Imperial Order.* Harrisburg, PA: Trinity Press International.

Hose, Martin. 1999. Post-Colonial Theory and Greek Literature in Rome. *Greek, Roman and Byzantine Studies* 40:303–26.

Howard-Brook, Wes, and Anthony Gwyther. 1999. *Unveiling Empire: Reading Revelation Then and Now.* Maryknoll, NY: Orbis.

Hoyt, Thomas, Jr. 1991. Interpreting Biblical Scholarship for the Black Church Tradition. Pages 17–39 in *Stony the Road We Trod: African American Biblical Interpretation.* Edited by Cane Hope Felder. Minneapolis: Fortress.

Huddart, David. 2006. *Homi K. Bhabha.* London: Routledge.

———. 2007. Homi K. Bhabha. *The Literary Encyclopedia.* http://www.litencyc.com/php/speople.php?rec=true&UID=5184.

Isager, Signe. 1990. Kings and Gods in the Seleucid Empire: A Question of Landed Property in Asia Minor. Pages 79–90 in *Religion and Religious Practice in the Seleucid Kingdom.* Edited by Per Bilde, Troels Engberg-Pedersen, Lise Hannestad, and Jan Zahle. Aarhus: Aarhus University Press.

James, Leslie R. 2000. Text and the Rhetoric of Change: Bible and Decolonization in Post–World War II Caribbean Political Discourse. Pages 143–66 in *Religion, Culture, and Tradition in the Caribbean.* Edited by Hemchand Gossai and Nathaniel Samuel Murrell. New York: St. Martin's.

———. 2010. The African Diaspora as Construct and Lived Experience. Pages 11–18 in *The Africana Bible: Reading Israel's Scriptures from Africa and the African Diaspora.* Edited by Hugh R. Page Jr. Repr., Minneapolis: Fortress.

Johnson, James Turner, ed. 1985. *The Bible in American Law, Politics, and Political Rhetoric.* Philadelphia: Fortress.

Johnson, Sylvester A. 2004. *The Myth of Ham in Nineteenth-Century American Christianity: Race, Heathens, and the People of God.* New York: Palgrave.

Jones, C. P. 1987. Stigma: Tattooing and Branding in Graeco-Roman Antiquity. *JRS* 77:139–55.

Jones-Warsaw, Koala. 1994. Toward a Womanist Hermeneutic: A Reading of Judges 19–21. *JITC* 22:18–35.

Joyner, Charles. 1995. "Believer I Know": The Emergence of African American Christianity. Pages 185–207 in *Religion and American Culture: A Reader*. Edited by David G. Hackett. New York: Routledge.

Kallet-Marx, Robert M. 1995. *Hegemony to Empire: The Development of the Roman Imperium in the East from 148 to 62 B.C.* Berkeley: University of California Press.

Kassam, Tazim R. 2007. Signifying Revelation in Islam. Pages 29–40 in *Theorizing Scriptures*. Edited by Vincent L. Wimbush. New Brunswick, NJ: Rutgers University Press.

Kee, Alistair. 2006. *The Rise and Demise of Black Theology*. Burlington, VT: Ashgate.

Kelleter, Frank. 2000. *Con/Tradition: Louis Farrakhan's Nation of Islam, the Million Man March, and American Civil Religion*. Heidelberg: Winter.

Kennedy, Valerie. 2000. *Edward Said: A Critical Introduction*. Cambridge: Polity.

Kim, Jean K. 1999. Uncovering Her Wickedness: An Inter(con)textual Reading of Revelation 17 from a Postcolonial Feminist Perspective. *JSNT* 73:61–81.

King, Martin Luther, Jr. 1997a. I Have a Dream. Pages 80–83 in *The Norton Anthology African American Literature*. Edited by Henry Louis Gates Jr. and Nellie McKay. New York: Norton.

———. 1997b. Letter from Birmingham Jail. Pages 1854–66 in *The Norton Anthology African American Literature*. Edited by Henry Louis Gates Jr. and Nellie McKay. New York: Norton.

King, Richard C., ed. 2000. *Postcolonial America*. Champaign: University of Illinois Press.

Kirk-Duggan, Cheryl. 2003. Let My People Go! Threads of Exodus in African American Narratives. Pages 123–43 in *Yet with a Steady Beat: Contemporary U.S. Afrocentric Biblical Interpretation*. Edited by Randall C. Bailey. SemeiaSt 42. Atlanta: Society of Biblical Literature.

Kooten, George H. van. 2007. The Year of the Four Emperors and the Revelation of John: The Pro-Neronian Emperors Otho and Vitellius and the Images and Colossus of Nero in Rome. *JSNT* 30:205–48.

Kraybill, J. Nelson. 1996. *Imperial Cult and Commerce in John's Apocalypse*. JSNTSup 132. Sheffield: Sheffield Academic.

Kristeva, Julia. 1980. *Desire in Language: A Semiotic Approach to Literature and Art*. New York: Columbia University Press.

Lampela, Anssi. 1998. *Rome and the Ptolemies of Egypt: The Development of Their Political Relations, 273–280 B.C.* Helsinki: Societas Scientarium Fennica.

Landry, Donna, and Gerald MacLean, eds. 1996. *The Spivak Reader: Selected Works of Gayatri Chakravorty Spivak*. New York: Routledge.

Laurence, Ray, and Joanne Berry, eds. 1998. *Cultural Identity in the Roman Empire*. London: Routledge.

Lazarus, Neil, ed. 2004. *The Cambridge Companion to Postcolonial Studies*. Cambridge: Cambridge University Press.

Lee, Archie C. C. 1999. Returning to China: Biblical Interpretation in Postcolonial Hong Kong. *BibInt* 7:156–73.

Levine, Lawrence W. 1997. Slave Songs and Slave Consciousness: An Exploration in Neglected Sources. Pages 57–87 in *African-American Religion: Interpretive Essays in History and Culture*. Edited by Timothy E. Fulop and Albert J. Raboteau. New York: Routledge.

Liew, Tat-siong Benny. *Politics of Parousia: Reading Mark Inter(con)textually*. BibInt 42. Leiden: Brill.

Lincoln, Bruce. 1989. *Discourse and the Construction of Society*. Oxford: Oxford University Press.

———. 2007. *Religion, Empire and Torture: The Case of Achaemenian Persia, with a Postscript on Abu Ghraib*. Chicago: University of Chicago Press.

Linton, Gregory L. 2006. Reading the Apocalypse as Apocalypse: The Limits of Genre. Pages 9–41 in *The Reality of Apocalypse: Rhetoric and Politics in the Book of Revelation*. Edited by David L. Barr. SymS 39. Atlanta: Society of Biblical Literature.

Logan, Shirley Wilson. 1999. *"We Are Coming": The Persuasive Discourse of Nineteenth-Century Black Women*. Carbondale: Southern Illinois University Press.

Long, Charles H. 1997. Perspectives for a Study of African-American Religion in the United States. Pages 21–35 in *African-American Religion: Interpretive Essays in History and Culture*. Edited by Timothy E. Fulop and Albert J. Raboteau. New York: Routledge.

Love, Velma. 2000. The Bible and Contemporary African American Culture 1: Hermeneutical Forays, Observations, and Impressions. Pages 49–65 in *African Americans and the Bible: Sacred Texts and Social Textures*. Edited by Vincent L. Wimbush. New York: Continuum.

Mabee, Charles. 1991. *Reading Sacred Texts through American Eyes: Biblical Interpretation as Cultural Critique.* StABH 7. Macon, GA: Mercer University Press.

———. 2000. African Americans and American Biblical Hermeneutics. Pages 103–10 in *African Americans and the Bible: Sacred Contexts and Social Textures.* Edited by Vincent L. Wimbush. New York: Continuum.

Macaulay, Thomas B. 1957. Minutes of 2 February 1835 on Indian Education. Page 729 in in *Macaulay, Prose and Poetry.* Edited by G. M. Young. Cambridge: Harvard University Press.

Malina, Bruce. 1995. *On the Genre and Message of Revelation: Star Visions and Sky Journeys.* Peabody, MA: Hendrickson.

Malkin, Irad. 1987. *Religion and Colonization in Ancient Greece.* Leiden: Brill.

———. 2004. Postcolonial Concepts and Ancient Greek Civilization. *Modern Language Quarterly* 65:341–64.

Martial. 2003. *Selected Epigrams.* Cambridge Greek and Latin Classics. Cambridge: Cambridge University Press.

Martin, Clarice J. 1989. The Chamberlain's Journey and the Challenge of Interpretations for Liberation. *Semeia* 47:105–35.

———. 1990. Womanist Interpretations of the New Testament: The Quest for Holistic and Inclusive Translation and Interpretation. *JSFR* 6, no. 2:41–61.

———. 1991. The *Haustafeln* (Household Codes) in African American Biblical Interpretation: "Free Slaves" and "Subordinate Women." Pages 206–31 in *Stony the Road We Trod: African American Biblical Interpretation.* Edited by Cain Hope Felder. Minneapolis: Fortress.

———. 2005. Polishing the Unclouded Mirror: A Womanist Reading of Revelation 18:13. Pages 82–109 in *From Every People and Nation: The Book of Revelation in Intercultural Perspective.* Edited by David Rhoads. Minneapolis: Fortress.

Matthews, Donald H. 1998. *Honoring the Ancestors: An African Cultural Interpretation of Black Religion and Literature.* New York: Oxford University Press.

Mattingly, D. J. 2011. *Imperialism, Power and Identity: Experiencing the Roman Empire.* Princeton: Princeton University Press.

Mazzaferri, Frederick David. 1989. *The Genre of the Book of Revelation from a Source-Critical Perspective.* Berlin: de Guyter.

Memmi, Albert. 1965. *The Colonizer and the Colonized.* New York: Orion.

Millar, Fergus. 1997. *The Emperor in the Roman World*. London: Duckworth.

———. 2002. *The Roman Republic and the Augustan Revolution*. Vol. 1 of *Rome, the Greek World, and the East*. Chapel Hill: University of North Carolina Press.

Miller, Margaret C. 1997. *Athens and Persia in the Fifth Century B.C.: A Study in Cultural Receptivity*. Cambridge: Cambridge University Press.

Miller, William Lee, Robert N. Bellah, and Martin E. Marty. 1998. *Religion and the Public Good: A Bicentennial Forum*. Macon, GA: Mercer University Press.

Moore, Stephen D. 2000. Postcolonialism. Pages 182–83 in *Handbook of Postmodern Biblical Interpretation*. Edited by A. K. Adam. St. Louis: Chalice.

———. 2001. Revolting Revelations. Pages 173–99 in *God's Beauty Parlor: And Other Queer Spaces in and around the Bible*. Stanford, CA: Stanford University Press.

———. 2005. Questions of Biblical Ambivalence under a Tree outside Delhi; or, the Postcolonial and the Postmodern. Pages 79–96 in *Postcolonial Biblical Criticism: Interdisciplinary Intersections*. Edited by Stephen D. Moore and Fernando F. Segovia. London: T&T Clark.

———. 2006. *Empire and Apocalypse: Postcolonialism and the New Testament*. Sheffield: Sheffield Phoenix.

———. 2007. The Revelation to John. Pages 133–56 in *A Postcolonial Commentary on the New Testament Writings*. Edited by Fernando F. Segovia and R. S. Sugirtharajah. London: T&T Clark.

———. 2011. Situating Spivak. Pages 15–30 in *Planetary Loves: Spivak, Postcoloniality, and Theology*. Edited by Stephen D. Moore and Mayra Rivera. New York: Fordham University Press.

Moore, Stephen D., and Fernando F. Segovia, eds. 2005. *Postcolonial Biblical Criticism: Interdisciplinary Intersections*. London: T&T Clark.

Moore-Gilbert, Bart. 1999. Postcolonial Cultural Studies and Imperial Historiography: Problems of Interdisciplinarity. *Interventions: International Journal of Postcolonial Studies* 13:397–411.

———. 2000a. *Postcolonial Theory: Contexts, Practice, Politics*. London: Verso.

———. 2000b. Spivak and Bhabha. Pages 451–66 in *A Companion to Postcolonial Studies*. Edited by Henry Schwarz and Sangeeta Ray. Malden, MA: Blackwell.

Morgan, Philip D., and Sean Hawkins, eds. 2004. *Black Experience and the Empire: The Oxford History of the British Empire Companion Series*. Oxford: Oxford University Press.

Morris, Ian, and Walter Scheidel, eds. 2010. *The Dynamics of Ancient Empires: State Power from Assyria to Byzantium*. Oxford: Oxford University Press.

Morrison, Toni. 1987. *Beloved*. New York: Knopf.

———. 1999. The Site of Memory. Pages 299–324 in *Out There: Marginalization and Contemporary Cultures*. Edited by Russell Ferguson, Martha Gever, Trinh T. Minh-ha, and Cornel West. Cambridge: MIT Press.

Morton, Stephen. 2003. *Gayatri Chakravorty Spivak*. Routledge Critical Thinkers. London: Routledge.

Moses, Wilson Jeremiah. 1993. *Black Messiahs and Uncle Toms: Social and Literary Manipulations of a Religious Myth*. Rev. ed. University Park: Pennsylvania State University Press.

Mostern, Kenneth. 2000. Postcolonialism after W. E. B. Du Bois. Pages 258–76 in *Postcolonial Theory and the United States: Race, Ethnicity, and Literature*. Edited by Amritjit Singh and Peter Schmidt. Jackson: University of Mississippi Press.

Mowry, Lucetta. 1952. Revelation 4–5 and Early Christian Liturgical Usage. *JBL* 71:75–84.

Myers, William H. 1991. The Hermeneutical Dilemma of the African American Biblical Student. Pages 40–56 in *Stony the Road We Trod: African American Biblical Interpretation*. Edited by Cain Hope Felder. Minneapolis: Fortress.

Naipul, V. S. 1967. *The Mimic Men*. New York: Macmillan.

Newman, Judith H. 1999. *Praying by the Book: The Scripturalization of Prayer in Second Temple Judaism*. EJL 14. Atlanta: Scholars Press.

Noll, Mark A. 1982. The United States as a Biblical Nation. Pages 41–55 in *The Bible in America: Essays in Cultural History*. Edited by Nathan O. Hatch and Mark A. Noll. New York: Oxford University Press.

———. 2002. *America's God: From Jonathan Edwards to Abraham Lincoln*. New York: Oxford University Press.

———. 2006. *The Civil War as a Theological Crisis*. Chapel Hill: University of North Carolina Press.

Nora, Pierre. 1989. Between Memory and History: Les Lieux de Mémoire. *Representations* 26:7–25.

Obama, Barack Hussein. 2008. A More Perfect Union. Online: http://www.huffingtonpost.com/2008/03/18/obama-race-speech-read-th_n_92077.html.

———. 2009. Inaugural Address. Online: abcnews.go.com/Politics/Inauguration/president-obama-inauguration-speech-transcript/story?id=6689022.

———. 2013. Inaugural Address. Online: https://www.whitehouse.gov/the-press-office/2013/01/21/inaugural-address-president-barack-obama.

Oduyoye, Mercy Amba. 1995. Reading from This Place: Some Problems and Prospects. Pages 33–51 in *Social Location and Biblical Interpretation from a Global Perspective*. Vol. 2 of *Reading from This Place*. Edited by Fernando F. Segovia and Mary Ann Tolbert. Minneapolis: Fortress.

O'Neale, Sondra A. 1993. *Jupiter Hammon and the Biblical Beginnings of African-American Literature*. Metuchen, NJ: Scarecrow.

O'Sullivan, John L. 1845. *United States Magazine and Democratic Review*. New York.

Palmer, Richard E. 1969. *Hermeneutics: Interpretation Theory in Schleiermacher, Dilthey, Heidegger, and Gadamer*. Evanston, IL: Northwestern University Press.

Parry, Benita. 2004. The Institutionalization of Postcolonial Studies. Pages 66–82 in *The Cambridge Companion to Postcolonial Studies*. Edited by Neil Lazarus. Cambridge: Cambridge University Press.

Patterson, Orlando. 1982. *Slavery and Social Death: A Comparative Study*. Cambridge: Harvard University Press.

Philipson, Robert. 2006. The Harlem Renaissance as Postcolonial Phenomenon. *African American Review* 40:145–60.

Pinn, Anthony. 2003. In the Raw: African American Cultural Memory and Theological Reflection. Pages 106–23 in *Converging on Culture: Theologians in Dialogue with Cultural Analysis and Criticism*. Edited by Delwin Brown. New York: Oxford University Press.

Plasa, Carl. 2000. *Textual Politics from Slavery to Postcolonialism*. Houndmills, Hampshire: Macmillan.

Pliny. 1938. *Natural History*. Translated by H. Rackham. LCL. Cambridge: Harvard University Press.

Plutarch. 1914. *Themistocles and Camillus, Aristides and Cato Major, Cimon and Lucillus*. Vol. 2 of *Lives*. Translated by Bernadotte Perrin. LCL. Cambridge: Harvard University Press.

Polybius. 1980. *Polybius on Roman Imperialism: The Histories of Polybius.* Translated from the text of F. Hultsch by Evelyn S. Shuckburgh. South Bend, IN: Regnery/Gateway.

Portier-Young, Anathea E. 2011. *Apocalypse against Empire: Theologies of Resistance in Early Judaism.* Grand Rapids: Eerdmans.

Powell, Colin. 2008. Interview on *Meet the Press,* October 19. Online: www.nbcnews.com/id/27266223/ns/meet_the_press/t/meet-press-transcript-oct/#.VPSSLbPF9UU.

Prakash, Gyan. 1995. *After Colonialism: Imperial Histories and Postcolonial Displacements.* Princeton: Princeton University Press.

Price, S. R. F. 1984. *Rituals and Power: The Roman Imperial Cult in Asia Minor.* Cambridge: Cambridge University Press.

Quayson, Ato. 2000. *Postcolonialism: Theory, Practice or Process?* Cambridge: Polity.

Raboteau, Albert J. 1980. *Slave Religion: The "Invisible Institution" in the Antebellum South.* New York: Oxford University Press.

———. 1995a. African Americans, Exodus and the American Israel. Pages 73–88 in *Religion and American Culture.* Edited by David G. Hackett. New York: Routledge.

———. 1995b. *A Fire in the Bones: Reflections on African American Religious History.* Boston: Beacon.

———. 2001. *Canaan Land: A Religious History of African Americans.* Oxford: Oxford University Press.

Ramsay, William Mitchell. 1904. *Letters to the Seven Churches of Asia and Their Place in the Plan of the Apocalypse.* London: Hodder & Stoughton.

Ray, Sangeeta. 2009. *Gayatri Chakravorty Spivak: In Other Words.* Oxford: Wiley-Blackwell.

Resseguie, James L. 2009. *The Revelation of John: A Narrative Commentary.* Grand Rapids: Baker Academic.

Rhoads, David, ed. 2005. *Every People and Nation: The Book of Revelation in Intercultural Perspective.* Minneapolis: Fortress.

Richardson, David. 2004. Through a Looking Glass: Olaudah Equiano and African Experiences of the British Atlantic Slave Trade. Pages 58–85 in *Black Experience and the Empire.* Edited by Philip D. Morgan and Sean Hawkins. Oxford: Oxford University Press.

Richardson, Marilyn. 1987. *Maria W. Stewart: America's First Black Woman Political Writer.* Bloomington: Indiana University Press.

Robinson, J. A. T. 2000. *Redating the New Testament.* Repr., Eugene, OR: Wipf & Stock.

Rodriguez, Jeanette, and Ted Fortier. 2007. *Cultural Memory: Resistance, Faith and Identity.* Austin: University of Texas Press.

Root, Margaret Cool. 2011. Embracing Ambiguity in the World of Athens and Persia. Pages 86–96 in *Cultural Identity in the Ancient Mediterranean.* Edited by Erich S. Gruen. Los Angeles: Getty.

Rossing, Barbara. 1999. *Choice between Two Cities: Whore, Bride and Empire in the Apocalypse.* Harrisburg, PA: Trinity Press International.

Rostovtzeff, M. I. 1963. The World Monarchy of Alexander the Great, and the Political History of Graeco-Oriental World in the Third Century B.C. Pages 242–57 in *Greece.* Oxford: Oxford University Press.

Rowland, Christopher. 1982. *The Open Heaven: A Study of Apocalyptic in Judaism and Early Christianity.* New York: Crossroad.

Runions, Erin. 2002. *Changing Subjects: Gender, Nature and Future in Micah.* Playing the Texts 7. Repr., London: Sheffield Academic.

Said, Edward W. 1979. *Orientalism.* New York: Vintage.

———. 1981. *Covering Islam: How the Media and the Experts Determine How We See the   Rest of the World.* New York: Pantheon.

———. 1983. *The World, the Text, and the Critic.* Cambridge: Harvard University Press.

———. 1993. *Culture and Imperialism.* New York: Knopf.

———. 2000. *Reflections on Exile and Other Essays.* Cambridge: Harvard University Press.

———. 2001. Reflections on American Injustice. *Media Monitors Network.* Online: http://www.mediamonitors.net/edward7.html.

Saillant, John. 2000. Origins of African American Biblical Hermeneutics in Eighteenth-Century Black Opposition to the Slave Trade and Slavery. Pages 236–50 in *African Americans and the Bible: Sacred Texts and Social Textures.* Edited by Vincent L. Wimbush. New York: Continuum.

Sanchez, David. 2008. *From Patmos to the Barrio: Subverting Imperial Myths.* Minneapolis: Fortress.

Scherrer, Steven J. 1984. Signs and Wonders in the Imperial Cult: A New Look at a Roman Religious Institution in the Light of Rev 13:13–15. *JBL* 103:599–610.

Schleiermacher, Friedrich. 1998. *Hermeneutics and Criticism and Other Writings.* Translated by Andrew Bowie. Cambridge: Cambridge University Press.

Schueller, Malini Johar. 2009. *Locating Race: Global Sites of Post-colonial Citizenship.* New York: State University of New York Press.

Schüssler Fiorenza, Elisabeth. 1991. *Revelation: Vision of a Just World.* Proclamation Commentaries. Minneapolis: Fortress.

———. 1998. *The Book of Revelation: Justice and Judgment.* 2nd ed. Minneapolis: Fortress.

———. 2007. *The Power of the Word: Scripture and the Rhetoric of Empire.* Minneapolis: Fortress.

Schwarz, Henry, and Sangeeta Ray, eds. 2000. *A Companion to Postcolonial Studies.* Malden, MA: Blackwell.

Scott, James C. 1995. *Domination and the Art of Resistance: Hidden Transcripts.* New Haven: Yale University Press.

Segovia, Fernando F. 1995a. And They Began to Speak in Tongues. Pages 1–11 in *Social Location and Biblical Interpretation in North American Perspective.* Vol. 1 of *Reading from This Place.* Edited by Fernando F. Segovia and Mary Tolbert. Minneapolis: Fortress.

———. 1995b. Cultural Studies and Contemporary Biblical Criticism: Ideological Criticism as Mode of Discourse. Pages 1–17 in *Social Location and Biblical Interpretation in Global Perspective.* Vol. 2 of *Reading from This Place.* Edited by Fernando F. Segovia and Mary Tolbert. Minneapolis: Fortress.

———. 1999a. Notes toward Refining the Postcolonial Optic. *JSNT* 75:103–14.

———. 1999b. Postcolonial and Diasporic Criticism in Biblical Studies: Focus, Parameters, Relevance. *Studies in World Christianity* 5:177–95.

———. 1999c. Postcolonialism and Comparative Analysis in Biblical Studies: Reply to A. C. C. Lee. *BibInt* 7:192–96.

Segovia, Fernando F., and Mary Ann Tolbert, eds. 1995a. *Social Location and Biblical Interpretation in North American Perspective.* Vol. 1 of *Reading from This Place.* Minneapolis: Fortress.

———. 1995b. *Social Locations and Biblical Interpretation in Global Perspective.* Vol. 2 of *Reading from This Place.* Minneapolis: Fortress.

Shohat, Ella. 1992. Notes on the "Post-Colonial." *Social Text* 31/32:99–113.

Singh, Amritjit, and Peter Schmidt, eds. 2000. *Postcolonial Theory and the United States: Race, Ethnicity, and Literature.* Jackson: University of Mississippi Press.

Smith, Abraham. 2004. Unmasking the Powers: Toward a Postcolonial Reading of 1 Thessalonians. Pages 47–66 in *Paul and the Roman*

Imperial Order. Edited by Richard A. Horsely. Harrisburg, PA: Trinity International.

Smith, Shanell T. 2014. *The Woman Babylon and the Marks of Empire: Reading Revelation with a Postcolonial Womanist Hermeneutics of Ambiveilence.* Minneapolis: Fortress.

Smith, Theophus. 1994. *Conjuring Culture: Biblical Formations of Black America.* Oxford: Oxford University Press.

Smith, Wilfred Cantwell. 1993. *What Is Scripture? A Comparative Approach.* Minneapolis: Fortress.

Spivak, Gayatri Charkravorty. 1974. Translation of Jacques Derrida's "Linguistics and Grammatology." *SubStance: A Review of Theory and Literary Criticism* 10:127–81.

———. 1985. Can the Subaltern Speak? Speculations on Widow-Sacrifice. *Wedge* 7–8:120–30.

———. 1986. Three Women's Texts and a Critique of Imperialism. Pages 243–61 in *"Race," Writing, and Difference.* Edited by Henry Louis Gates Jr. Chicago: University of Chicago Press.

———. 1987. *In Other Worlds: Essays in Cultural Politics.* London: Methuen.

St. Clair, Raquel. 2007. Womanist Interpretation. Pages 54–62 in *True to Our Native Land: An African American New Testament Commentary.* Edited by Brian Blount. Minneapolis: Fortress.

———. 2008. *Call and Consequences: A Womanist Reading of Mark.* Minneapolis: Fortress.

Stam, Juan. 1978. El Apocalipsis y el Imperialismo: Book of Revelation and Social, Political, Economic and Religious Aspects of the Roman Empire in *Capitalismo: Violencia y Anti-Aida: La Opresion de las Mayorias y la Domestication de los Dioses: Ponencias del Encuentro Latino-Americano de Cien.* Edited by Elsa Tamez and Saul Trinidad. San José, Costa Rica: Editorial Universitaria Centroamericana.

Starnes, Casey. 2009. Ancient Visions: The Roots of Judeo-Christian Apocalypse. Pages 27–46 in *End of Days: Essays on the Apocalypse from Antiquity to Modernity.* Edited by Karolyn Kinane and Michael A. Ryan. Jefferson, NC: McFarland.

Stave, Shirley, ed. 2006. *Toni Morrison and the Bible: Contested Intertextualities.* New York: Peter Lang.

Stout, Harry S. 1982. Word and Order in Colonial New England. Pages 19–34 in *The Bible in America: Essays in Cultural History.* Edited by Nathan O. Hatch and Mark Noll. New York: Oxford University Press.

Suetonius. 2000. *The Lives of the Twelve Caesars.* Translated by Catharine Edwards. Oxford: Oxford University Press.

Sugirtharajah, R. S., ed. 1998. *The Postcolonial Bible.* Sheffield: Sheffield Academic.

———. 1999. *Asian Biblical Hermeneutics and Postcolonialism: Contesting the Interpretations.* Sheffield: Sheffield Academic.

———. 2001. *The Bible and the Third World: Precolonial, Colonial and Postcolonial Encounters.* Cambridge: Cambridge University Press.

———. 2002. *Postcolonial Criticism and Biblical Interpretation.* Oxford: Oxford University Press.

———. 2005. Postcolonial Biblical Interpretation. Pages 535–52 in *The Modern Theologians: An Introduction to Christian Theology since 1918.* Edited by David F. Ford with Rachael Muers. 3rd ed. Malden, MA: Blackwell.

———, ed. 2006. *The Postcolonial Biblical Reader.* Malden, MA: Blackwell.

Taylor, Lily Ross. 1927. The "Proskynesis" and the Hellenistic Ruler Cult. *Journal of Hellenic Studies* 47:53–62.

———. 1931. *The Divinity of the Roman Emperor.* Middletown, CT: American Philological Association.

Taylor, Paul C. 2008. Post-Black, Old Black. *African American Review* 41:625–40.

Thiselton, Anthony C. 1992. *New Horizons in Hermeneutics: The Theory and Practice of Transforming Biblical Reading.* Grand Rapids: Zondervan.

Thompson, Leonard L. 1990. *Book of Revelation: Apocalypse and Empire.* New York: Oxford University Press.

———. 1998. *Revelation.* Abingdon New Testament Commentaries. Nashville: Abingdon.

Thompson, Steven. 1985. *The Apocalypse and Semitic Language.* Cambridge: Cambridge University Press.

Thurman, Howard. 1949. *Jesus and the Disinherited.* Nashville: Abingdon.

Townes, Emilie M. 1993. *Womanist Justice, Womanist Hope.* AARAS 79. Atlanta: Scholars Press.

———. 1995. *In a Blaze of Glory: Womanist Spirituality as Social Witness.* Nashville: Abingdon.

Tweed, Thomas A., ed. 1997. *Retelling U.S. Religious History.* Berkeley: University of California Press.

Valeri, Mark, and John F. Wilson. 1985. Scripture and Society: From Reform in the Old World to Revival in the New. Pages 13–38 in *The*

Bible in American Law, Politics, and Political Rhetoric. Edited by James Turner Johnson. Philadelphia: Fortress.

Varisco, Daniel Martin. 2007. *Reading Orientalism: Said and the Unsaid.* Seattle: University of Washington Press.

Waetjen, Herman C. 1995. Social Location and the Hermeneutical Mode of Integration. Pages 75–94 in *Social Location and Biblical Interpretation in North American Perspective.* Vol. 1 of *Reading from This Place.* Edited by Fernando F. Segovia and Mary Ann Tolbert. Minneapolis: Fortress.

Walker, Alice. 1983. *In Search of Our Mother's Gardens: Womanist Prose.* Orlando: Harvest.

Wallace, Robert W., and Edward Monroe Harris, eds. 1996. *Transitions to Empire: Essays in Greco-Roman History, 360–146 B.C., in Honor of E. Badian.* Norman: University of Oklahoma Press.

Wan, Sze-Kar. 2008. Signification as Scripturalization. Pages 105–14 in *Theorizing Scriptures: New Critical Orientations to a Cultural Phenomenon.* Edited by Vincent L. Wimbush. New Brunswick, NJ: Rutgers University Press.

Webster, Jane. 1997. Necessary Comparisons: A Postcolonial Approach to Religious Syncretism in the Roman Provinces. *World Archaeology* 28:324–38.

Webster, Jane, and Nicholas J. Cooper, eds. 1996. *Roman Imperialism: Post-Colonial Perspectives: Proceedings of a Symposium Held at Leicester University in November 1994.* Leicester, England: School of Archaeological Studies, University of Leicester.

Weeks, Louis. 1985. God's Judgment, Christ's Command: Use of the Bible in Nineteenth-Century American Political Life. Pages 61–77 in *The Bible in American Law, Politics, and Political Rhetoric.* Edited by James Turner Johnson. Philadelphia: Fortress.

Weems, Renita J. 1988. *Just a Sister Away: A Womanist Vision of Women's Relationship in the Bible.* San Diego: LuraMedia.

———. 1991. Reading *Her Way* through the Struggle: African American Women and the Bible. Pages 57–77 in *Stony the Road We Trod: African American Biblical Interpretation.* Edited by Cain Hope Felder. Minneapolis: Fortress.

Whitfield, James M. 1997. America. Pages 402–5 in *The Norton Anthology of African American Literature.* Edited by Henry Louis Gates Jr. and Nellie Y. McKay. New York: Norton.

Wiesehöfer, Josef. 2010. The Achaemenid Empire. Pages 66–98 in *The Dynamics of Ancient Empires: State Power from Assyria to Byzantium.* Edited by Ian Morris and Walter Scheidel. Repr., Oxford: Oxford University Press.

Williams, Delores S. 1987. Womanist Theology: Black Women's Voices. *Christianity and Crisis* 47:66–70.

———. 1993. *Sisters in the Wilderness: The Challenge of God-Talk.* Maryknoll, NY: Orbis.

Williams, Patrick. 1998. *Ngugi wa Thiong'o.* Manchester: Manchester University Press.

Williams, Patrick, and Laura Chrisman. 1994. *Colonial Discourse and Post-Colonial Theory: A Reader.* New York: Columbia University Press.

Wills, David W. 1997. The Central Themes of American Religious History: Pluralism, Puritanism, and the Encounter of Black and White. Pages 7–20 in *African American Religion: Interpretive Essays in History and Culture.* Edited by Timothy E. Fulop and Albert J. Raboteau. New York: Routledge.

Wilson, Christian J. 1993. The Problem of the Domitianic Date of Revelation. *NTS* 39:587–605.

Wimbush, Vincent L. 1991. The Bible and African Americans: An Outline of an Interpretative History. Pages 81–97 in *Stony the Road We Trod: African American Biblical Interpretation.* Edited by Cain Hope Felder. Minneapolis: Fortress.

———, ed. 2000a. *African Americans and the Bible: Sacred Texts and Social Textures.* New York: Continuum.

———. 2000b. Introduction: Reading Darkness, Reading Scriptures. Pages 1–43 in *African Americans and the Bible: Sacred Texts and Social Textures.* Edited by Vincent L. Wimbush. New York: Continuum.

———, ed. 2008. *Theorizing Scriptures: New Critical Orientations to a Cultural Phenomenon.* New Brunswick, NJ: Rutgers University Press.

———. 2012. *White Men's Magic: Scripturalization as Slavery.* New York: Oxford University Press.

———, ed. 2013. *MisReading America: Scriptures and Difference.* New York: Oxford University Press.

Woolf, Greg. 1994. Becoming Roman, Staying Greek: Culture, Identity and the Civilizing Process in the Roman East. *Proceedings of the Cambridge Philological Society* 40:116–43.

Worth, Roland J. 1999. *The Seven Cities of the Apocalypse and Roman Culture.* New York: Paulist.

Wright, Jeremiah. 2003. Sermon. Online: http://hiphopandpolitics.word-press.com/2009/06/17/1233/.

Yarbro Collins, Adela. 1977. The Political Perspective of the Revelation of John. *JBL* 96:241–56.

———. 1984. *Crisis and Catharsis: The Power of the Apocalypse.* Philadelphia: Westminster.

———. 2001. *The Combat Myth in the Book of Revelation.* Repr., Eugene, OR: Wipf & Stock.

Young, Robert J. C. 2001. *Postcolonialism: An Historical Introduction.* Oxford: Blackwell.

———. 2003. *Postcolonialism: A Very Short Introduction.* Oxford: Oxford University Press.

Zakai, Avihu. 1992. *Exile and Kingdom: History and Apocalypse in the Puritan Migration to America.* Cambridge: Cambridge University Press.

Zanker, Paul. 1988. *The Power of Images in the Age of Augustus.* Translated by Alan Shapiro. Ann Arbor: University of Michigan Press.

Index of Primary Sources

INDEX OF NAMES

CPSIA information can be obtained at www.ICGtesting.com
Printed in the USA
LVOW07s1301090216

474332LV00001B/34/P